IN MEMORY OF:

   Ransom and Ann Oetzel

PRESENTED BY:

Mr. and Mrs. Terry Oetzel
and
Family

Women's
Almanac

Women's Almanac

VOLUME 2: Society

Edited by Linda Schmittroth
& Mary Reilly McCall

AN IMPRINT OF GALE

Women's Almanac

Edited by Linda Schmittroth and Mary Reilly McCall

Staff

Julie Carnagie, *U·X·L Associate Developmental Editor*
Carol DeKane Nagel, *U·X·L Managing Editor*
Thomas L. Romig, *U·X·L Publisher*

Shanna P. Heilveil, *Production Assistant*
Evi Seoud, *Assistant Production Manager*
Mary Beth Trimper, *Production Director*

Margaret A. Chamberlain, *Permissions Associate (Pictures)*

Pamela A. E. Galbreath, *Art Director*
Cynthia Baldwin, *Product Design Manager*

Linda Mahoney, *Typesetting*

Library of Congress Cataloging-in-Publication Data

Women's almanac / edited by Linda Schmittroth and Mary Reilly McCall.
   p. cm.
Includes biographical references and index.
ISBN 0-7876-0656-1 (set: alk. paper); ISBN 0-7876-0657-x (v. 1);
ISBN 0-7876-0658-8 (v. 2); ISBN 0-7876-0659-6 (v. 3)

   1. Women—Miscellanea. 2. Women—History—Miscellanea.
    3. Almanacs. I. Schmittroth, Linda. II. McCall, Mary Reilly.

HQ1111.W73 1996
305.4'09 — dc20

96-25681
CIP

Printed in the United States of America

10 9 8 7 6 5 4 3 2

*This book is dedicated to some of the leaders of tomorrow—
Sara Schmittroth and the members of Girl Scout Troop #1399:
Stephanie Cetnar, Jackie Douglas, Laura Hendrickson,
Ashley Jenkins, Sheena Maggard, Margie McCall,
Jayla McDavid, Monti Miller, Erin Morand, Rachel Morand,
Rameka Parham, Courtney Phillips, and Amy Yunker*

Contents

Bold type indicates volume number.
Regular *type indicates page number.*

Volume 2: Society

Reader's Guide

Women's Almanac features a comprehensive range of historical and current information on the life and culture of women in the United States and around the world. Each of the 25 subject chapters in these three volumes focuses on a specific topic relevant to women, such as education, civil rights, and social concerns. The *Women's Almanac* does more than highlight the accomplishments of women in a variety of fields, time periods, and cultures. It offers insight into history and attitudes, so that readers can understand just how remarkable some of these accomplishments truly are.

Additional Features

Women's Almanac contains biographical boxes on prominent women relating to the subject being discussed, sidebar boxes examining related events and issues of high interest to students, more than 200 black-and-white illustrations, and 20 statistical tables. Each of the three volumes also contains a glossary of terms used throughout the text and a cumulative subject index.

Acknowledgments

Special thanks are due for the invaluable comments and suggestions provided by U•X•L's *Women's Almanac* advisors:

Annette Haley, Librarian/Media Specialist at Grosse Ile High School in Grosse Ile, Michigan; Mary Ruthsdotter, Projects Director of the National Women's History Project in Windsor, California; and Francine Stampnitzky, Children's/Youth Adult Librarian at Elmont Public Library in Elmont, New York.

Special thanks also is extended to the panel of readers, whose comments in many areas have strengthened and added insight to the text: Marlene Heitmanis, Kathleen Reilly, and Robert Reilly. Marlene Heitmanis is the coordinator of an at-risk program at a Michigan middle school. She holds bachelor's and master's degrees in teaching and an education specialist degree. She commented on the appropriateness of the text and the reading level. Kathleen Reilly holds a bachelor's degree in anthropology and a master's degree in teaching English as a second language. She commented on grammar, culture, and feminist issues. Robert Reilly holds a doctoral degree in English. He is a professor emeritus of the University of Detroit, where he taught American literature for 33 years. He commented on grammar, literature, history, and philosophy.

Thank you, too, to Teresa San-Clementi for fine tuning the fine and applied arts information, and to Bob Russette for theater and Broadway musical information.

Comments and Suggestions

We welcome your comments on *Women's Almanac* as well as your suggestions for topics to be featured in future editions. Please write: Editors, *Women's Almanac,* U•X•L, 835 Penobscot Bldg., Detroit, Michigan 48226-4094; call toll-free: 1-800-877-4253; or fax: 313-961-6348.

Photo Credits

The Granger Collection, New York: Suffragettes (top); Corbis-Bettmann: ERA demonstration at Lincoln Memorial (bottom); AP/Wide World Photos: Benazir Bhutto (left).

Photographs and illustrations appearing in *Women's Almanac* were received from the following sources:

Corbis-Bettmann: Volume 1: pp. vii, 17, 34, 67, 99, 119, 137, 170; Volume 2: pp. 252, 359, 391, 412; Volume 3: pp. 534, 591, 595, 677, 744; AP/Wide World Photos: Volume 1: pp. xiii, xvii, 23, 50, 54, 59, 66, 88, 93, 101, 104, 114, 139, 146, 154, 177, 181, 183, 197, 213, 215; Volume 2: pp. 246, 257, 259, 270, 271, 273, 275, 277, 278, 279, 283, 284, 290, 302, 303, 315, 321, 331, 334, 335, 337, 361, 366, 376, 380, 383, 387, 410, 433, 438, 441, 442, 443, 467; Volume 3: pp. 507, 512, 518, 537, 549, 552, 558, 560, 561, 565, 566, 587, 593, 601, 604, 611, 612, 627, 629, 631, 637, 638, 649, 653, 654, 686, 705, 706, 709, 725, 730, 736, 740, 749, 751; UPI/Corbis-Bettmann: Volume 1: pp. xxvii, 61, 75, 110, 138, 140, 186, 194, 195, 219; Volume 2: p. 422; Volume 3: pp. 632, 731; Archive

Words to Know

A

Abolition: A movement in American history (1775–1864) in which people (abolitionists) worked to legally end the practice of slavery.

Activist: A person who has a strong belief and takes action to make that belief become an accepted part of society, either through law or government policy.

Agenda: A set of goals that a person or group tries to complete.

Allies: Nations or groups who fight on the same side during a war.

Anchor: In the television news media, the person who either narrates (tells) or coordinates (organizes) a program on which several correspondents give news reports.

Apartheid: An official South African policy that denied blacks and other nonwhites equality with whites in politics, law, and the economy.

Artifacts: Objects made by human beings, especially tools and utensils, often studied by later societies.

Astrology: The study of the stars and planets in the belief that they have an influence on events on earth and in human affairs.

Autobiography: A factual story that a person tells about his or her own life.

B

Baptism: In many Christian churches, this is the sacrament of joining or being initiated into the church; it usually involves the pouring of water over the new member to symbolize the washing away of sin.

Barbarians: People who do not behave in accepted civilized ways. For instance, the French and German tribes that overran Rome in about A.D. 400 were considered barbarians by the Romans.

Blockade: The use of ships, planes, and soldiers to seal off traffic to and from a coastline or city. The blockade cuts off the enemy's supply of food and weapons.

Blueprint: A written plan or drawing for how something should be built.

Boycott: The refusal to purchase the products of an individual, corporation, or nation as a way of bringing about social and political pressure for change.

C

Cabinet: A select group of people who advise the head of government.

Campaign: With reference to politics, an action undertaken to achieve a political goal.

Capitalism: An economic system in which goods and services are exchanged in a free market and are priced according to what people are willing to pay for them. Companies producing those goods and services are privately owned.

Censorship: The examination of filmed or printed material to ensure there is nothing objectionable in it.

Census: An official count of the population, conducted in the United States every ten years.

Chauvinist: A person who believes in the superiority of his or her own gender.

Choreographer: A person who creates the pattern of steps for a dance.

Christian: A person who believes that Jesus Christ is God, and that he lived on earth in human form.

Civil Rights movement: A social movement of the late 1950s and 1960s to win equal rights for African Americans.

Civil disobedience: Nonviolent acts that disrupt the normal flow of society, such as bus boycotts and sit-ins.

Civilian: A person who is not in the military.

Classic: A literary work of such quality that it continues to be read long after its original publication date.

Clearinghouse: A central location for the collection and sharing of information and/or materials.

Coeducational: An adjective describing an educational system in which both boys and girls (or men and women) attend the same institution or classes.

Code of law: A written list of rules that apply to all people. Laws can be enforced by the ruler or the government, and those who break the law can be tried and punished.

Collage: An art form that combines many different media and which may include paper, fabric, objects, text, and glass or metal.

Colonial period: The time in U.S. history between the first permanent English settlements in the early 1600s to the signing of the Declaration of Independence in 1776 when America was considered a colony of England.

Colonist: A person who settles in a new land and declares that the new land belongs to an already existing country.

Combat: The actual fighting that occurs during a war, including hand-to-hand fighting between soldiers, fights between pilots in planes, and fights between enemy ships.

Commission: An order for an artist to create a piece of art for a wealthy patron.

Communism: A form of government whose system requires common ownership of property for the use of all citizens. All profits are to be equally distributed and prices of goods and services are usually set by the state. Communism also refers directly to the official doctrine of the former Soviet Union.

Concerto: A musical composition for an orchestra that features one or more solo instruments.

Conservative: This term describes a philosophy or belief that the status quo, or the current system, should remain unchanged unless a very good argument is put forward for the change. Conservatives tend to prefer a small federal government and careful spending of public money.

Convention: A formal meeting of an organization's members.

Credit union: An organization somewhat like a bank that is owned by its members.

Crossover: A recording or album of one particular style, such as gospel or rap, that also becomes a hit on the popular music charts.

Curricula: All the courses of study offered by an educational institution. The singular form of the word is curriculum.

D

Dark Ages: The period (450–900) after the collapse of the Roman Empire, when violence, ignorance, and superstition was common.

Debut: Pronounced day-byoo; a first performance. An actor or dancer opens her career with a debut performance.

Delegation: A person or group of persons elected or appointed to represent others. A delegation to a national party convention represents all the voters of the state from which it came.

Democracy: A system of government in which the people elect their rulers.

Desegregate: To open a place such as a school or workplace to members of all races or ethnic groups. Desegregation usually happens after laws are passed rather than as a result of voluntary action taken by an institution.

Developed countries: A category used by the United Nations for countries that have extensive industry and a high standard of living. Developed countries and areas include all of North America, Europe, parts of the former Soviet Union, Japan, Australia, and New Zealand.

Developing countries: Countries that are not highly industrialized. Developing countries include all of Africa, all of Asia except Japan, all of Latin America and the Caribbean, and all of Oceania except Australia and New Zealand. Also known as the Third World or less developed countries.

Discrimination: Unfair practices, laws, or treatment of certain people based on a person's social class, gender, or race rather than on the person's merits.

Displaced homemakers: Women whose primary activity has been homemaking and who have lost their main source of income because of divorce, separation, widowhood, their husband's inability to work, or long-term unemployment.

Doctrine: A set of beliefs that guides how a person views the world and how she or he behaves.

Documentary: A nonfiction (true-to-life) film that tries to present information in a dramatic and entertaining way.

Domestic and decorative arts: The type of knowledge thought appropriate for young women in European society from the Dark Ages to modern times. These arts include caring for and beautifying the home, child care, gardening and food preparation, and self-improvement through art and music.

Dowry: Money, property, or goods that a bride's family gives to a bridegroom or his family at the time of a wedding.

E

Embassies: The buildings that governments maintain in foreign countries to conduct diplomatic business.

Endowed: To be provided with income or a source of income. Sometimes wealthy people endow colleges, providing the school with a source of income. The college then does not have to rely entirely on tuition payments.

Enlightenment: A period of cultural richness in Europe during the eighteenth century that called for critical examination of previously unchallenged doctrines and beliefs.

Evangelical: An adjective that refers to the Gospels of the New Testament in the Bible; an evangelist seeks to win converts to Christianity by teaching about the Gospels.

Exodus: A massive moving of people from one area to another.

Exploited: The act of using a person or resource without permission or without adequate payment.

F

Feminism: The belief that women are equal to men in terms of physical and mental ability, and that women's accomplishments should be equally praised in history and society.

Forum: A group that conducts an open discussion.

Frontier: The edge of known territory or what is considered civilized territory. When the Europeans first came to America, they considered the land west of the Appalachian Mountains the frontier. Next it was the land west of the Mississippi River. Finally, the frontier was the territory west of the Rocky Mountains.

Front line: The site of a battle where two sides meet to fight.

G

Gender equity: Fair treatment of both men and women.

Genre: A type of literary form, such as a poem, story, novel, essay, or autobiography. Sometimes genre refers to the groups within a literary form. For instance, novels may be historical, mystery, thriller, spy, or romance.

Great Depression: A period of economic hardship in U.S. history, from 1929 to about 1940. Many companies went out of business, and many people were without jobs.

Greco-Roman: Relating to both ancient Greece and Rome.

Guilds: Formal organizations of skilled workers that dominated trade and crafts in the Middle Ages (500–1500). Young people were apprenticed to guild members, who taught them a skill. Guilds had rules about days and times a business could be operated, prices that could be charged, and the number of new apprentices taken on each year.

I

Illiteracy: Illiteracy is defined differently in different countries. Sometimes it means the ability to read and write only simple sentences. In some countries, people who have never attended school are considered illiterate.

Immigrant: A person who leaves one country and settles in another.

Impressionism: A style of painting made popular in the late 1800s in France. Impressionists watched how light illuminated forms and then used color to create that image. Their work was very different from that of traditional realist painters, who represented scenes with great accuracy.

Incest: A sexual act between closely related people such as a father and daughter, a mother and son, a sister and brother.

Income: Money received by persons from all sources. Some of these sources can include wages, payments from government such as welfare or Social Security benefits, and money received from rental property.

Indentured servants: A person bound by contract to work for another for a certain length of time; during the early period of American history, both black and white indentured servants were commonly used and were usually forced to work for seven years before they gained their freedom.

Industrial Revolution: A period of history that began in England about 1750 and lasted until about 1870. The period was characterized by great growth in business and cities and greater dependence on machinery and inventions, which replaced hand tools and individual labor.

Inflation: An economic term referring to a rise in the cost of living. In an inflationary period, the cost of goods and services rises faster than wages increase.

Information Age: A period of time when a country's economy depends more on the exchange of information than on the production of goods.

J

Judaism: A religion based on belief in one God and a moral life based on the teachings of the Torah, or the Old Testament of the Bible.

Judeo-Christian: The religious tradition that forms the basis of the Christian churches. It includes the belief in one divine God and the need to live a good life in order to reach eternal salvation in heaven after death.

L

Labor unions: An organization of workers formed to bargain with employers over wages, hours, and working conditions.

Liberal left: A political belief that the federal government has a duty to make changes happen in society. Liberals favor government managed health care and social programs and strict environmental regulations.

Literate: The ability to read and write.

Lobby: In politics, the act of trying to persuade an elected or appointed government official to favor a particular policy. Washington, D.C., has thousands of lobbyists who argue for causes such as gun control.

Lyricist: The person who writes the words (lyrics) to a song. Many lyricists work with a composer, who creates the music to go with the words.

M

Mainstream: The beliefs and customs of the majority of society.

Maternity leave: Time off from work to have and care for a baby.

Medieval: An adjective that refers to the Middle Ages, which took place in Europe from about 500 to 1500.

Middle Ages: The period (500–1500) when the struggle for power gradually resolved itself into the creation of kingdoms ruled by a king and his noblemen. The period was a highly religious one, and learning and the arts reappeared as the times of peace lengthened.

Midwife: A trained health-care worker, most often a woman, who assists during childbirth and cares for newborns.

Militia: Civilians who join together to form an unofficial army, usually to protect their homes from invasion by an enemy.

Minimum wage: A payment per hour that is set by the government; employers cannot pay their workers less than the minimum wage.

Mural: A painting done on a wall. During the Renaissance (1450–1600), murals were done on wet plaster. Modern murals are often done on the cinder block walls of public structures or on the brick of a neighborhood building.

N

Network: A large chain of interconnected radio or television broadcasting stations.

Networking: The sharing of information and resources among a group of individuals in the same profession or interest area.

New World: The term used to refer to the North and South American continents. The Europeans (from the Old World) "discovered" the Americas in the late 1400s, and claimed the land for their king back home. The New World became colonies of the Old World.

Nontraditional: A new or different way of thinking or acting. For example, nontraditional jobs for women still include being a mechanic or the head of an automobile manufacturing plant.

O

Obstetrics: The branch of medicine concerned with pregnancy and childbirth.

Order: An official religious group dedicated to a specific purpose.

P

Pacifist: A person who is opposed to war or any use of force against another person.

Paganism: A religious system that does not accept the existence of one true god. Instead, pagans may worship animals, their own ancestors, or nature.

Parliament: An assembly of representatives, usually of an entire country, that makes laws.

Patent: A grant made by a government to an inventor that gives only the inventor the right to make, use, and sell her invention for a certain period of time.

Patriarchy: Social organization marked by the supremacy of the father in the clan or family, the legal dependence of wives and children, and the tracing of descent through the father's side of the family.

Pension: An amount of money given to a person by an organization on a regular basis, usually after a person retires. Career military people receive a pension from the U.S. government.

Philanthropists: Wealthy people who donate to charity or who try to make life better for others.

Philosopher: A scholar who is concerned with the principles that explain the nature of the universe and human thought and behavior.

Picket lines: To picket is to stand outside a place of employment during a strike. A picket line consists of more than one person picketing.

Piecework: Work paid for by the piece. Today this type of work is still done by women in the home, as a "cottage industry."

Policies: Plans or courses of action of a government, political party, school, or business intended to influence and determine decisions, actions, and other matters.

Political prisoners: People who are without legal rights and are held by a government that has no right to imprison them.

Poverty: The condition of being poor. The U.S. government defines poverty according to levels of money income that vary by age and family size.

Preparatory: Relating to study or training that serves as a preparation for advanced education. College preparatory classes prepare a student to handle college-level work.

Prodigy: An extremely talented child who shows an understanding or ability far beyond his or her age.

Producer: One who supervises and finances a public entertainment.

Progressive: A political or social belief that existing systems and organizations should be reevaluated from time to time and that new ways of doing things should be adopted if they are better.

Prohibition: A law, order, or decree that forbids something.

Public interest: A phrase used to identify concerns that affect the public as a whole.

R

Racism: Discrimination based on race.

Rape: The crime of forcing another person by spoken or implied threats of violence to submit to sex acts, especially sexual intercourse.

Ratification: The political process of passing an amendment to the U.S. Constitution. In the United States, thirty-six states must approve an amendment before it is passed into constitutional law.

Renaissance: The period from about 1450 to about 1750 that saw a great flowering in knowledge of all kinds, including the arts, sciences, music, literature, and philosophy.

Representative: In politics, a type of government in which people have the right to vote for their rulers. The rulers in turn represent or look after the interests of the people.

Rhetoric: The art of using language in a persuasive way that is not necessarily supported by facts.

S

Sacred: Something or someone that is holy or associated with a religion.

Saint: A person who has been officially recognized through the process of canonization as being worthy of special reverence.

Scholarly: Related to advanced learning.

Segregated: Separated or apart from others. Sex-segregated schools have either all boys or all girls; usually refers to government laws and social customs that keep white and black people apart.

Seminary: A school. The term is used today to mean a school for the training of priests, ministers, or rabbis. In the past, it referred to a private school of higher education for women.

Sex discrimination: Treating a person differently based only on his or her sex.

Sexism: Discrimination based on gender.

Sexual harassment: A practice that implies a person will lose his or her job, scholarship, or position unless he or she is willing to trade sexual favors.

Social government: This general phrase refers to some modern governments that believe they must play a strong role in protecting their citizens' health, safety, and educational systems. Other governments believe that individuals in the society must contribute and protect these things.

Socialism: An economic system under which ownership of land and other property is distributed among the community as a whole, and every member of the community shares in the work and products of the work. Socialists may tolerate capitalism as long as the government maintains influence over the economy.

Speakers' bureau: People within a group or club that give speeches regarding the group or club's goals, mission, or activities to an audience.

Stereotype: A distorted, one-sided image of a person or idea. Stereotypes include the strong, silent hero and the dizzy, blond heroine.

Steroids: Chemical compounds that may be useful for treating some medical conditions, but are sometimes misused by athletes to enhance their performance.

Still-life: A type of painting in which the subject is not moving. Flowers and fruit are favorite subjects of still-life painters.

Stream of consciousness: A writing technique that reflects the thought process of a character. The writing may include sentence fragments, unconnected ideas, and confused thinking. The technique is used to give the reader insight into how a character feels and makes decisions.

Strike: A refusal by employees in a particular business or industry to work. The goal is usually to force employers to meet demands for better pay and working conditions.

Subordinate: The idea that one person is less valuable or important than another. For instance, slaves are subordinate to their masters, and they must obey them. In some societies women are still subordinate to men.

Suffrage: The legal right to vote. In U.S. history, it usually refers to the movement to gain a woman's right to vote in elections of officials to public office.

Sweatshop: A factory in which employees work long hours for low wages under poor conditions.

T

Technology: Using the ideas of science to make tasks easier. Technology began with the invention of stone tools. The development of computers is one of the most important recent advances in technology.

Temperance movement: A social movement in the United States that started in the early 1870s in the West. Its goal was to make liquor production and consumption illegal.

Theology: The study of God and religious writings.

Tour of duty: The amount of time an enlisted man or woman spends in the military. Usually tours of duty or "hitches" run from two to four years.

U

Underrepresentation: The inadequate or insufficient representation of a certain group of people. For instance, in the 1960s, women and people of color were underrepresented on the police forces of most American cities

Universal suffrage: The right of an entire population, regardless of race or sex, to vote.

V

Vaudeville: An early form of American musical theater that was a collection of separate acts with no connecting theme.

Further Reading

A

Adair, Christy, *Women and Dance: Sylphs and Sirens,* New York University Press, 1992.

Agonito, Rosemary, *History of Ideas on Woman: A Sourcebook,* Perigee Books, 1977.

Alcott, Louisa May, *Work: A Story of Experience,* Roberts Brothers, 1873, reprinted, Viking Penguin, 1994.

Anderson, Bonnie S., and Judith P. Zinsser, *A History of Their Own: Women in Europe from Prehistory to the Present,* Harper & Row, 1988.

Ash, Russell, and Bernard Higton, *Great Women Artists,* Chronicle Books, 1991.

B

Basinger, Jeanine, *A Woman's View: How Hollywood Spoke to Women, 1930-1960,* Alfred A. Knopf, 1993.

Beauvoir, Simone de, *Le Deuxieme Sexe,* Gallimard, 1949, translation published as *The Second Sex,* Knopf, 1953.

Blos, Joan W., *A Gathering of Days: A New England Girl's Journal, 1830-32: A Novel,* Scribner, 1979.

Boston Women's Health Collective, *The New Our Bodies, Ourselves: A Book By and For Women,* Touchstone Books, 1992.

Bowers, Jane, and Judith Tick, eds., *Women Making Music: The Western Art Tradition, 1150-1950,* University of Illinois Press, 1986.

Brennan, Shawn, ed., *Women's Information Directory,* Gale Research, 1993.

C

Cantor, Dorothy W., and Toni Bernay, with Jean Stoess, *Women in Power: The Secrets of Leadership,* Houghton Mifflin, 1992.

Carabillo, Toni, Judith Meuli, and June Bundy Csida, *Feminist Chronicles: 1953-1993,* Women's Graphics, 1993.

Chadwick, Whitney, *Women, Art, and Society,* Thames and Hudson, 1990.

Clapp, Patricia, *Constance: A Story of Early Plymouth,* Lothrop, Lee & Shepard, 1968.

D

DeWitt, Lisa F., *Cue Cards: Famous Women of the Twentieth Century,* Pro Lingua Associates, 1993.

E

Edwards, Julia, *Women of the World: The Great Foreign Correspondents,* Houghton Mifflin, 1988.

Evans, Sara M., *Born for Liberty: A History of Women in America,* The Free Press, 1989.

F

Fallaci, Oriana, *Interview with History,* Houghton Mifflin, 1976.

Faludi, Susan, *Backlash: The Undeclared War Against American Women,* Crown Publishers, 1991.

Farrer, Claire R., *Women and Folklore,* University of Texas, 1975.

Fernea, Elizabeth Warnock and Basima Qattan Bezirgan, eds., *Middle Eastern Muslim Women Speak,* University of Texas Press, 1977.

Fischer, Christiane, ed., *Let Them Speak for Themselves: Women in the American West, 1849-1900,* E. P. Dutton, 1978.

Fisher, Maxine P., *Women in the Third World,* Franklin Watts, 1989.

Fox-Genovese, Elizabeth, *Within the Plantation Household: Black and White Women of the Old South,* University of North Carolina, 1988.

Fraser, Antonia, *The Warrior Queens,* Alfred A. Knopf, 1989.

Fraser, Antonia, *The Weaker Vessel,* Alfred A. Knopf, 1984.

Friedan, Betty, *The Feminine Mystique,* Dell Publishing, 1963.

G

Gilden, Julia, and Mark Friedman, *Woman to Woman: Entertaining and Enlightening Quotes by Women About Women,* Dell Publishing, 1994.

Goodrich, Norma Lorre, *Heroines: Demigoddess, Prima Donna, Movie Star,* HarperCollins, 1993.

H

Haskell, Molly, *From Reverence to Rape: The Treatment of Women in the Movies,* Holt, Rinehart and Winston, 1973.

Hymowitz, Carol, and Michaele Weissman, *A History of Women in America,* Bantam Books, 1978.

K

Kosser, Mike, *Hot Country Women,* Avon, 1994.

Kraft, Betsy Harvey, *Mother Jones: One Woman's Fight for Labor,* Clarion Books, 1995.

Kramarae, Cheris, and Paula A. Treichler, *Amazons, Bluestockings and Crones: A Feminist Dictionary,* Pandora Press, 1992.

L

Lerner, Gerda, *The Creation of Feminist Consciousness: From the Middle Ages to Eighteen-seventy,* Oxford University Press, 1993.

Levey, Judith S., *The World Almanac for Kids: 1996,* World Almanac Books, 1995.

Lobb, Nancy, *Sixteen Extraordinary Hispanic Americans,* J. Weston Walch, Publisher, 1995.

Lunardini, Christine, Ph.D., *What Every American Should Know About Women's History: 200 Events that Shaped Our Destiny,* Bob Adams, Inc., 1994.

M

Macdonald, Anne L., *Feminine Ingenuity: Women and Invention in America,* Ballantine Books, 1992.

Maio, Kathi, *Popcorn and Sexual Politics: Movie Reviews,* The Crossing Press, 1991.

McLoone, Margo, and Alice Siegel, *The Information Please Girls' Almanac,* Houghton Mifflin, 1995.

Mead, Margaret, *Male & Female: A Study of the Sexes in a Changing World,* William Morrow, 1977.

Mills, Kay, *A Place in the News: From the Women's Pages to the Front Pages,* Columbia University Press, 1991.

Morgan, Robin, ed., *Sisterhood Is Global: The International Women's Movement Anthology,* Anchor Press/Doubleday, 1984.

Moses, Robert, and Beth Rowen, eds., *The 1996 Information Please Entertainment Almanac,* Houghton Mifflin, 1995.

N

Nelson, Mariah Burton, *Are We Winning Yet?: How Women Are Changing Sports and Sports Are Changing Women,* Random House, 1991.

Netzer, Dick, and Ellen Parker, *Dancemakers: A Study Report Published by the National Endowment for the Arts,* National Endowment for the Arts, 1993.

P

Paterson, Katherine, *Lyddie,* Dutton, 1991.

Pederson, Jay P., and Kenneth Estell, eds., *African American Almanac,* UXL, 1994.

Post, Elizabeth L., *Emily Post's Etiquette,* 14th ed., Harper & Row, 1984.

R

Ranke-Heineman, Uta, *Eunuchs for the Kingdom of Heaven: Women, Sexuality, and the Catholic Church,* Viking Penguin, 1991.

Rubinstein, Charlotte Streifer, *American Women Artists from Early Indian Times to the Present,* Avon Books, 1982.

Ryan, Bryan, and Nicolas Kanellos, eds., *Hispanic American Almanac,* UXL, 1995.

S

Schmittroth, Linda, ed., *Statistical Record of Women Worldwide,* 2nd ed., Gale Research, 1995.

Schneir, Miriam, ed., *Feminism: The Essential Historical Writings,* Random House, 1973.

Sherr, Lynn, and Jurate Kazickas, *Susan B. Anthony Slept Here: A Guide to American Women's Landmarks,* Times Books, 1994.

Sklar, Kathryn Kish, *Catharine Beecher: A Study in American Domesticity,* W. W. Norton: 1976.

Smith, Robert, *Famous Women: Literature-Based Activities for Thematic Teaching, Grades 4-6,* Creative Teaching Press, 1993.

Stratton, Joanna L., *Pioneer Woman: Voices from the Kansas Frontier,* Simon & Schuster, 1981.

T

Taylor, Debbie, *Women: A World Report,* Oxford University Press, 1985.

Trager, James, *The Women's Chronology: A Year-by-Year Record, from Prehistory to the Present,* Henry Holt and Company, 1994.

Trotta, Liz, *Fighting for Air: In the Trenches with Television News,* Simon & Schuster, 1991.

U

Uglow, Jennifer S., ed., *The International Dictionary of Women's Biography,* Continuum, 1982.

U.S. Bureau of the Census, *Historial Statistics of the United States. Colonial Times to 1970,* U.S. Dept. of Commerce, 1975.

W

Witt, Linda, Karen M. Paget, and Glenna Matthews, eds., *Running As A Woman: Gender and Power in American Politics,* The Free Press, 1994.

Wright, John W., ed., *The 1996 Universal Almanac,* Andrews and McMeel, 1995.

Z

Zientara, Marguerite, *Women, Technology & Power: Ten Stars and the History They Made,* AMACOM, 1987.

9

Women's Movements: Suffrage to ERA

The history of women's rights in the United States is a story that began in 1607, when the first permanent settlers arrived from England. With them the colonists brought English Common Law. Under this law, married women were not only the property of their husbands, they could not own property themselves, could not obtain a divorce even from the cruelest of husbands, and could not sue for custody of their children. Under English Common Law, neither married nor single women could vote in local, state, or federal elections.

Thus, English Common Law is at the heart of the American women's movement. English Common Law also explains in part why it took more than three hundred years for women to earn the right to vote. Many customs and legal practices had to be challenged and overturned before women could take part equally in society.

The women's movement in the United States is marked by three distinct periods: the Women's Rights movement, the Suffrage

Timeline of Events in Women's Movements

1789 The first election is held in the United States, but only white men could vote.

1830s–1860s Women become active in the Abolition movement to free slaves.

1833 The first national temperance convention is held in Philadelphia, Pennsylvania. Many of the temperance workers who attend the conference are women.

1870 The Fifteenth Amendment to the U.S. Constitution is passed, giving black men the right to vote.

1848 The Women's Rights Convention is held in Seneca Falls, New York.

1919 The Nineteenth Amendment to the U.S. Constitution is passed; following ratification the next year, it allows women of all races to vote in elections.

1960s Women become active in the Civil Rights movement that would encourage the passage of laws requiring fair treatment to African Americans.

1963 Betty Friedan publishes the *The Feminine Mystique,* which sparks the Women's Rights movement.

1963 As a result of the report published by the President's Commission on the Status of Women, the Equal Pay Act of 1963 is passed and marks the first time the U.S. government agrees that women should receive the same pay as men.

1966 The National Organization for Women (NOW) is founded to fight sexual discrimination in all aspects of society.

1972 The U.S. Congress passes the Equal Rights Amendment (ERA) by a vote of 84 to 8.

1982 The ERA is defeated when it failed to get the necessary ratification by 36 U.S. states.

(right to vote) movement, and the Equal Rights movement. In the first stage, the Women's Rights movement of the mid-1800s, women began to question the numerous social and legal restrictions placed upon them. Many women were convinced that once they had won the right to vote they could then make other laws that would improve their lives. Following in the late 1800s was the nationwide push for suffrage. Women working for voting rights began to organize. The Equal Rights movement, from the early 1960s to the present, continues to strive for equality in laws, workplace practices, pay, education, and society in general.

The First U.S. Election

In 1789, the United States held its first election and the voters named General George Washington their first president. Unlike elections today, when all citizens can vote, only a very few of the American population could actually cast ballots.

When the U.S. Constitution was written in 1787, it did not recognize two-thirds of the American population as citizens with the right to vote. Black men did not win the right to vote until after the Civil War (1861–65), when the Fifteenth Amendment to the U.S. Constitution was ratified in 1870. Women of all races did not receive the right to vote until the passage of the Nineteenth Amendment in 1919. Native Americans living on reservations were not guaranteed the full rights of citizenship, including the right to vote, until 1968!

The story of how women won their right to vote in local, state, and federal elections is a long one. It has its heroes, its villains, its successes and failures. But like many stories, when one chapter ends, another begins. When women received the right to vote in 1919, the stage was set for several new chapters to be written in the story of women's rights.

American Abolition

Almost as soon as the first slave ships dropped anchor off the North American shore, there were Americans who spoke in favor of abolishing the practice of slavery. These people were called "abolitionists."

The American Abolition movement was based in the northern states, since the economics of the southern states depended on the free labor of slaves on its large plantations. The movement to end slavery really grew during the 1830s when politicians, ministers, and journalists began to talk and write about the cruelties of slavery. Their duty, as they saw it, was to make the American public aware of the moral evils and physical cruelties of slavery.

In 1833, when Great Britain outlawed slavery, becoming the role model for the rest of the Western world, Americans began to debate the issue intensely. This same year, the American Anti-Slavery Society was formed by a group of religious people in Philadelphia, Pennsylvania, called Quakers. The society became the largest and most influential of the abolitionist groups, and although the group had both male and female members, only male members could hold decision-making roles. Many Quaker women interested in abolition who resented not being allowed to make any decisions joined together to form their own branch of the society. They called it the Female Anti-Slavery Society.

As a result, the antislavery message spread, and by 1837 more than one thousand abolitionist societies were operating in America. Of their fifteen thousand members, more than one-half were women.

Angelina Grimké on Women's Rights in Society

Following are excerpts from a letter written by Angelina Grimké, an activist in the Abolition and Women's Rights movements before the Civil War:

"I recognize no rights but human rights—I know nothing of men's rights and women's rights. . . . It is my solemn conviction [belief], that, until this principle of equality is recognized and embodied in practice, the church can do nothing effectual [that works] for the permanent reformation of the world. . . .

"I believe it is a woman's right to have a voice in all the laws and regulations by which she is to be governed, whether in the Church or State; and that the present arrangements of society, on these points, are a violation of human rights, a rank usurpation [taking] of power, a violent seizure and confiscation [withholding] of what is sacredly and unalienably hers."

At first, the women contributed in quiet ways, donating money and attending speeches. As they became more involved, the women became bolder and more outspoken. Some, like Angelina and Sarah Grimké of South Carolina, became public speakers, an unheard of occupation for women at that time. Others, like Lucretia Mott and Elizabeth Cady Stanton, began comparing the status of African American slaves to that of women: both were property of their white male masters.

Mott and Stanton pointed to women's legal status as proof of their enslavement: they still could not vote, own property, win a divorce, or sue for custody of their children. The American Abolition movement was a fertile breeding ground for those who would eventually spearhead the first women's movement. The Abolition movement taught these women about large-scale organization, public speaking, fund-raising, and remaining focused on and committed to an issue.

The tension between the male and female abolitionists peaked in the late 1840s. The male leaders of the American Anti-Slavery Society wanted to focus on freeing the slaves, and agreed that after accomplishing this goal, they would consider the question of women's rights. The men believed that after years of working to bring the American people to a passion against slavery, the public was ready to end slavery, but it was not ready to allow women to vote.

Although the women abolitionists continued to work for the end of slavery, they never again felt completely a part of the antislavery movement. Instead, they felt betrayed by their male colleagues, and vowed to begin their own effort to win voting and legal rights for all women.

The Temperance Movement

Another group that eventually took part in the Women's Rights movement were the members of the Temperance movement. The American Society for the Promotion of Temperance was founded by a group of women in Philadelphia, Pennsylvania, in 1826. It was a time when daily drinking was quite acceptable and beer or liquor was served with lunch and dinner. It was also a time of deep religious belief, however, and public drunkenness did not fit the image of a moral society.

The Temperance movement, committed to ending the sale and consumption of liquor, attracted women supporters from all levels of society. These mothers, wives, and sweethearts were concerned about the effects of alcohol on their male relatives and friends. Their reform effort was called a "grassroots" movement because it grew from the bottom up, starting in the small villages and farm communities of New England and spreading to other areas and finally to the national government. In 1833, the first national temperance convention was held in Philadelphia, and temperance workers from many states attended. Because their movement was well organized, it persuaded the U.S. Congress to prohibit the sale of alcohol to Native Americans in 1834. By 1851, Maine had become the first state to ban liquor entirely, a practice called prohibition.

The Temperance movement really took off when the women pioneers of the West discovered it. The most famous of the temperance workers was Carrie Nation, who stood six feet tall and used an ax handle to smash liquor bottles on her visits to saloons. The drinkers in the saloon found her arguments and her ax handle convincing.

The Temperance movement was important because as women became involved in this public form of protest, they felt freer to question other aspects of society. When they heard of the activist agenda for gaining voting and social rights for women, many of these temperance workers went on to become suffrage and women's rights activists.

Women's Rights

In America, there have always been women who rebelled. For example, Anne Hutchinson challenged the male Puritan rule in Massachusetts during the 1600s, and Abigail Adams challenged the Constitutional Convention to "remember the Ladies" as they formed the new U.S. government in the 1780s. However, it was not until the 1840s that American women began rebelling as a group by speaking, writing, and organizing around what they saw as the inequality of women in America.

Lucretia Mott was one of the founding members of the Suffrage movement.

Mott and Stanton Join Forces

The American Suffrage movement's founding moment may have been the meeting of Lucretia Mott and Elizabeth Cady Stanton in 1840 at the World Anti-Slavery Conference held in London, England. They had time to get acquainted and share their views during the meeting because women were barred from the conference floor. In their conversations, Mott and Stanton began to wonder why they were fighting for the rights of black slaves instead of for their own legal and social rights.

Mott and Stanton began to speak out, comparing the plight of women with that of slaves. At first, their speeches fell on deaf ears and their writings on blind eyes. Soon, however, some women in the American Abolition movement did see the similarities between the slaves' and women's legal status; eventually, Mott and Stanton's ideas were being discussed in mainstream society. Although many observers ridiculed the idea of women's rights, the seed had been sown in the American consciousness, and the subject of women's rights was becoming an acceptable topic of conversation.

One of the events underlying the American women's movement was the increasing number of women who worked outside the home. Although many middle-class women still tended their homes and families, poorer and immigrant women were working in the mills and manufactories or "factories" in the Northeast. Women had no legal rights to make complaints against their employers or about their working conditions, and married women had no right to their pay since it was considered their husbands' property.

Spurred on by this unfairness, women began in 1836 until its enactment in 1848, women to work for the passage of the Married Woman's Property Act in New York State. While the law addressed only property ownership and not the right to wages, the women considered its 1848 passage a victory. The legislation became a model for later, similar action in other states.

Seneca Falls Convention Is Held

Mott and Stanton's campaign for women's rights culminated in the first Women's Rights Convention in Seneca Falls, New York, held on July 19 and 20, 1848. They used the organizational skills they had learned as abolitionists to plan the meeting and attract a crowd of more than three hundred. In her opening address, Stanton linked the rights of women with the basic ideas of the founding fathers who had written the U.S. Declaration of Independence and the U.S. Constitution. As a result, Stanton and her colleagues drafted their own declaration and called it the Declaration of Rights and Sentiments (see box).

The convention mobilized women all over the United States by giving the vague uneasiness they had felt about their political and legal status a voice. Speeches at the convention had called for women to have equal rights in terms of pay, property rights, freedom of speech, education, and other areas of American society. The speakers ended by calling for women's right to vote. American women now had a goal to win the vote and legislate legal rights to property and pay. Then, they believed, social equality would follow.

One of the early leaders of the movement was Lucy B. Stone, an abolitionist lecturer who had attended Oberlin College in Ohio, one of the few colleges open to women and African Americans. Stone was an impassioned and eloquent speaker whose speeches won many over to the cause of women's rights. Sojourn-

Abolitionist Lucy B. Stone

er Truth, another great lecturer on the women's circuit, was especially believable because she was an ex-slave speaking both for abolition and women's rights.

Because most of the women's rights promoters were also wives and mothers, they struggled to balance their private lives with their lives as public speakers, writers, and educators. Some, like Lucy Stone, married men who acted as equal partners in the marriage. Others, like Stanton, were married to men who pursued their own careers and left their wives to manage the children and household on their own.

Women's suffragette Elizabeth Cady Stanton

Stanton-Anthony Partnership

One of Stanton's friends and helpers was Susan B. Anthony. Their two distinct personalities blended into a remarkable partnership that would do much to further the cause of women's rights. On many of her visits to Stanton's home in Seneca Falls, Anthony would tend to the children so that Stanton, the "deep thinker" of the partnership, could devote herself to writing. Anthony's genius was her organizational skill. She not only set up systems for running Stanton's house, but also for running the women's movement. Many of Anthony's organizing techniques were learned in her abolitionist days, but others she developed herself, including the practice of canvassing, or going door-to-door seeking support for a cause, which is still used by political workers today. In 1860, largely due to Stanton and Anthony's efforts, New York State passed a law giving married women the right to keep their own wages and the right to own property.

The women's movement continued to grow stronger and more credible in the eyes of the American public, until the Civil War (1861–65) began. Everything was put on hold while the North and South battled for four long years. During the war, the southern slaves were freed when President Abraham Lincoln signed the Emancipation Proclamation in 1863. Shortly after the war, the Northern slaves were freed with the passage of the Thirteenth Amendment. Thus the former abolitionists found themselves without a cause. As a result, they redefined their mission, and turned their energy and organizational skills to winning the vote for former male slaves.

When the Civil War was over, the women in the Abolition movement again asked the male abolitionists to throw their weight behind the cause of equal rights for women. Once again the male abolitionists declined. They would not dilute their efforts to win the vote for former male slaves. Women were told that it was "the Negroes' hour," and that they should wait.

Women's Movement Splinters

The women, embittered and angry, tried to rally, but they began to argue

What If You Had No Legal Rights?

Imagine living in a society in which you have no voice. You cannot vote for representatives in the government—other people do that. You cannot start a lawsuit and hope to win because everyone on the jury will vote against you. You cannot hold a job without your spouse's approval, and if you are employed, your wages belong to your spouse. Your home and children are not yours—in the eyes of the law, they belong to your spouse even though your spouse may be a negligent parent—and even the clothes you wear belong to your spouse.

If you are an unmarried person, you must work for your keep. You have your choice of low-paying, backbreaking work in a factory or mill, or you can be a low-paid teacher, nurse, or secretary. You cannot complain about the unfairness of the system because the law will not support you, and if you do complain, you will probably lose your job.

You do not exist in the eyes of the law. The law does not hear your voice nor recognize any of your claims. You are helpless and must rely on the good nature and wisdom of those around you.

This helplessness was the status of women in America until changes were made in property laws, and until women won the right to vote.

---

among themselves. Some women, like Stanton and Mott, became even more radical and wanted to advocate not only voting rights but also certain unpopular social rights like divorce. Others, like Stone, believed that the movement should focus on winning the vote for black men first and then tend to women's issues. As a result, the women's movement splintered. Stanton, Mott, and Anthony formed the National Woman's Suffrage Association, while Stone and her followers formed the American Women Suffrage Association.

Stanton's Nationalists continued to advocate voting rights as the door to social equality. She believed that once women had a legal voice, they could challenge the laws and social customs that made them less than equal citizens. However, critics of the group said that the Nationalists either lacked focus or that they focused on too many unpopular issues.

One of the most dynamic speakers drawn to the Nationalists was Victoria Woodhull, the first woman to run for the U.S. presidency, which she did in 1872. Woodhull was a supporter of free love, or love outside of marriage, in a time when marriage was considered sacred. Her presence, however, cost the Nationalists many middle-of-the-road supporters.

Declaration of Rights and Sentiments

Following are excerpts from The Declaration of Rights and Sentiments, delivered by Elizabeth Cady Stanton at the Seneca Falls Convention in 1848:

"We hold these truths to be self-evident: that all men and women are created equal; that they are endowed by their Creator with certain unalienable [legal] rights; that among these are life, liberty, and the pursuit of happiness....

"The history of mankind is a history of repeated injuries and usurpations [assuming someone else's responsibilities] on the part of man toward woman, having in direct object the establishment of an absolute tyranny [power] over her. To prove this, let facts be submitted to a candid [honest] world:

"He has never permitted her to exercise her unalienable right to the elective franchise.

"He has compelled her to submit to laws, in the formation of which she had no voice....

"He has made her, if married, in the eye of the law, civilly dead....

"He has taken from her all right in property, even to the wages she earns.

"He has so framed the laws of divorce, as to what shall be the proper causes, and in the case of separation, to whom the guardianship of the children shall be given, as to be wholly regardless of the happiness of women...

"After depriving her of all rights as a married woman, if single, and the owner of property, he has taxed her to support a government which recognizes her only when her property can be made profitable to it.

"He has monopolized nearly all the profitable employments....

"He has denied her the facilities for obtaining a thorough education, all colleges being closed against her.

"He allows her in Church, as well as State, but a subordinate position.

"He has created a false public sentiment by giving to the world a different code of morals for men and women....

"He has usurped the prerogative of Jehovah himself, claiming as his right to assign for her a sphere of action, when that belongs to her conscience and to her God.

"He has endeavored, in every way that he could, to destroy her confidence in her own powers, to lessen her self-respect, and to make her willing to lead a dependent and abject life."

(Excerpted in part from *A History of Women in America* by Carol Hymowitz and Michaele Weissman, New York: Bantam Books, 1978.)

Stone's Americans believed they were much more likely to win the vote for women if they made this their only cause. They focused their energy on establishing local and state groups that would collect signatures on petitions and lobby politicians for the right to vote. Some critics, however, said that by just concentrating on the women's vote, Stone and her followers ignored too many of the social injustices suffered by poor and single women. All told, the split between the feminist groups lasted more than twenty years.

The Nineteenth Amendment

In 1878, Senator Arlen A. Sargent of California introduced the Nineteenth Amendment to the U.S. Constitution. This was the first women's suffrage amendment, and it was finally passed, unedited, more than four decades later. The amendment, which was actually written by Susan B. Anthony, reads:

> The right of citizens of the United States to vote shall not be denied or abridged by the United States or any State on account of sex. Congress shall have the power, by appropriate legislation, to enforce the provisions of this article.

The Nineteenth amendment, which came to be known as the Susan B. Anthony Amendment, was considered by Congress and rejected every year between 1878 and 1918. Before it was finally passed in 1919, another nationwide women's movement had to take place.

Susan B. Anthony is one of the most famous suffragettes.

Suffrage

In 1890, the two wings of the U.S. women's movement decided it was time to set aside their differences and unite to pass the Anthony Amendment. They formed a new group, called the National American Woman Suffrage Association (NAWSA). Stanton was elected its first president, and with its formation the Suffrage movement was launched.

It was an excellent time to band together. Women had made great strides since the end of the Civil War in 1865. Many attended high school and college,

The First Woman Pictured on U.S. Money

In 1979 and 1980, the U.S. government minted a new one-dollar coin for circulation. For the first time in U.S. history, a general circulation coin carried the picture of a woman (that is, a real woman who had actually lived, not the stylized Liberty figureheads pictured on some coins). The woman who made history—seventy-three years after her death—was Susan B. Anthony, author of the Nineteenth Amendment, which gave American women the right to vote. The coin portrayed Anthony in profile, her hair drawn back into a bun and her plain dress buttoned to the throat.

Being pictured on currency is an honor usually given only to U.S. presidents. The exceptions, up until 1979, were Alexander Hamilton ($10 bill), Benjamin Franklin ($100 bill), and Salmon P. Chase ($10,000 bill). Hamilton was a vice president and the founder of the U.S. Treasury Department. Franklin was an ambassador and one of the framers of the U.S. Constitution. Chase was a chief justice of the U.S. Supreme Court and a secretary of the treasury.

Anthony, who never held elective office, was honored for her contributions to women's rights.

---

so educated women were becoming the norm. The social interests of women were coordinated under the General Federation of Women's Clubs, an umbrella organization of some two hundred clubs and twenty thousand female members. These clubs met women's social needs and gave their organizational abilities a focus—social reform. The social reform centered around prisons, education, the poor, and politics. Women were also gaining visibility and power through the Temperance movement. Through these gains, women seemed to have won the right to participate socially in society, but they were still ridiculed when they demanded the right to participate politically.

New Leaders Emerge

By the end of the nineteenth century, Anthony, Stanton, and Stone were the old guard. Their approach focused on a broad federal amendment that would grant the right to vote nationally. But newer leaders of the Women's Rights movement were emerging, and they favored a state-by-state approach to winning suffrage. One of these new leaders was Carrie Chapman Catt. Catt and her contemporaries favored campaigning in a particular state until suffrage was won, and then moving their campaign to another state. Under this approach, Colorado was the first state to grant women universal suffrage (the ability to vote without restriction) in 1893. The Territory of Wyoming had granted women suffrage in 1869 without the prompting of the NAWSA.

Of course, this state-by-state approach caused some confusion. In some U.S. states, women could and did vote, while in others they had yet to win the right to vote. The overall effect was that until all women could vote, they could not mobilize into one large voting bloc in order to pass legislation and elect representatives favorable to women's rights.

Like the leadership, the membership of women's groups was changing. New voices were being heard, ones that embraced socialism, pacifism (nonviolence), and labor unionism. These new voices broadened the appeal of the Suffrage movement to include those outside the mainstream: the poor and immigrant workers who were underpaid and working in unsafe conditions, and religious groups that deplored violence.

About midway through its state-by-state campaign, in states that had not yet granted women the right to vote, NAWSA president Carrie Chapman Catt decided that the process was too slow and that it needed to be changed. With the help of other NAWSA leaders, she developed a strategy to win passage of the Anthony Amendment, giving herself six years to succeed.

In states where women could already vote, Catt counted on their ability to elect representatives sympathetic to women's suffrage. In other states, she organized local women's groups that would ring doorbells, circulate petitions, hold ral-

Carrie Chapman Catt became one of the new leaders in the Suffrage movement.

lies, give speeches, protest outside of male political meetings, and write and distribute leaflets describing the advantages of giving women the vote.

As the years went by and suffrage was granted very slowly, one state at a time, the women used stronger measures to bring attention to their cause. In 1915, Alice Paul, one of the most famous leaders of the movement, thought of using automobiles to bring the suffrage message to Americans. With the help of suffragists in every state, Paul organized a motorcade that traveled from San Francisco, California, to Washington, D.C. With the motorcade came a petition urging Con-

Women display the Mile of Signatures in front of the League of Women Voters headquarters in Washington, D.C.

gress and the president to give women the right to vote. This petition measured eighteen thousand feet long and carried the names of five-hundred thousand Americans.

When publicity stunts like the motorcade failed to win the vote, women stepped up their campaign in Washington, D.C. They began to picket the White House, holding up signs that asked, "Mr.

President, How Long Must Women Wait for Liberty?" When arrested for protesting and other acts of civil disobedience, the women went on hunger strikes.

Alice Paul fasted for twenty-two days after being arrested and imprisoned in a Virginian workhouse. She and others considered themselves political prisoners, bullied and confined by a system in which they had no voice. The authorities responded by making Paul undergo a mental examination and then force feeding her. Paul's courage and dedication inspired many other suffragettes to confront the established system.

All this was going on while World War I (1914–18) raged. When the war began, most Americans had considered it a European conflict. But in 1916, the German navy sank a passenger ship called the *Lusitania,* which carried 128 Americans. Suddenly the German threat seemed much closer to home, and Americans began to believe that they had to join the war. "Fight for democracy" became the rallying cry, as the United States officially entered the war in 1917.

Catt and Paul pointed out that it was ironic that American soldiers were being sent to Europe to fight for democracy while democratic rights were being denied to female citizens at home. After the war, the suffragettes used the work that women had done for the war effort as an argument for giving them voting rights. These women had worked as Red Cross volunteers, navy secretaries, army nurses, delivery van drivers, and farmhands. Catt believed that women had done their bit to

Women's Vote: Adoption by States*

Year	State
1869	Wyoming (territory)
1890	Wyoming (state)
1893	Colorado
1896	Utah
	Idaho
1910	Washington
1911	California
1912	Arizona
	Kansas
	Oregon
1913	Alaska (territory)
1914	Montana
	Nevada
1917	New York
1918	Michigan
	Oklahoma
	South Dakota

*Some states had given women selected voting rights before 1869. This table lists states that passed general suffrage for women, where no conditions were applied.

make the world safe for democracy and that they had earned the full rights of citizenship. Enough men in Washington, D.C., agreed, and in 1919 Congress voted for the Anthony Amendment. Fittingly, the amendment was introduced by Jeannette Rankin, a newly elected representative from Montana and the first woman to serve in the U.S. Congress.

Window on the World: England

The struggle of English women to win the vote parallels that of American women. The English women's struggle lasted from about 1830 to 1930, with the starting point being the passage of the Great Reform Act of 1832. This act gave the vote to more English men (previously only Englishmen who owned a certain amount of property could vote), but it did nothing for women. So women began to organize to win their own rights.

As in America, English women were active in social causes such as the anti-slavery movement and social reforms that benefited poor people. Like their American sisters, they were outraged at being excluded from the decision-making processes by their male colleagues. In response, Anne Knight (1786–1862) and others formed the Female Political Association. Their goal was women's suffrage.

Along the way to winning voting rights, these female activists helped open English colleges to women, gained property rights for married women, and opened more professions to single women. As time passed, the English suffragettes grew impatient. They employed such tactics as public demonstrations and protests. Like their American counterparts, they were arrested and force fed when they went on hunger strikes. But the English struggle was more violent and destructive than the American one. English suffragettes and their supporters broke windows, damaged mail boxes, and cut telegraph wires. Their destructiveness and the government's response came to a head in 1913 and 1914, when more than one thousand suffragettes went to prison for their actions.

World War I (1914–18) plunged England into war, and its female citizens into new jobs such as nursing and factory and clerical work. At the war's end, the English prime minister honored these women, many of whom had been suffragettes, by saying, "There were thousands of such women, but a year ago we did not know it." After the war, in 1920, the British Parliament passed the woman's voting act.

After Congress passed it, the amendment started its ratification process. Finally, on August 26, 1920, the Nineteenth Amendment was ratified by the necessary thirty-six states and became part of the U.S. Constitution.

America Enters the Modern Era

In the years between 1920 and 1960, the United States fought in two wars (World War II from 1939 to 1945 and the

League of Women Voters

The League of Women Voters was formed in 1919 to educate Americans about the election process. The league does not endorse candidates for office. Instead, it collects and publishes information about all the candidates, including his or her background and answers to several questions of concern to voters. This helps voters decide which candidate is most likely to best serve in the public interest.

The League of Women Voters is the outgrowth of the National American Woman Suffrage Association, which had worked to win the vote for women between 1880 and 1920. Today the league helps to arrange and host presidential debates before televised audiences. The organization still operates much as it did 75 years ago, with state and local chapters and a national headquarters. It has about 150,000 dues-paying members nationwide.

Korean War from 1950 to 1953). Television was born and so was the space age. Suburbs grew up, and so did the automotive industry. Civil rights became an issue as African Americans tried to exercise their political rights in the Deep South. The "Red Scare" and the "cold war" blossomed as fear of a communist takeover of the U.S. government led to extreme fear and public trials of thousands of American citizens. It was a time of great social, industrial, and economic change.

These four decades were also a time of great change for women. Many voted for the first time, and many more attended college and began careers as secretaries, teachers, nurses, and librarians. Now that their right to vote was secure, the NAWSA organization evolved into the League of Women Voters (see box), allowing women to remain socially and politically active.

During World War II, some women joined the military serving as nurses, drivers, and administrators. Several million American women also worked in factories, so the men could go off to fight. After working in the factories, many women discovered that they liked having a job and a career. Others returned to the socially accepted occupations of motherhood and family life, now taking place in the newly developing suburbs.

Civil Rights Movement

Between 1920 and 1960, a movement had grown up to win civil rights for black Americans. While the law said that blacks could vote, many in the South were denied voting rights. Southern states and communities had instituted poll taxes (a fee charged to people who wanted to vote) and other conditions that prevent-

Window on the World: European Pacifism

About the middle of the 1800s, a new movement began to influence public thought in many European countries. The movement was called "pacifism." Pacifists were people who believed that war was morally wrong, no matter what the reason for fighting. These people refused to serve in their country's military or to support the war effort in any way.

Pacifism grew out of people's dismay with how European political affairs were being conducted in the 1800s. The growth of nationalism (the belief in the superiority of one's own country) created many disputes over territory. The Crimean War (1853–56) was an example of a dispute over territory. Both Russia and Turkey (and its ally, England) fought for control of the Crimean peninsula, a strip of land that extends into the Black Sea. Some of these small wars would eventually evolve into larger conflicts, which was the case in World War I (1914–18). What started out as a conflict between Serbia and Austria spread into a war that enveloped Europe.

In the 1800s, women did not serve as soldiers, but they were beginning to serve as nurses and saw much of the horror of battle. At home, they supported the war effort by working in factories and taking clerical jobs. As they saw and learned more of the nature of war, they objected to it more and more strongly.

In 1854, Frederika Bremer appealed to European women to form a "peace league." Bremer, a Swedish woman working for equal rights at home, was responding to the Crimean War. Austrian suffragist Bertha von Suttner wrote a book in 1889 called *Lay Down Your Arms!* About the same time, Alfred Nobel, the Swedish physicist, established the Nobel Peace Prize. Nobel had invented dynamite for use in clearing mines. But once he saw how dynamite was being used as a war weapon, he pledged his huge fortune to those dedicated to peace.

Suffragettes in England, Hungary, Germany, France, and the Netherlands all spoke out for pacifism. Some historians credit these early women pacifists with sowing the seeds that would grow into the League of Nations and the United Nations (UN). Both organizations were founded after world wars, and both were dedicated to international peacekeeping.

ed many African Americans from voting. At the same time, in many American communities, both North and South, blacks were discriminated against by the "separate but equal," or the Jim Crow, laws. They were made to sit separately from whites at public places and were educated in separate schools.

In 1948, President Harry S Truman integrated the U.S. military, and for the first time black and white Americans served in the same fighting units. School desegregation was occurring about this time, as blacks and liberal whites challenged the "separate but equal" education that southern states claimed to give black children. And as they were in the days of abolition, women throughout the United States were actively involved in every phase of the Civil Rights movement.

These women used the tools developed during the Suffrage movement to further their new cause. They passed petitions to collect signatures of those in favor of doing away with poll taxes. They knocked on doors to pass out literature and educate white and black voters alike. They attended rallies and marched in the streets with banners. They spoke to crowds and recruited others like themselves to support the cause.

In the end, the Civil Rights Act of 1964 was passed during the administration of President Lyndon B. Johnson. Much of the credit goes to the lobbying efforts of such famous black leaders as Martin Luther King Jr. and A. Philip Randolph. But some of the praise must go to the women who worked for the cause of equal civil rights for all Americans.

The Vietnam Era

The 1960s was a special time in the United States in other ways, too. The country had recovered from World War II dur-

Betty Friedan's book sparked the beginning of the feminist movement in the United States.

ing the 1950s. It had confronted the danger of communism and survived. Industry was back on course and the country was prosperous. But the settled, satisfied feeling of the 1950s gave way to a period of great social dispute during the 1960s. America's involvement in the Vietnam War did much to make U.S. citizens question the wisdom of military involvement in foreign conflicts. Students on college campuses in particular were outspoken against America's role in Vietnam. Among the other questions addressed were the social rights of American subgroups such as blacks and women (see box).

Feminism and Equal Rights

During the 1960s, women made up more than one-half of the U.S. population. However, they were still not afforded the same rights as white males. As a result, women began to respond to a concept called feminism that had emerged in the United States and Europe during World War II. Feminism is a belief that women are equal to men in terms of intellect and ability and that women's accomplishments should be equally praised in history and society.

At first feminism was a belief shared by a few intellectuals on college campuses and in the publishing industry and the arts. Then, in February 1963, a disturbing book called *The Feminine Mystique* was published. The book, written by Betty Friedan, presented the findings of a study Friedan had conducted with women all over the United States. She found that many of the women she questioned felt sad and unfulfilled despite having a seemingly happy marriage and home life. Friedan's subjects said that they loved their husbands and their children, but that they also longed for an identity of their own, separate from being someone's wife or mother.

Friedan's book touched a nerve. She had stated what many women were asking themselves: why are our jobs, our lives, and our education so different from those of the men around us? Like the women who worked for the Abolition movement, women involved in the Civil Rights movement began to compare the "separate but equal" status of blacks with their own status in society.

President's Commission on the Status of Women

The same year *The Feminine Mystique* was published, the President's Commission on the Status of Women published its report titled *American Women.* The report, which was ordered by President John F. Kennedy in 1962 and funded by the U.S. government, described women's working life. It argued for an end to sex discrimination in jobs, for the availability of quality child care, and for equal pay. In a way, the commission's report said officially what Friedan had said unofficially: women who want a career belong in the workplace, and it is society's duty to help them get there.

The Kennedy Administration saw the passage of the Equal Pay Act of 1963, marking the first time the U.S. government had asserted that women should have the same working conditions as men. The early 1960s also saw a new grassroots movement in which women across the country began to meet in small groups for the purpose of "consciousness raising." In these informal groups, women talked about their lives and their concerns, and slowly brought to consciousness their unhappiness over what they saw as their unequal social status.

Women Question Their Role

Many women went a step further by using their small consciousness-raising groups as a step toward political change. Some felt that mainstream society could not be changed fast enough to satisfy them. As a result, these women started their own institutions such as free medical clinics that focused on women's health issues and free legal clinics where women could receive help in challenging laws that restricted access to jobs, education, and divorce.

One aspect of the women's movement during the 1960s and 1970s was a strong questioning of the social roles women were taught to play in society. In general, women believed they were conditioned to be passive, to allow men to make decisions and take the lead in all aspects of public life. Women also believed that society encouraged them to be dependent upon men by restricting the better-paying jobs to males. One response to this dissatisfaction with the traditional "feminine" role was the growth of assertiveness training. The training often took place in the consciousness-raising groups, but later moved to community college campuses as it gained credibility. Assertiveness training taught women how to speak out for themselves and how to be persistent and effective in claiming what they saw as their fair rights.

NOW Establishes a "Feminist Agenda"

In addition to the individual questioning going on in many women's minds, there was also a national consciousness being raised. The Kennedy Administration's report on the unequal employment status of women sparked much indignation, or anger. In 1966, the National Organization for Women (NOW) was formed.

Bra-burning symbolizes women's liberation.

NOW's purpose was to fight sexual discrimination wherever it was found.

Two years later, the Women's Equity Action League was founded to make sure America's educational system was treating women fairly by seeing that female students received equal opportunities in the classroom and that higher education opportunities were open to them. In 1971, the National Women's Political Caucus was established to promote female candidates for local, state, and national offices. While hundreds of thousands of American women embraced feminism to some degree, many others disagreed with it (see box).

A "feminist agenda" resulted from all of the women's questioning and challenging. This agenda, which changed and grew over the next twenty years, included:

- the right of women to obtain, hold, and be promoted in any and all jobs

- the right of women to equal educational opportunities

- the right of women to decide if and when to have a family, and to be able to limit the number of children born

- the right of women to be safe on public streets and in their homes

- the right of women to be treated as valuable members of society

While these rights might seem like common sense today, they were still somewhat shocking in the 1960s. For instance, many men still objected to women working, and really objected to women being promoted to positions above them. Women were not considered as equal candidates for roles as police officers, soldiers, fire fighters, doctors, ministers, or politicians, and they were steered into traditional feminine careers during high school and college. Birth control was still not discussed openly during the 1960s, and abortion was illegal. Women who were the victims of rape were often treated by the courts as if they had "asked for it," and the police generally ignored women's complaints about abusive husbands.

Equal Rights Amendment

Once the agenda became clear, it became a rallying point for women across the United States. The work of the local and national women's groups culminated in the passage of the Equal Rights Amendment (ERA) in 1972. While Congress passed the amendment by a vote of 84 to 8, its ratification by the necessary 36 U.S. states remained in question for many years because antifeminist groups fought to defeat it. The amendment that aroused such heated controversy read:

> Equality of rights under the law shall not be denied or abridged by the United States or any state on account of sex.

For the next ten years, feminist and women's groups would work at the state level for passage of the ERA. Among the more famous women working for its passage were Bella Abzug, a U.S. representative and founder of Women's Equality Day, a celebration of the Nineteenth

Antifeminist Backlash

In 1979, an organization called Concerned Women for America was founded. Its purpose was to protect, preserve, and promote traditional American values. In particular it stressed the value of the traditional roles of women as wife, mother, and homemaker.

Other women found a voice in the various religious-affiliated organizations that responded to what they perceived as the threat of feminism to traditional American life. The first large antifeminist organization was the National Right to Life Committee, formed in 1970 by the Catholic Church. Its goal was to stop the liberalization, or spread, of abortion laws. Another organization was the Moral Majority, founded in 1979 by the Religious Roundtable. A third, Pro-Life Action League, was founded by a former Catholic seminarian (a man studying to become a priest). The American Life Lobby was also founded to oppose abortion and the use of birth control.

Perhaps the most famous opponent of feminism is Phyllis Schlafly. Even before her involvement in women's issues, Schlafly had a busy public life supporting a number of conservative causes and political candidates. She had worked as a researcher for Senator Joe McCarthy, cofounded the Cardinal Mindsezenty Foundation to stop communism, been an active member of the John Birch Society (an anticommunist group), and supported Barry Goldwater's Republican run for the presidency in 1964. In 1972, Schlafly openly opposed the Equal Rights Amendment (ERA), and formed an organization to stop its ratification. She called her group "Stop ERA." Schlafly fought against the ERA because she believed it would require women to perform combat duty in the armed forces. She also feared women would lose their right to receive financial support form their husbands if the ERA passed.

People who opposed the feminist agenda also took other steps to preserve American society as they knew it. They supported certain candidates for office, they opposed the use of textbooks with a feminist message, and they challenged the courts in cases involving divorce, abortion, and child custody.

Amendment's ratification; Shirley Chisholm, a U.S. representative and the first black woman to run for president; Betty Friedan, author of *The Feminine Mystique* and former NOW president; Wilma Scott Heide, president of NOW from 1971 to 1973; and Gloria Steinem, publisher of *Ms.* magazine, the first large-circulation publication about women's issues.

ERA leaders from left: Steinem, Abzug, Chisholm, and Friedan holding a press conference.

The ERA was ultimately defeated in 1982, when it failed by three states to win ratification in the ten-year deadline allotted by Congress (this was the first U.S. amendment subjected to a deadline). While the ERA was dead, at least for a time, it had served as a way of energizing the issue of women's rights. During its ten-year bid for ratification, the United States had seen its first female governor of the New York Stock Exchange, Dr. Juanita Kreps, in 1972; the first female navy pilots (they entered training in 1973); the first female counselor to a U.S. president, Anne Armstrong, in 1973; and the first female chaplain to the U.S. Air Force,

Lorraine K. Potter, also appointed in 1973. The country also saw the first female house reporter for United Press International (UPI), a national news service, Helen Thomas, appointed in 1974; the first woman film producer to win an Oscar, Julia Phillips in 1974 for *The Sting;* the first female Episcopal priest, Jacqueline Means, ordained in 1977; and the first female Indianapolis 500 (car race) winner, Janet Guthrie, in 1977. Other firsts include the first ten female NASA candidates, selected in 1977; the establishment of the National Women's Hall of Fame in Seneca Falls, New York, in 1979; the first women to be awarded a television station license in 1980; the Explorers Club, a previously all-male club, admitting its first two female members, NASA astronaut Kathryn Sullivan and oceanographer Sylvia Earle in 1981; and the first female U.S. Supreme Court judge, Sandra Day O'Connor, appointed in 1981.

An Expanded "Feminist Agenda"

In the years since the ERA failed to gain ratification, the women's movement has branched out to fight against pornography, discrimination in credit and finance (women could be denied credit cards and home mortgages), and sexual harassment at work and school. They have also fought for family leave for new fathers, flexible working hours, medical benefits for families, child care, battered women's shelters, and stalking laws. (Stalking is an obsessive display of unwanted attention directed toward a particular person.) NOW and other women's groups have remained active, but many have joined the political mainstream by forming political action committees (PACs). PACs are lobbying groups whose job it is to convince legislators to consider certain laws and amendments.

Although the women's movement has achieved a great deal since the 1840s, there is still much work to be done. Inequality between men and women is still evident in jobs, finances, and other aspects of American life. Until women achieve full equality with men, the women's movement will continue to be a major part of American society.

10

Politics: The Voter and Officeholder

Politics are "arrangements whereby one group of persons is controlled by another."

*—Feminist writer
Kate Millett*

The American political system includes the formal institutions of government—Congress (the House of Representatives and the Senate), the Supreme Court, and the various departments that make up the Executive Branch of our government (such as the Federal Bureau of Investigation and the Environmental Protection Agency). The course of American politics is affected by the way groups of citizens (often called interest groups) compete for influence over those formal institutions.

American women were essentially denied a role in the country's politics until the twentieth century. Women were not welcomed in the government arenas where decisions affecting their lives were made. Nor were they encouraged to make their views known. They were not even allowed to vote until 1920.

The situation has finally begun to change, though. By the late twentieth century, women had made many strides in elected and appointed positions. In the 1992 elections, women were elected in record numbers to serve in both the state legislatures and in the U.S. Senate and House of Representatives.

Timeline: American Women in Politics

1756 Mrs. Josiah Taft of Uxbridge, Massachusetts, casts the first recorded vote by an American woman. She is granted this privilege of voting for a tax increase because her husband is dead and her son is a minor.

1840 Dorothea Dix champions government support for the care of the mentally ill. She is the first woman lobbyist at the national level.

1872 Victoria C. Woodhull is nominated to run for the U.S. presidency by the National Equal Rights Party.

1916 Jeannette Rankin of Montana is the first woman elected to the U.S. Congress.

1919 The League of Women Voters is founded.

1919 The Nineteenth Amendment to the Constitution is passed by Congress. After nearly one hundred years of struggle, women are granted the right to vote. The amendment is ratified in 1920.

1920 Charlotte Woodward, age 93, votes in the 1920 election. She is the only woman who attended the 1848 Seneca Falls Convention to live long enough to cast a vote.

1922 Rebecca L. Felton is the first woman to serve in the U.S. Senate. Sworn in to fill a vacancy, she serves for one day before giving up her seat to a newly elected man.

1925 Nellie Tayloe Ross of Wyoming replaces her dead husband and serves as the nation's first woman governor.

When the 103rd Congress began its term in January 1993, women made up about 10 percent of the voting members. For the first time in history, 47 women served in the House of Representatives (24 newly elected), and 7 women served in the Senate (4 newly elected; the number of women senators rose to 8 in 1995). Women also made gains at the state level of government, where they made up 22 percent of legislators in 1993. How women went from securing the vote to achieving some voice in national decision making—however small it still may be—is an interesting story.

American Women Voters

The passage of the Nineteenth Amendment to the Constitution in 1919, which finally granted American women the right the vote, caused many politicians to fear that women would use their right to vote against elected officials who did not support legislation favorable to women. Congressmen hurried to show their support for so-called "women's issues," such as health and education. In 1921 Congress passed the Sheppard-Towner Act which became the first health care act that provided federal govern-

1926 Bertha Landes is elected mayor of Seattle, Washington, the first time a woman is elected mayor of a major city. Concha Ortiz y Pino de Kleven is elected to the New Mexico state legislature, the first Latina to serve at that level of government.

1932 Frances Perkins becomes the first woman cabinet officer when President Franklin Roosevelt appoints her secretary of labor.

1935 Mary McLeod Bethune is appointed by Roosevelt to his cabinet as a consultant.

1936 Eleanor Roosevelt succeeds in transforming the role of first lady from a decorative to an activist position.

1945 Eleanor Roosevelt is the only woman appointed to the U.S. delegation to the newly formed United Nations. She is a prime advocate for the United Nations Declaration of Human Rights.

1950 U.S. Senator Margaret Chase Smith delivers her speech titled "A Declaration of Conscience."

1953 Former U.S. representative from Connecticut (1943–47) and playwright Clare Boothe Luce is one of the first women to represent the United States in a major diplomatic post when she is appointed U.S. ambassador to Italy.

---

ment funds for maternal (mother) and infant health care.

While Congress was passing the legislation it thought women wanted, the women's groups that had fought so hard for the right to vote began arguing among themselves and eventually split up. One group supported legislation to protect women workers from working too many hours. Another group argued that women were the same as men and didn't need special protection. That group fought for passage of a newly written piece of legislation—the Equal Rights Amendment (ERA). It was introduced in 1923.

Meanwhile, several election cycles passed, and the expected "women's vote" didn't materialize. For two decades after the passage of the Nineteenth Amendment, women did not vote in large groups for any particular candidate or agenda. Congressmen took note of the squabbling among the women's groups and the small numbers of women voters. As a result, Congress dropped its support for women's issues. The Sheppard-Towner Act was allowed to expire. For congressional representatives, it was back to business as usual, until World War II (1939–45) changed American politics forever.

Timeline: American Women in Politics

1964 Civil rights activist Fannie Lou Hamer founds the Mississippi Freedom Democratic Party and leads its members to the Democratic National Convention in Atlantic City, New Jersey. In front of a national television audience, they protest the seating of an all-white Mississippi delegation to the convention.

1964 U.S. Senator Margaret Chase Smith is the first American woman ever considered a serious potential presidential candidate after she receives the second highest number of votes at the electoral convention.

1965 Patsy Takemoto Mink is the first Asian American woman elected to the House of Representatives.

1968 Shirley Chisholm becomes the first black congresswoman.

1971 The National Women's Political Caucus is founded.

1972 Shirley Chisholm runs for president.

1972 Congress passes the Equal Rights Amendment (ERA) after intensive lobbying by feminists. It eventually fails to be ratified.

1972 Frances Jean Miles Westwood is elected chair of the Democratic National Committee, becoming the first woman chair of a major political party.

1974 Mary Louise Smith is elected chair of the Republican National Committee.

1974 Ella Grasso of Connecticut is the first woman to be elected governor in her own right (she did not succeed her husband).

1977 Patricia Harris is the first black woman to serve in a cabinet office when she is

The Post-War Years

During and after the war, American women began to enter the labor force in large numbers. By the 1960s they had begun to take a greater interest in politics. Both working women and homemakers began to see that more attention needed to be paid to issues like child care, family leave, fair treatment in the workplace, and equal access to education and financial credit. As the economy changed and more and more women had to work, it became apparent that women needed access to birth control so that they would not suffer economic disaster due to unplanned pregnancies. Reproductive rights, an issue not often discussed in Congress, came out in the open for debate, and women's issues were on the table for full discussion. Just as important, the few women seeking public office would now be able to speak out in favor of women's issues in their campaigns without appearing self-centered.

appointed secretary of Housing and Urban Development by President Jimmy Carter.

1982 Loretta Glickman is elected mayor of Pasadena, California, the first black woman to serve as mayor of a city with a population of more than one hundred thousand.

1984 Democrat Geraldine Ferraro is the first woman in American history to run as a vice-presidential candidate for a major political party.

1985 Wilma Mankiller becomes the first female Principal Chief of the Cherokee (Native American) Nation.

1987 Representative Pat Schroeder is the second woman in American history to

be seriously considered a potential presidential candidate.

1989 Ileana Ros-Lehtinen of Florida is the first Cuban American elected to Congress.

1992 Barbara Boxer and Dianne Feinstein are elected U.S. senators from California. For the first time in U.S. history, a state is represented by two female senators at the same time. Carol Moseley-Braun is the first African American woman elected to the U.S. Senate. Nydia Velazquez of New York is the first Puerto Rican elected to the House of Representatives.

1993 Lucille Roybal-Allard of California is the first Mexican American woman elected to the House of Representatives.

There are few studies of women's voting behavior before 1968. In fact, few really cared how women voted. What studies had been done showed that when married women did vote, they tended to vote the same as their husbands.

By the late 1960s, as the woman's movement heated up, this situation was changing. Women activists were proclaiming a new era for women. By 1968, women were voting at about the same rate as men for the first time. And many

believed that women were about to exercise their right to vote to achieve their own ends. Indeed, the beginning of the 1980s signalled that a definite gender gap in women's voting behavior had entered the national consciousness, and by 1984 more women than men were voting in national elections.

The Gender Gap

The differences between the ways in which men and women vote are referred

Vice-presidential candidate Geraldine Ferraro

The gender gap took on a life of its own as pollsters and consultants joined the search for differences in voting behavior and policy preferences between the sexes . . . . The data seemed solid enough . . . to keep the image of an emerging women's bloc [group united for a common action] before the public's eyes in the years leading up to the next [1984] presidential election.

The gender gap in voting patterns persuaded the Democratic Party to risk running a woman vice-presidential candidate, Geraldine Ferraro, in the 1984 race for the presidency. However, the Republican Party was also aware of differences in women's voting behavior, and took pains to appeal to women to vote for Ronald Reagan, who eventually did win. In 1988, Republican George Bush won 51 percent of women's votes after emphasizing he was "a family man."

The idea of women, who make up 53 percent of voters, banding together to create a unified voting bloc excites some people and makes others nervous because women are now in a position to determine the outcome of elections. This was shown in the 1992 presidential election, in which women voters preferred Democratic candidate Bill Clinton (who won) to either Republican George Bush or Independent Ross Perot.

Democrat or Republican: Voting on the Issues

Prior to the 1970s, most women were not interested in supporting one political party over another. This made women nonpartisan. Today, however, it is known that women are somewhat more

to as the gender gap. The gender gap has been observed in every election since 1980, when more women than men voted for Democrat Jimmy Carter. Although Carter lost to Ronald Reagan, women activists reasoned that if women did vote differently from men, and if these activists could provide evidence of that difference to the media, legislators seeking women's votes might be more willing to take up women's issues. Members of the National Organization for Women (NOW) hurried to provide the media with evidence of the gender gap. According to the authors of *Running As a Woman:*

likely than men to vote for a Democrat than a Republican. One explanation given for this is that the Democratic Party is regarded as the party of big government. Big government is responsible for programs such as welfare, food stamps, and public assistance. Women are more likely than men to benefit from these programs because they are paid less than men and are often single parents. Women continue to be divided over issues such as abortion and the Equal Rights Amendment (ERA). In 1980 the Republican Party overturned its forty-year-old support of abortion rights and the ERA. As a result, women who support abortion rights and/or the ERA might favor a Democratic candidate.

Women tend to vote against military involvement and capital punishment, and for gun control. Women as a group also tend to vote to control industries like prostitution, gambling, and drug dealing.

Although voters are coming to believe that there are some issues women candidates are better able to address because of their life experiences, women will not vote for a woman just because of her sex. According to Ann Richards, former governor of Texas: "[Women] are not stupid. They vote for the candidate they think is going to give them the best government."

Political Organizations

Throughout the 1800s, before women succeeded in getting the right to vote, they had built up numerous orga-

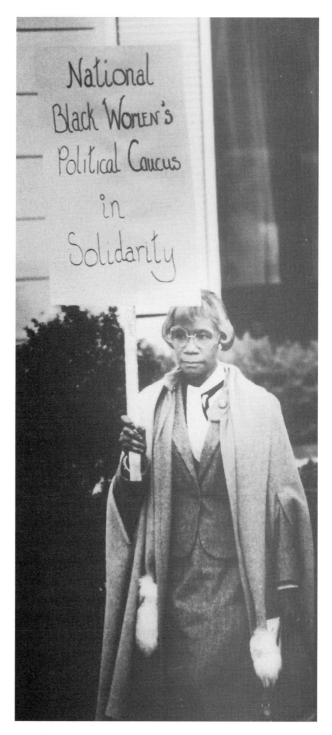

Former U.S. Representative Shirley Chisholm

Window on the World:
Golda Meir, Prime Minister of Israel

Golda Meir was born Golda Mabovitz in Kiev, Ukraine, in 1898. At the age of eight she immigrated to the United States with her family. She grew up in Milwaukee, Wisconsin, and married Morris Meyerson (whose last name she changed to Meir in 1956) in 1917. The following year the couple, who were Jewish, moved to Palestine in the Middle East. The British, who controlled Palestine, were working toward establishing a national homeland for the Jewish people there. When the couple arrived in Palestine, they joined a farming village. In 1948, following World War II, Palestine was divided into three states, one of which became the Jewish nation of Israel.

Meir served as minister of labor in the newly formed nation from 1949 to 1956. In 1969 she became prime minister, a position she held until 1974. Israeli president David Ben-Gurion called her "the ablest man in my cabinet." When she died in 1978 at the age of eighty, Shimon Peres, the Chairman of Meir's Labor Party, called her a "stalwart lioness . . . one of the greatest women in Jewish and world history."

In a conversation with journalist Oriana Fallaci in 1972, while she was still prime minister, and was later published in *Interview With History,* Meir reflected back on her career as a pioneer woman in Israeli politics. She stated that she had "never suffered on account of men because I was a

nizations based on their interest in social welfare, health, and education. By the time suffrage was granted in 1919, women were experts at organizing, and their organizations had given them training in political leadership.

League of Women Voters

Politically inclined women formed the League of Women Voters in 1919. It was devoted to educating the voting public—both men and women—about the candidates and issues. It also lobbied for legislation that would benefit everyone,

not just women. In 1922 the governor of New York called the members of the league "a menace to our free institutions and to representative government." It was not until the 1970s that the league finally took up issues having to do with women's rights, and many women who were active in the organization went on to run for public office.

National Women's Political Caucus

By 1970, thousands of women had become involved in politics. They sat at typewriters, passed out campaign litera-

woman. Men have never given me special treatment but neither have they put obstacles in my way. Of course I've been lucky, of course not all women have had the same experience. . . . To be successful, a woman has to be much more capable than a man. Whether she dedicates herself to a profession or dedicates herself to politics." Meir continued by saying, "There aren't many women in our parliament, something that bothers me a lot. And these few women, let me assure you, are by no means less capable than men. . . . So it's ridiculous that toward women there still exist so many reservations, so many injustices, that when a list is being drawn up for the elections, for example, only men's names get chosen."

ture for male candidates, and fetched coffee and donuts. Because they were responsible for stuffing and mailing envelopes, the female workers were known as "lickers and stickers." Then in 1971 four prominent feminists—Bella Abzug, Shirley Chisholm, Betty Friedan, and Gloria Steinem—organized the National Women's Political Caucus (NWPC).

The NWPC was the first organization that encouraged women to run for political office. Cofounder Friedan proclaimed a new era in which women

refused "to be manipulated any longer" by white males holding all the power. "What unites women across the lines of race, class, generation and man-made party politics is the demand for participation ourselves: our own voice in the big decisions affecting our lives."

The NWPC was responsible for sending the largest number of women in history to both the Democratic and Republican National Conventions. Where both parties had previously ignored women, they could no longer do so.

Window on the World: Indira Gandhi, Prime Minister of India

Indira Gandhi (1917–1984) was the daughter of Jawaharlal Nehru, a prime minister of India, and a niece of Vijaya Lakshmi Pandit, first female president of the United Nations. She was a follower of the pacifist Mohandas K. (Mahatma) Gandhi. Both her father and Mahatma Gandhi (no relation) were legendary men who challenged the hold of the British Empire on India. Because of her father's dangerous political activities, Gandhi was sent to study in Switzerland when she was eight years old. At age thirteen, she returned home and founded her own army, called the Monkey Brigade. It consisted of six thousand children who carried messages and sometimes even attacked the British soldiers' barracks.

In 1942, Gandhi married a young lawyer from Bombay, India, and they had two sons. When Gandhi's father became prime minister of India in 1947, she left her husband to go and live with him. She became known as "the first lady of India." On her father's death in 1964, Gandhi was elected his successor in congress. Two years later, she became prime minister, serving until 1977 and then making a comeback in 1980. She was assassinated four years later by political rivals.

Gandhi is often compared to Israel's Golda Meir in terms of their personal lives. Both sacrificed their marriages to rule over their countries. Journalist Oriana Fallaci, who interviewed both women extensively, wrote, "The strain and injustice of being a woman were demonstrated precisely by the two women who had arrived at the top of the pyramid. And it was painful and infuriating [to me] to discover that a man with a destiny can follow it without giving up his family, without giving up love. A woman cannot."

In an interview with Fallaci in 1972, Gandhi commented on Indian politics:

Political Action Committees (PACS)

Political action committees (PACs) are committees formed by interest groups to see that money donations go to candidates for office who will support the positions of the interest groups. PACs are allowed by law to give more money to candidates than an individual can.

Today there are about fifty PACs that help fund women candidates running for national office. Two prominent PACs are EMILY's List and WISH.

EMILY's List

EMILY stands for Early Money Is Like Yeast (it grows). The group was found-

"Today ... people no longer want to be represented," she noted. "Each wants to speak for himself and participate directly—it's the same for the Negroes, for the Jews, for women. So not only Negroes and Jews, but also women are part of a great revolt of which one can only approve. Women sometimes go too far, it's true. But it's only when you go too far that others listen.

"In India women have never been in hostile competition with men—even in the most distant past, every time a woman emerged as a leader, perhaps as a queen, the people accepted her. As something normal and not exceptional. Let's not forget that in India the symbol of strength is a woman: the goddess Shakti. Not only that— the struggle for independence here has been conducted in equal measure by men and by women. And when we got our independence, no one forgot that."

ed in 1985 to assist female Democratic candidates in their quest for election to political office. By 1992 EMILY's List had raised $6 million for women candidates.

WISH

WISH (Women in the Senate and House) is a fairly new organization that helps Republican women candidates get elected to Congress or governorships by contributing time or money to their campaigns. WISH requires that the candidates they support be in favor of abortion rights (pro-choice), even though the Republican Party takes an antiabortion stand.

American Women Politicians

American women had to fight throughout the nineteenth century to establish their right to even speak in public. Once they accomplished that task, they used what authority they had to speak on behalf of children, families, and the poor. For a woman to speak out in public to secure political power for herself would have been considered improper and unladylike. The belief that if a woman were going to speak in public at all it should be on behalf of the less fortunate was firmly in place by the time suffrage was granted.

Leaders of women's rights groups had been certain that once they attained the right to vote, women would become interested in running for political office. They were doomed to disappointment, however. Not only did women not rush to join the political life, they scarcely turned out to cast their votes. The few who did run for office were welcomed neither by voters nor by the men already in power.

Women in Elective or Appointed Offices: The Early Days

By 1931 there were only seven women in Congress (out of a total of 535 senators and representatives). Six were in the House, three of whom had been appointed to fulfill their dead husbands' terms or elected to succeed their husbands. The only female senator was also a widow. Most of the women in Congress projected "a mature grand-motherly image," and few of them had any prior office-holding experience or other qualifications.

This became the long-standing pattern for women in high political office. They were often widows who were appointed to Congress or state governorships to complete the unexpired terms of their husbands, or they were elected to office based on the voters' recognition of the names of their male relatives.

Why Women Run for Political Office Today

Many American women who are politically active today did not start out with the intention of running for office. Instead, they noticed a specific problem in their city, state, or even in the country. When it seemed no one was going to do anything to resolve it, the women found themselves organizing campaigns to get themselves elected to office and solve the problems. Senator Pat Schroeder of Colorado got involved in politics in the 1970s because she was unhappy with how President Richard Nixon was handling the Vietnam War (1954–75) and environmental issues. As a result, she campaigned for election to the House of Representatives in 1972 and won.

Lynne Yeakel of Pennsylvania ran for the U.S. Senate in 1992 against Senator Arlen Specter because she was angry at the prominent role he played in the interrogation of Anita Hill (discussed on

Sandra Day O'Connor: First Woman Supreme Court Justice

Sandra Day O'Connor made history in September 1981 when she became the first woman to sit on the U.S. Supreme Court. The Supreme Court is the highest body in the judicial branch of government. It is the court of final appeals for people who want their cases redecided.

O'Connor was born in Texas in 1930 and grew up on her family's cattle ranch on the Texas-New Mexico border. She attended college and law school at Stanford University in California, graduating third in her class.

After graduation in 1952, O'Connor found that no law firm would hire her because she was a woman. As a result, she entered public service, first working as a deputy county attorney in California and later as an assistant attorney general in Arizona. O'Connor also worked as a lawyer in Germany, where her husband was stationed with the U.S. Army. At one point, she operated her own law firm. She was also active in the Republican Party and was an Arizona state senator for several terms. O'Connor was then elected to a judgeship and later appointed to the Arizona Court of Appeals.

In July 1981, O'Connor was nominated to replace retiring Associate Justice Potter Stewart on the U.S. Supreme Court. President Ronald Reagan, who nominated O'Connor, praised her as a person of "unique qualities of temperament, fairness, and intellectual capacity." Her nomination was opposed by antiabortion groups, who thought her past judgments were not strong enough against abortion. Nevertheless, the nomination passed through the U.S. Senate, and in September 1981, she took her seat on the Supreme Court.

page 280). Although she had thought about running for office before, "it took the image of seeing those men making those decisions and controlling our future to get me to do it," Yeakel said. Similarly, Carol Moseley-Braun said: "I would not have run for the Senate had the Senate not gone on television."

U.S. representative Pat Schroeder participates in a 1995 congressional hearing on religion in public schools.

The modern crop of political women is no longer content to remain in women's traditional roles. They have worked alongside men and have seen that they are equally capable of running for and occupying a political office. Women are experiencing particular success in running for office at the state and local levels. Most of those positions are part-time occupations, which women find they can adapt to their existing family and work responsibilities. These offices can also be stepping stones to national offices. By 1986, the average woman candidate for Congress was able to point to fifteen years of office-holding experience.

Running for office at the federal level is where the real problems begin for women. Those offices are considered the most desirable, in part because they pay more and carry more influence. But the financial cost of campaigning is a tremendous hurdle.

Why Women Don't Run for Office

To many women, the world of politics is strange and uncomfortable. Attacks by the press and opponents are a common—and unwelcome—experience. Women have traditionally avoided cutthroat competition. The media is often guilty of stereotyping competitive women, calling them pushy, loud, aggressive, strident, and worse.

Women politicians admit that running for political office can be rough. However, they also admit that it can be exhilarating. California congressional representative Nancy Pelosi sums up these feelings: "[Running for office is] brutal. It's tough. You are going for power. It's never been just given away. It's highly competitive trying to take power, and as long as you understand that and are ready to take a punch square in the face, then you'll love it."

Getting Money to Run for Office Isn't Easy

Running for office is an extremely expensive proposition. Many women who have chosen to run for political office say the decision was especially hard because it meant committing the family's money to a political campaign. Between 1990 and 1992, the average cost of a Senate race was $3 to $4 million. The cost to run for a seat in the House of Representatives ranged from $400,000 to $1 million or more, and the cost goes up for every election. Madeleine Kunin, former governor of Vermont, noted: "I think your strength as a candidate depends on how well you can raise money. . . . If you don't raise it, you are in trouble."

A woman candidate must ask herself if she is willing to risk her children's college tuition money, her home, or retirement money on such an undertaking. Female candidates have often found it hard to get funding from the same sources that male politicians have tapped—such as large corporations and wealthy individuals. The reason for this is that people and companies who support political candidates have been unwilling to commit money to a candidate they feel has little chance of winning, and women were perceived as having little chance of winning.

The first fund-raising event that resulted in big money for a female candidate took place in 1990. Ann Richards raised $400,000 in one night to use in her bid for the governorship of Texas. At Richards's fund-raising event, a star attraction had been the presence of the extremely influential Senator Sam Nunn. With Nunn supporting Richards's campaign, people and corporations felt safe enough to provide funding.

U.S. senator Carol Moseley-Braun speaks at a NOW convention for the election of women candidates

Media Scrutiny Is Dismaying

Women politicians are often concerned with the scrutiny (intense examination) to which they and their spouses are subjected by individuals and by the media. Back in 1917, when Jeannette Rankin voted against involvement in World War I, the *New York Times*'s headline read: "One Hundred Speeches Were Made—Miss Rankin, Sobbing, Votes No." (She was not the only one who voted no.) When Pat Schroeder cried briefly after announcing in 1987 that she would not run for president, she made media headlines all over the country.

"[They] just decided that's the only thing I've ever done that counted," she said. In 1984, when Geraldine Ferraro campaigned for the vice presidency, the financial affairs of her husband were laid out by the media in detail.

All areas of a woman's private life and that of her spouse become issues in her political career. If she spends a lot of time away from home, as she certainly must, rumors may start that her marriage is in trouble or she is having extramarital affairs. Female politicians complain that they are constantly asked: "Where's your husband?" Male politicians, on the other hand, are rarely asked: "Where's your wife?"

The 1992 Elections

The Grilling of Anita Hill

Nearly all of the eleven women who ran for the U.S. Senate in 1992 used the name of Anita Hill in their campaign literature. Hill had testified in 1991 before an all-male Senate Judiciary Committee. She charged that President George Bush's nominee for the Supreme Court, Clarence Thomas, had sexually harassed her when she worked for him. Her television testimony was watched by tens of millions of people. Hill was treated with disrespect by the male senators who questioned her, and the media tore her apart. Many women were stung into political action by the televised spectacle, and as a result, those women helped elect the largest number of women to the Senate than ever before in history.

These women, however, almost didn't get the chance to hear Hill's charges. The Senate Judiciary Committee, which decides whether to approve or reject the nomination of a Supreme Court candidate, concluded that Hill's charges were not worth pursuing, even though she cast doubt on the fitness of Thomas to hold such an important position. Without hearing Hill's testimony, the committee set a date to vote on the nomination.

Then two journalists got ahold of the story and released it on the radio and in a newspaper. Next, seven angry female members of the House of Representatives marched to a Senate office building to voice their protest that Hill was not being allowed to testify. The congresswomen were told they were "strangers" who could not come in. When the media picked up this story, the Judiciary Committee changed its mind, and a hearing was held to allow Hill to testify. This was a unique event for at least two reasons: first, because women rarely brought charges against powerful men; and second, because such an event had never before been televised.

After Hill's testimony, she was questioned by members of the all-white, all-male Judiciary Committee (Hill and Thomas are both African American). During questioning, Hill was referred to as a "woman scorned," implying that she was seeking revenge against Thomas for an unhappy love affair. Insulting statements were made about her motives for coming forward. Public reaction was mixed—some people believed Hill and others didn't. But many were angered by the committee's original refusal to hear her out and by their treatment of Hill once she was permitted to testify. This anger was visible in the 1992 elections.

Although Thomas was eventually confirmed and sworn in as a Supreme Court justice, activists and women who had never before been politically involved swung into action. Some decided to run for office, and women's organizations that supported female candidates received tremendous monetary donations and experienced a significant rise in memberships. Many men simply did not understand why women were so angry about the Hill-Thomas hearings. A saying made popular by the event was, "the men just don't get it." That is to say, Hill's questioners had no sensitivity to or knowledge of how widespread workplace harassment is.

During the 1992 elections, women candidates claimed they would bring different views to the process of making public policy. They said they knew what women and the family needed. They declared that "business as usual" was a thing of the past. When the election results were tallied, female representation in the U.S. Senate tripled, to 6 percent. Women increased their numbers in the U.S. House of Representatives by nearly 70 percent, from 29 to 47 out of a total of 435.

The debate continues, however, as to the significance of the 1992 election of greater numbers of women to high political office. Will the pattern continue, or was it a fluke? Some analysts say that women will be making real progress only when they make up 50 percent of the membership of both the U.S. House of Representatives and the U.S. Senate. The Center for the American Woman and Politics says that at the rate we are going, we can expect equal representation of women in the U.S. House and Senate in about four hundred years.

Speaking in a Different Voice

In the past, most women who held political office were unwilling to speak out on behalf of women's issues. However, women running for office at the end of the twentieth century were more willing to stress their differences from male candidates. They were more willing to address the issue of using political power to benefit women. These female candidates stressed that they could bring a different point of view because their life experiences have been different from men's.

Women are usually perceived by the public as caring, peace-loving, honest, attentive, and willing to work together. These are the qualities that once bound them to the home. Today, many people argue that these are the qualities that are needed in policy-making.

Recent studies done by the Center for the American Woman and Politics show that women politicians have been using what power they do possess to push for change on issues important to their gender. Those issues include: absentee fathers, sexual harassment, breast cancer research, reproductive rights, child care, support for single mothers, domestic violence, rape, hiring practices, and equal pay for equal work.

Black Women and Political Power

While white women were speaking out against slavery and in favor of women's rights in the 1800s, the male heads of the American Anti-Slavery Society wanted to focus on freeing the slaves. They agreed that after accomplishing this goal, they would consider the question of women's rights. However, they failed to do so.

African American women made up only 29 percent of the country's black elected officials in 1993, and those women were mostly located among the lowest positions in local government. Of the forty black members of Congress in 1993, only nine were women.

Hispanic American Women and Political Power

Calls to action during the Civil Rights movement in the 1960s and 1970s were heard by Hispanic American women as well as African American women. Farm workers such as Jesse Lopez de la Cruz, Lupe Anguiano, and Dolores Huerta joined labor organizer Cesar Chavez to improve working conditions for Hispanic American farm laborers. These women and other Hispanic Americans helped to inspire a massive, nationwide grape boycott in the late 1960s to protest poor working conditions. They have emerged as strong leaders, especially in the labor movement and in local politics in the southwestern states.

Notable Political Women

Eleanor Roosevelt

Eleanor Roosevelt came to the White House as the wife of Franklin Delano Roosevelt, the thirty-second president of the United States. Before assuming the role of first lady, Roosevelt had been a teacher, social worker, and newspaper columnist. After bearing five children between 1905 and 1916, she turned her attention to politics, becoming active in the League of Women Voters and other organizations. When her husband became active in New York State politics, she became his advisor. Roosevelt used her position to speak on behalf of people who had long been overlooked—women, the unemployed, and blacks.

During her sixteen years as first lady, Roosevelt was an advocate of many of the New Deal programs begun by her husband. Through the New Deal, the U.S. government became involved for the first time in providing jobs on a large scale through the Public Works Act. Social security, unemployment, and medical benefits also became government concerns during the New Deal era. The time was ripe for social programs of this nature because the country was struggling to recover from the devastating Great Depression that lasted from 1929 to 1940. During this period, millions of Americans were out of work.

With her clear vision of social justice, Roosevelt redefined the role of first lady from a decorative to an activist position. She also helped to advance the cause of female politicians. Among her friends were trailblazers Molly Dewson, Frances Perkins, Helen Gahagan Douglas, and Mary McLeod Bethune. After her husband's death in 1945, Roosevelt went on to serve as a U.S. delegate to the United Nations.

Molly Dewson Becomes First Female Political Boss

Molly Williams Dewson (1874–1962) is called the first female political boss. A political boss is a person who uses her power and influence to advance the causes of her political party. She acquired her interest in history and government from her invalid father, and her aunt was a leader in the prison reform movement. Dewson herself graduated in 1897 from Wellesley College. Her classmates predicted that she would one day be president of the United States. Upon her graduation she accepted a job as secretary of an influential Boston reform group. Its goal was finding ways to turn housework into a profession. Thus began a long career in politics.

Dewson was an old hand at heading up political organizations. She was appointed by Franklin Roosevelt, then governor of New York, to head the Women's Division of the Democratic National Committee. Her talent made women a recognizable force in Democratic political circles. Dewson is credit-

Eleanor Roosevelt was the first president's wife to play a visible role in America's politics.

ed with organizing eight thousand women into the Women's Division and getting them out to help elect Roosevelt as president. She was also notable for being the country's leading authority on minimum wage laws.

Frances Perkins Becomes the First Female Cabinet Member

Frances Perkins (1880–1965) was also a friend of Eleanor Roosevelt. She witnessed the Triangle Shirtwaist Factory fire in 1911, which killed 146 workers, most of them women. Thereafter, she devoted herself to improving the health,

Frances Perkins became an important member of Franklin Roosevelt's cabinet.

when she was elected to the House of Representatives in 1944. She is especially remembered for a dramatic speech she gave on behalf of homemakers upset over the high price of groceries. Two things were remarkable about her speech. The first was that at the time, it was still highly unusual for a woman to want to draw attention to herself in the corridors of male power. The second was that she was one of the first powerful women to speak out for women's economic interests.

Douglas served three terms in the House and then decided to run for the Senate in 1950. She was among the first female politicians to draw on a women's network for financial and other help in running for office. Her friend Eleanor Roosevelt was among her backers. However, Douglas lost to Richard Nixon, who ran a vicious campaign against her. She never again ran for public office after the loss, returning instead to the Broadway stage.

Mary McLeod Bethune Is Appointed to Roosevelt's "Black Cabinet"

Mary McLeod Bethune (1875–1955) was appointed by Franklin Roosevelt to his cabinet as a consultant on the basis of her reputation as an educator and black leader. Roosevelt was a progressive in the area of social issues. He favored equal rights for blacks long before the Civil Rights movement of the late 1950s. But he was president at a time when blacks did not serve at high levels of government. Roosevelt decided to change that, so he created a second, unof-

safety, and working conditions of American laborers. She was employed as a social worker and served as industrial commissioner of New York before being appointed by Franklin Roosevelt to serve in his cabinet. As his secretary of labor, Perkins helped make laws to create unemployment insurance, Social Security, and the minimum wage.

Helen Gahagan Douglas Is Elected to the House

Helen Gahagan Douglas (1900–1980) was a dramatic actress and very comfortable being the center of attention

Window on the World: Daw Aung San Suu Kyi

Daw Aung San Suu Kyi (1945–) was awarded the Nobel Peace Prize for her nonviolent struggle to bring democracy to her native Burma. She is the daughter of U Aung Sang, the highly regarded founder of modern Burma who was assassinated in 1947, when Aung San Suu Kyi was only two years old. At the age of seventeen she moved to India, and later went to England, where she attended Oxford University, married, and had two children.

In 1988, Aung San Suu Kyi returned to Burma for the first time since 1960 to care for her dying mother. While she was there Burma's brutal military government (which had been ruling with an iron fist since 1962) killed more than three thousand demonstrators at a pro-democracy rally. Horrified by the disregard for human life, Aung San Suu Kyi began writing and delivering speeches against the dictatorship and formed with other Burmese activists the National League for Democracy (NLD).

The government, seeing that the NLD had quickly amassed a huge following and unwilling to risk international criticism, promised to hold fair elections in 1990. Disbelieving, Aung San Suu Kyi and the NLD continued to agitate. In July 1989, the government made good on its long-time threat to jail Aung San Suu Kyi, and they placed her under house arrest in her mother's home. She was spared her life only because the eyes of the world were on Burma, particularly after Aung San Suu Kyi was awarded the Nobel Prize in 1991.

The government did hold elections in 1990, but, to no one's surprise, disregarded the outcome (the NLD won 80 percent of the vote). The military government—which had changed the country's name to Myanmar in 1990—is still firmly in control. They finally released Aung San Suu Kyi in 1995, after holding her prisoner for six years. Still active in the democracy movement in Myanmar, Aung San Suu Kyi is regarded by her fellow citizens as a courageous symbol of hope for a better future.

---

ficial group of cabinet officers to give him advice about social affairs. The members of this unofficial cabinet were prominent black educators and civic leaders.

Born in South Carolina, Bethune was the fifteenth child of former slaves. She learned to read and write at a missionary school, a five-mile walk from her home. She worked as a teacher before starting her own school for black girls. This school eventually evolved into Bethune-Cookman College, which is still open today.

When Roosevelt launched the National Youth Administration (NYA) in the

Women in the CIA and FBI

During times of peace, the United States government continues to protect its interests through spying and surveillance. Two government agencies that have been given the official task of keeping an eye on suspected enemy activity are the Central Intelligence Agency (CIA), which focuses on harmful activities overseas, and the Federal Bureau of Investigation (FBI), which operates within the United States.

Women belong to both the CIA and the FBI. While some are happy with their jobs, others charge that they are passed over for promotion and not given assignments in the field (within the enemy's reach). In 1995, a group of female agents filed a lawsuit against the CIA. The CIA responded by offering the women promises of promotions and a sum of money for damages.

The women remain unsatisfied. They believe the discrimination within the CIA runs deep; they tell stories of how their supervisors still pressure them for dates. However, things may be looking up for women at the CIA. After the lawsuit, a woman and former navy assistant secretary, Nora Slatkin, took over the number three job in the agency.

---

height of the Depression, he appointed Bethune a special consultant. She became one of the few blacks—and the only black woman—to hold an influential post in Roosevelt's government. The NYA was intended to force fair representation and participation of African Americans in society. Under Bethune's guidance, the NYA saw to it that 150,000 black boys and girls were able to attend high school, and 60,000 were able to attend college. Bethune also saw to it that blacks were given jobs in government. By the 1940s, Bethune was recognized as a leader of American black women and young people. Her focus was on ending racial discrimination rather than on promoting women's issues.

Margaret Chase Smith Is Elected to the Senate

Margaret Chase Smith (1897–1995) entered the House of Representatives in 1940 after the death of her husband. She successfully ran for the Senate in 1948, becoming the first woman elected who was not the widow of a senator.

Smith was highly respected by her male colleagues and became a role model for female politicians who followed her. She is especially notable for her independence and her willingness to disagree with her political party when her conscience required her to do so. When Senator Joseph McCarthy falsely claimed in 1950 that hundreds of government employees were communists and traitors to their country, Smith condemned him in a famous speech that came to be known as "A Declaration of Conscience." Unlike many other members of Congress, Smith was not afraid to speak out against McCarthy.

Also notable among the early female politicians were Edith Nourse Rogers of Massachusetts, Frances Bolton of Ohio, and Katharine St. George of New York. Rogers was the longest-serving woman in the history of the House, holding the office from 1925 to 1960. Bolton, a member of the House from 1940 to 1969, headed up the very important House Committee on Foreign Affairs. St. George was a strong supporter of the Equal Rights Amendment (ERA). She served from 1946 to 1964.

Other than these few outstanding examples, women for the most part were still regarded as riding on the coattails of men. Most of the first women to serve in Congress had gotten into office because of the influence of a powerful male relative and were not taken seriously by their male colleagues. Then along came Martha Wright Griffiths.

Martha Wright Griffiths Wins the Respect of the Senate

Martha Wright Griffiths (1912–) of Michigan served in the House of Representatives for twenty years. During that time, she was largely responsible for the inclusion of equal employment opportunities for women in the Civil Rights Act of 1964. She also fought for passage of the ERA and left her mark on the country's tax code, Social Security, and pension laws.

Griffiths's contributions to welfare reform and national health insurance in the 1970s brought those issues into the national consciousness. (Those issues were still being debated in the late 1990s.) She was admired by all her colleagues, even those who disagreed with her.

Women and the Clinton Administration

President Bill Clinton, who took office in January 1993, appointed several women to highly visible and powerful positions. Among his appointments were Janet Reno, the first female attorney general of the United States; Donna Shalala, who is secretary of Health and Human Services; and Ruth Bader Ginsburg, the second woman to be appointed to the U.S. Supreme Court.

Clinton's administration was forced, however, to decrease the once-extensive role of First Lady Hillary Rodham Clinton. During the campaign for the presidency, many people were upset at how highly visible and ambitious Mrs. Clinton seemed. Former President Richard Nixon commented on Mrs. Clinton's presences during the campaign by saying that "if the wife comes on too strong and intelligent, it makes the husband look like a wimp."

When Clinton assumed office, he appointed his wife to oversee the drafting of a new national health insurance

Window on the World:
Benazir Bhutto, Prime Minister of Pakistan

Benazir Bhutto (1953–), elected prime minister of Pakistan in 1988, was the first woman ever to head an elected government in an Islamic nation. Earlier she had received degrees from two famous foreign colleges—Radcliffe College in the United States and Oxford University in England.

Bhutto's father served as prime minister of Pakistan beginning in 1971; he was overthrown and imprisoned in 1977. Bhutto appeared at rallies in support of her father, but he was executed in 1979. A military dictatorship took over the country and Bhutto was placed under house arrest, then was imprisoned, and finally was forced into exile in England.

Bhutto was allowed to return to Pakistan in 1986 and became the head of the political party her father had founded. Two years later, she was elected prime minister. In 1990, Pakistan's president, who was a holdover from the military dictatorship, removed her from office, charging her and her followers with corrupt government and abuse of power.

However, she was reelected prime minister in 1993. Bhutto has vowed that this time she will remain in power.

Bhutto is leader of a country whose population rose from 50 million in 1960 to 130 million in 1996. Pakistan struggles with overpopulation, political instability, and violent divisions among religious and ethnic groups.

The prime minister's critics charge that she has done very little to improve the status of women in Pakistan. Aside from Bhutto herself, women play no role in public life there. Supporters say that she faces special obstacles as the first woman to head the government of a Muslim country in a culture where women have been repressed, and they praise her for keeping democracy alive in Pakistan.

Bhutto has adopted a woman's agenda. That agenda includes separate women's police stations and courts (Pakistan is a country where the sexes are segregated), a 10 percent quota for government jobs (women will hold 10 percent of government jobs), and expanded education for girls.

plan. Some voters became upset over the large part Mrs. Clinton seemed to be playing in decision-making when she had not been elected by the voters to any office. As a result, the health insurance plan disappeared from view, and Mrs. Clinton began to perform the more traditional duties of first ladies, such as visiting foreign countries and speaking out on behalf of children.

Women Leaders Around the World: Then and Now

The European Tradition

A few women throughout history have been able to get around the leadership limitations placed on them. Some, such as the brilliant politician Elizabeth I of England (1533-1603) and the warrior Catherine the Great of Russia (1729-1796) ruled as queens. Other women who were members of the upper class exercised power in the courts of kings, acting as friends and unofficial advisors. (These women were sometimes referred to as "the power behind the throne.") Some women acted as representatives of male relatives when a male ruler was not available. Others were even given their own lands to govern by their families. These women were the exception to the rule, however.

Revolutions in Europe during the eighteenth century put an end to even these few opportunities for women. In countries where queens still ruled, as Victoria did in England, they did so with the advice of male ministers. Women from wealthy families might hold positions at court, but these positions did not involve the exercise of power. Nor did women influence government policy. The French put an end to women's influence in 1793 by outlawing all political activity by women. Throughout Europe, women's participation in politics came to be seen as a disturbing move into male territory. It had to be stopped—and it was.

Elizabeth I was one of history's most influential leaders.

Modern Times: Queens and Members of Parliament

At the end of the twentieth century, six queens reigned in Europe. Although they are royalty, they hold no political power. They are: Queen Elizabeth II of Great Britain, Queen Sofia of Spain, Queen Beatrix of The Netherlands, Queen Margrethe II of Denmark, Queen Silvia of Sweden, and Queen Fabiola of Belgium.

In 1995, the United Nations reported that between the years 1975 and 1993, the proportion of women lawmakers worldwide actually fell, from 12.5 percent to 10.1 percent. As a matter of fact, nearly

Window on the World:
Corazon "Cory" Aquino President of the Philippines

Former Philippines president Corazon Aquino was born in 1933 to a wealthy family in Manila, the Philippines. She graduated from the College of Mount St. Vincent in New York City in 1953, and a year later she married Benigno S. Aquino Jr. He later became the political rival of Philippine President Ferdinand Marcos and was assassinated in 1983. Aquino blamed Marcos for her husband's assassination.

Marcos led the Philippines for twenty years. During his rule, the country went into massive debt. It is said that he borrowed billions of dollars from foreign banks and put the money into his own bank account.

The whole world was astonished when Aquino was elected president of the Philippines in 1985, and great things were expected of her. When she had been in office for about two years, the *New York Times* said: "Her achievements cry out for applause. The Philippine Republic is now the liveliest democracy in Asia."

Under Aquino's rule, the Philippines experienced some economic growth. However, she was not able to keep all of her promises, and some critics charge that she badly mismanaged the country. They claim that in her attempts to pay back the debts run up by Marcos, she laid the burden on the backs of the country's poorest people.

Aquino chose not to run again for office in 1992. In her last state of the nation address, she said she had done her best. The Philippine Republic has many problems, which make governing difficult. Always a poor country, more than 40 percent of its population is less than fourteen years old, and more than one-half of all children who enter school drop out before they reach the sixth grade.

one hundred countries have no women lawmakers at all. The Scandinavian countries, however, consistently appear at the top of the list in terms of female political representation. In 1994, for example, Sweden's parliament was 42 percent female.

The decline in the number of women serving in parliaments followed the collapse of communism in Europe and the growth of democracy there and in Africa. Under communism, women were included in government positions. In some countries, quotas of as high as 30 percent were established for women. When communism fell and free elections were held, women were not chosen by political parties to run for office.

Among the 106 countries that are members of the United Nations and hold free elections, the United States ranks forty-third in the number of national seats held by women. This figure was lower than that of developing countries (such as in Africa), Russia and many Eastern European countries, and the Latin American countries. Canada ranked twenty-first.

Although women have become more politically active in recent years, there is still much that needs to be done. It is important that countries give all their citizens the opportunity to participate in how the government is run, no matter what sex, race, or religion those people are. True equality cannot be achieved until all people have equal representation in local, state, national, and world governments.

11

Women's Organizations

"I could not, at any age, be content to take my place in a corner by the fireside and simply look on. Life was meant to be lived."

—Eleanor Roosevelt,
First Lady and social activist

Hundreds of organizations have formed around women and the issues that are of concern to them. Some of the groups presented in this chapter were founded and are run by women. Others are government or university programs that focus on women's specific needs. While a complete list would be too long for this work, your local library does have books in the reference section that give the names and addresses for many more women's organizations.

The organizations listed in this chapter are grouped together under the general issue on which their activities focus. They are arranged alphabetically under one of the following subheads:

- art and cultural organizations
- education organizations
- ethnic organizations
- feminist organizations
- labor organizations

- legal organizations
- military organizations
- political organizations
- professional/industry/business organizations
- religious organizations
- science/technology organizations
- social/health organizations
- sports organizations

Art and Cultural Organizations

American Folklore Society
Women's Section
George Mason University
Department of English
Fairfax, VA 22030
(703)323-2220

Peggy Yocum, Chairperson

Purpose: The Women's Section of the American Folklore Society is made up of individuals and institutions who are interested in collecting, discussing, and publicizing folklore about women from throughout the world, with an emphasis on North American women.

Coalition of Women's Art Organizations
123 East Beutel Road
Port Washington, WI 53074
(414)284-4458

Purpose: Members of this advocacy group are professional artists and representatives of art organizations. They work to protect and improve the rights of all artists, but especially the rights of women artists, by alerting them to issues in their fields.

Feminist Writers' Guild
174 West Melrose
Chicago, IL 60657
(312)929-1326

Jorjet Harper, Administrator

Purpose: The guild offers an opportunity for women writers to gather, offer support, and share information about the "politics of publishing," including educational aspects and political action. The guild bestows the Annual Woman of Promise Award to a previously unpublished author.

International League of Women Composers
Southshore Road, Box 670
Point Peninsula
Three Mile Bay, NY 13693
(315)649-5086

Elizabeth Hayden Pizer, Chairperson

Purpose: The league was established by female composers from twenty-five countries to help them obtain more commissions (writing music for a specific purpose such as a movie), recordings, and performances. The league holds concerts, sponsors radio series, and encourages new talent through the Search for New Music Competition.

National Association of Women Artists
41 Union Square West, Room 906
New York, NY 10003
(212)675-1616

Ann Hermanson, Executive Secretary

Purpose: Members of this group are professional women artists, such as sculptors, printmakers, and painters in oil, acrylic, and paper works. The association sponsors national and foreign travel and shows for its members as well as holds an annual awards program.

Women Make Movies

462 Broadway, Suite 500
New York, NY 10013
(212)925-0606

Debra S. Zimmerman, Director

Purpose: This group is comprised of individuals who are devoted to the development of a strong multicultural feminist media that accurately reflects the lives of women. The group assists emerging artists, acts as a clearinghouse for women's films and videos, and encourages audiences to explore the changing and diverse roles that women play in modern society.

Education Organizations

Alpha Kappa Alpha, Inc. (AKA)

5656 South Stony Island Avenue
Chicago, IL 60637
(312)684-1282

Allison Harris, Executive Director

Purpose: This is the first sorority (a social or service organization of women members, usually on college campuses) for black women. Its members focus on activism in the areas of job discrimination, affirmative action, employment training, access to nontraditional jobs, equal pay, poverty, economic development, teenage pregnancy, education, child care, and leadership development.

American Association of University Professors (AAUP)

Committee on the Status of Women in the Academic Profession
1012 14th Street Northwest, Suite 500
Washington, DC 20005
(202)737-5900

Leslie Lee Francis, Associate Secretary

Purpose: The AAUP uses laws to promote the fair treatment of women in academic advancement. The laws they cite have to do with preventing sex discrimination in colleges and universities. The group has been involved in legal battles by providing expert witnesses for legal cases and by operating its Legal Defense Fund to pay the legal fees of teachers.

American Association of University Women (AAUW)

1111 16th Street Northwest
Washington, DC 20036
(202)785-7700

Anne L. Bryant, Executive Director

Purpose: This group works for the advancement of women by promoting lifelong learning, research, lobbying, women's studies programs, and competitions.

American Federation of Teachers

Women's Rights Committee
Human Rights Department
555 New Jersey Avenue Northwest

Washington, DC 20001

(202)879-4400

Barbara Van Blake, Director

Purpose: Members of the Women's Rights Committee recommend action on women's issues to the rest of the American Federation of Teachers membership. Topics of interest to the committee include integrating women's history into the core curriculum (subjects regularly taught), sexual harassment, child-care options, and pay equity. They also lobby Congress, do research, and maintain a speakers' bureau.

Delta Kappa Gamma Society International

P.O. Box 1589

Austin, TX 78767

(512)478-5748

Theresa Fachek, Staff Director

Purpose: This group was founded to advance and improve college/university education, to endow (give on a regular basis) scholarships and fellowships, and to honor women who have given distinctive service to education.

Feministas Unidas

2101 East Coliseum Boulevard

Ft. Wayne, IN 46805

(219)481-6836

Stacey Schlau, President

Purpose: This group examines the portrayal of Hispanic women in literature and acknowledges Hispanic women's contribution to literature. Members of Feministas Unidas include feminist scholars working in Hispanic, Luso-Brazilian (Brazilians of Portuguese descent), Chicana, or Puerto Rican studies. The group also works with the Modern Language Association (MLA), the largest U.S. organization of professors teaching college English, literature, and writing.

Ethnic Organizations

Association of Asian Studies (AAS)

Committee of Women in Asian Studies (CWAS)

State University of New York at Albany

Department of History

Albany, NY 12222

(518)442-4800

Sucheta Mazumdar, Chair

Purpose: This group brings together those women and men within the Association of Asian Studies membership who are interested in women's issues, especially issues affecting Asian women, and those members involved in research on gender.

Black Professional Women's Network

123 West 44th Street, Suite 2E

New York, NY 10036

(212)302-2924

Paulette M. Owens, President

Purpose: This network provides information about employment, health care, and finances to black and Hispanic women professionals, managers, and technical employees.

Comision Femenil Mexicana Nacional (CFMN)

379 South Loma Drive
Los Angeles, CA 90017
(213)484-1515

Maggie Cervantes, President

Purpose: This group advocates Hispanic women's rights and works to advance Hispanic women politically, socially, economically, and educationally. The group maintains the Chicana Service Center and a group home for Mexican American women and teens.

Institute for Women's Studies in the Arab World

Beirut University College
475 Riverside Drive, Room 1846
New York, NY 10115
(212)870-2592

Julinda Abu Nasr, Director

Purpose: The institute conducts research, provides facts and statistics, produces publications, and sponsors action programs to improve the condition of women and children in the Arab world.

North American Indian Women's Association

9602 Maestor's Lane
Gaithersburg, MD 20879
(301)330-0397

Ann French, Contact

Purpose: The association promotes intertribal communication, awareness of the Native American culture, and the betterment of Indian family life, health, and education. Members of the association are women, eighteen years and older, who belong to Native American tribes recognized by the U.S. government.

Pan Pacific and Southeast Asia Women's Association of the U.S.A.

Box 1531, Madison Square Station
New York, NY 10159
(212)228-5307

Ann Allen, President

Purpose: This association promotes cooperation among women of Asia and the Pacific region for the study and improvement of social, economic, and cultural conditions of these areas. The group studies Asian and Pacific affairs; offers friendship, hospitality, and assistance to women who come to the United States from this region; and presents educational programs, awards, and scholarships to women of Asian descent.

Feminist Organizations

Ms. Foundation for Women

141 Fifth Avenue, Suite 6-S
New York, NY 10010
(212)353-8580

Marie C. Wilson, Executive Director

Purpose: The foundation's goals are to eliminate sex discrimination in all areas of society and to improve the status of women and girls. The foundation provides money and support to local activists (a person who works in support of a cause) who are fighting sex discrimination.

Labor Organizations

AFL-CIO
Women's Activities
815 16th Street Northwest
Washington, DC 20006
(202)637-5272

Cynthia McCaughan, Coordinator

Purpose: AFL-CIO stands for American Federation of Labor-Congress of Industrial Organizations. Its Women's Activities group works with national and international labor unions to help carry out the civil rights and women's rights policies of the AFL-CIO in workplaces.

International Ladies' Garment Workers' Union (ILGWU)
1710 Broadway
New York, NY 10019
(212)265-7000

Jay Mazur, President

Purpose: This organization, founded in 1900, represents women and other workers in the apparel industry.

United Federation of Teachers
Women's Rights Committee
260 Park Avenue South
New York, NY 10010
(212)598-6879

Pearl Wolf, Chairperson

Purpose: The committee, part of the United Federation of Teachers, provides its members with curriculum information on teaching women's history, publishes a newsletter on women's issues, and organizes Women's History Month, held in March.

Legal Organizations

American Bar Association
Section on Individual Rights and
    Responsibilities
Committee on Rights of Women
1800 M Street Northwest
Washington, DC 20036
(202)822-6644

Leslie Harris, Co-chairperson

Purpose: Members of this committee work to educate people in the legal profession (lawyers, judges, and court workers) about legal issues that affect women. Members also work to improve the status of women within the profession.

Equal Rights Advocates
1663 Mission Street, Suite 550
San Francisco, CA 94103
(415)621-0672

Nancy L. Davis, Executive Director

Purpose: Equal Rights Advocates is a public interest law center that specializes in sex discrimination cases. The issues involved in the cases include discrimination against women in nontraditional work, sexual harassment, pregnancy-based discrimination, and equal pay.

Federation of Women Lawyers
Judicial Screening Panel
2000 P Street Northwest, Suite 515
Washington, DC 20036
(202)822-6644

Estelle H. Rogers, Director

Purpose: Members of this group are female attorneys. They serve on the

Female attorneys who are members of the Federation of Women Lawyers screen candidates for federal judgeships.

screening panel that investigates and evaluates candidates who are under consideration for federal judgeships. Emphasis is placed on the potential nominee's "demonstrated commitment to equal justice under the law." The panel's comments are conveyed to the U.S. Senate Committee on the Judiciary and taken into consideration before federal judges are appointed.

Hollywood Women's Political Committee

3679 Motor Avenue, Suite 300
Los Angeles, CA 90034
(310)287-2803

Lara Bergthold, Executive Director

Purpose: This nonpartisan political action committee, or PAC (a lobbying group that uses donations to influence how public officials vote on certain issues), is made up of women involved in the entertainment industry and related fields. They raise money for federal political candidates, grassroots (local) organizations, and statewide initiatives that pledge to represent the group's interests, which include nuclear disarmament, increased environmental protection, improved public education, and expanded civil rights for women.

Institute for the Study of Matrimonial Laws

11 Park Pl., Suite 1116
New York, NY 10007
(212)766-4030

Sidney Siller, President

Purpose: The institute studies the United States's laws on divorce, alimony (financial support for ex-spouses), child custody, and child and grandparent visitation. The goal of this organization is to help create a national legal code that reflects the needs and situations of modern families.

National Center for Lesbian Rights

1663 Mission Street, Fifth Floor
San Francisco, CA 94103
(415)621-0674

Roberta Achtenberg, Executive Director

Purpose: The National Center for Lesbian Rights is a public interest law firm that specializes in cases involving sexual orientation (homosexual) discrimination, particularly those involving lesbians (women who are sexually attracted to other women). Issues center around child custody and foster parenting, employment, housing, military service, and medical and life insurance.

Women's Sports Foundation

Eisenhower Park
East Meadow, NY 11554
(800)227-3988

Donna Lopiano, Executive Director

Purpose: The foundation encourages and supports the participation of women in sports activities for their health, enjoyment, and mental development. Members of the foundation educate the public about athletic opportunities and the value of sports for women. They support enforcement of a national law called the Title IX Amendment of the 1972 Equal Education Act and the Amateur Sports Act. This law prohibits sex discrimination in federally funded education and sports programs.

Military Organizations

American GI Forum Women

9948 South Plaza, Apartment 1-D
Omaha, NE 68127
(402)593-1248

Marianne Martinez, Chairperson

Purpose: This organization offers comfort and information to women, aged fourteen or older, who are related to members of the American GI Forum of the United States. (GI stands for Government Issue and refers to a member of the military.) Both the American GI Forum and the American GI Forum Women focus especially on relatives and GIs of Hispanic origin.

Vietnam Women's Memorial Project

2001 S Street Northwest, Suite 302
Washington, DC 20009
(202)328-7253

Diane Carlson Evans, Chairperson and Founder

Purpose: Members of this project work to identify and document women who served during the Vietnam War (1969–73) and educate the American public about the contributions of women during the Vietnam War. The project was instrumental in the erection of a memorial to Vietnam-era servicewomen in Washington, D.C., in 1994.

Political Organizations

EMILY's List

1112 16th Street Northwest, Suite 750
Washington, DC 20036
(202)887-1957

Ellen Malcolm, President

Purpose: EMILY stands for Early Money Is Like Yeast. This political network for women is part of the Democratic Party and raises campaign funds for the election of pro-choice women candidates to office. "Pro-choice" means a candidate supports a pregnant woman's right to choose an abortion.

Evangelical and Ecumenical Women's Caucus

P.O. Box 209
Hadley, NY 74110
(518)696-2406

Florence Brown, Executive Director

Purpose: The goal of this caucus is to encourage evangelical women to work for change in their churches and in society. Members of this group are Christian feminists from churches, seminaries, and colleges. Since evangelicals believe strongly in the Bible, members of the caucus believe that the Bible, when properly understood, supports the basic equality of the sexes, the basis of the feminist movement.

League of Women Voters of the United States

1730 M Street Northwest
Washington, DC 20036
(202) 429-1965

Gracia Hilman, Executive Director

Purpose: This volunteer organization of U.S. citizens eighteen years and older promotes political responsibility through informed and active participation of citizens in government. Members study political issues and offer the general public educational material about these issues. Local chapters of the group gather and publish information about local candidates running for office. The league is nonpartisan (it is not affiliated with any political party), and it does not endorse candidates.

National Federation of Democratic Women

828 Lemont Drive
Nashville, TN 37216
(615)244-4270

Gwen McFarland, Executive Officer

Purpose: The goal of the federation is to develop local and national women leaders to work as officials and candidates in the Democratic Party.

National Federation of Republican Women

310 First Street Southeast
Washington, DC 20003
(202)547-9341

NOW is a women's group that seeks to end sexual discrimination in all areas of society.

Huda Jones, President

Purpose: Members of the federation encourage women's participation in every level of the Republican Party. Participation ranges from candidacy to educating communities on the Republican Party's stand on issues affecting U.S. society.

National Organization for Women (NOW)

1000 16th Street Northwest, Suite 700
Washington, DC 20036
(202)331-0066

Patricia Ireland, President

Purpose: NOW seeks to end prejudice and discrimination against women in government, industry, employment, churches, political parties, the judiciary (court system), labor unions, education, science, medicine, law, religions, "and every other field of importance in American society." NOW supported passage of the Equal Rights Amendment (ERA), and promotes enforcement of federal laws that prohibit sex discrimination. NOW also engages in lobbying and legal cases and sponsors student essay contests.

Professional/Industry/ Business Organizations

American Agri-Woman

Route 2, Box 193
Keota, IA 52248
(515)636-2293

Sandy Greiner, President

Purpose: This women's farm and ranch organization works to promote a positive image of farmers and ranchers to the public. The group supports family farms, advocates reasonably priced food products, and works with lawmakers and consumer groups to encourage fair treatment of farmers.

American Association of Women Dentists

401 North Michigan Avenue
Chicago, IL 60611-4267
(312)245-1084

Christine Norris, Executive Director

Purpose: Members, who are female dentists and dental students, encourage other young women to pursue academic degrees in dentistry and work to advance the status of women already involved in the dental profession.

American Business Women's Association

9100 Ward Parkway
P.O. Box 8728
Kansas City, MO 64114
(816)361-6621

Carolyn B. Elman, Executive Director

Purpose: This group provides opportunities for businesswomen through education, leadership, networking support, and national recognition. Members include women who own and operate their own businesses, and women in professions, government, education, retailing, manufacturing, and service companies.

American College of Nurse-Midwives

1522 K Street Northwest, Suite 1000
Washington, DC 20005
(202)289-0171

Ronald E. Nietzsche, CCO

Purpose: This college helps registered nurses who wish to offer gynecological services and care for mothers and babies throughout the maternity cycle. The group certifies midwives (women trained to assist women giving birth) and conducts research.

American News Women's Club

1607 22nd Street Northwest
Washington, DC 20008
(202)332-6770

Jane T. Lingo, Contact

Purpose: This organization is a networking service for women who write

The American Nurses Association campaigns for better working conditions.

news for all media (newspapers, television, and radio), government agencies, and nonprofit organizations or who free-lance (sell their work to different employers as it's needed).

American Nurses Association

1101 14th Street Northwest, Suite 200
Washington, DC 20005
(202)842-4375

Donna R. Richardson, Director of Government and Agency Relations

Purpose: This association advances the nursing profession by fostering high standards of nursing practice, by improving working conditions for nurses, and by lobbying the U.S. Congress about issues affecting nurses and public health in general.

American Psychiatric Association

Association of Women Psychiatrists
9802 Farnham Road
Louisville, KY 40223
(502)588-6185

Kathy Garvin, Executive Assistant

Purpose: The group's purpose is to form an international network of women psychiatrists; to provide support for women practicing as psychiatrists; to advance women into leadership positions within the psychiatric profession; to advocate women's mental health issues; to lobby the U.S. Congress on mental health laws; and to have an impact on the policies and procedures that govern how women are treated by the mental health system in the United States.

American Society of Women Accountants

1755 Lynnfield Road, Suite 222
Memphis, TN 38119-7235

Allison Conte, Executive Director

Purpose: This society acts as a network and support group for women accountants and educators and conducts education and research, training seminars, and recognition programs.

American Women in Radio and Television (AWRT)

1101 Connecticut Avenue Northwest, Suite 700
Washington, DC 20036
(202)429-5102

Donna Cantor, Executive Director

Purpose: The AWRT offers educational and recognition programs and sponsors the AWRT Educational Foundation, all of which supports women working in administrative, creative, or executive positions in radio or television stations (including cable and network TV).

Association of Women in Architecture

7440 University Drive
St. Louis, MO 63130
(314)621-3484
Betty Lou Custer, Executive Officer

Purpose: Members of this organization are women involved in architecture or the allied arts (related fields such as structural engineering or building construction). The organization acts as a forum for women to share ideas and encourage others to enter the architecture profession.

Association of Women Gemologists

P.O. Box 1844
Pearland, TX 77588
(713)485-1606

Anna Miller, Director

Purpose: The association provides a network for women gemologists (jewelers who work with gemstones, such as diamonds or rubies) and provides information about the industry.

Association for Women Geoscientists

10200 West 44th Avenue, Suite 304
Wheat Ridge, CO 80033
(303)422-8527

Jane Willard, President

Purpose: Members of this group encourage the participation of women in geology, geophysics, petroleum engineering, geological engineering, hydro (water) geology, paleontology (study of fossils), and geochemistry (earth and soil chemistry). They exchange technical, professional, and educational information. The group also helps in job searches, gives scholastic awards, and recruits high school students into college programs.

Association for Women in Mathematics

Wellesley College
Box 178
Wellesley, MA 02181
(617)237-7517

Tricia Cross, Executive Director

Purpose: The group seeks to improve the status of women in the mathematical profession and to make students aware of opportunities in the field. Members include mathematicians and math students employed by universities, government, and private industry.

Association for Women in Social Work

University of Pennsylvania
Women's Center
119 Houston Hall
3417 Spruce Street
Philadelphia, PA 19104-8611

Elena M. DiLapi, Director

Purpose: This group is a national organization of individuals who offer support to women in the field of social work, especially those who practice from a feminist/womanist philosophy.

Association for Women Veterinarians

32205 Allison Drive
Union City, CA 94587
(415)471-8379

Chris Stone Payne, Secretary

Purpose: This group presents scholarships and awards to women veterinary students and veterinary professionals.

Committee of 200

625 North Michigan Avenue, Suite 500
Chicago, IL 60611-3477
(312)751-3477

Lydia Lewis, Executive Director

Purpose: The group supports women entrepreneurs (a person who starts and runs a new business) and seeks ways to strengthen the influence of women business leaders. Members of this group are women executives who are recognized as leaders in their industries.

Institute of Electrical and Electronic Engineers (IEEE)

Task Force on Women and Minorities
1111 19th Street, Suite 608
Washington, DC 20036
(202)758-0017

Vin O'Neill, Administrator of Professional Programs

Purpose: IEEE members are engineers and scientists who work in or study electrical engineering, electronics, or related fields. The organization offers lectures, supports study groups, and maintains a library. It also offers recognition, awards, and scholarships. The IEEE Task Force on Women and Minorities focuses on ways to increase the number of women and minorities in the electrical engineering and electronics profession.

International Association of Physical Education and Sport for Girls and Women

University of Delaware
Carpenter Sports Building
Newark, DE 19716
(302)831-2644

Barbara J. Kelly, Executive Officer

Purpose: This association seeks to bring together women working in physical education. The association also conducts research, encourages the exchange of members between countries, and supports organizations that encourage women's services. Members are from organizations in fifty-four countries with an interest in physical education for girls and women.

International Association of Women Ministers

579 Main Street
Stroudsburg, PA 18360
(717)421-7751
Carol S. Brown, Treasurer

Purpose: The association offers support for women ministers and conducts research on the status of women in the ministry, with the idea of helping women broaden their role. Members are women from twenty countries. They are ordained, licensed, or authorized by any evangelical denomination (religions based strictly on the Bible) to preach or are women who are preparing for the ministry.

International Nanny Association

P.O. Box 26522
Austin, TX 78755
(512)454-6462

Janet Shannon, General Manager

Purpose: Members include nannies, nanny employers, educators, and nanny placement agencies. The association's services include promoting in-home professional child care and acting as a clearinghouse for information about the profession.

National Association of Women in Horticulture

P.O. Box 1483
Mt. Dora, FL 32757
(904)383-8811

Lori Brown, Executive Secretary

Purpose: This group serves as a networking vehicle for women holding professional positions in horticulture (the raising of plants). It offers scholarships and a Woman of the Year award.

National Association of Women Lawyers

750 North Lake Shore Drive
Chicago, IL 60611
(312)988-6186

Patricia O'Mahoney,
    Executive Director

Purpose: The National Association of Women Lawyers is a support network for women lawyers who have been admitted to practice in any state or territory of the United States. The group maintains seventeen committees that study and research aspects of the law as it applies to women.

Ninety-Nines, International Women Pilots

Will Rogers Airport
P.O. Box 59965
Oklahoma City, OK 73159
(405)685-7969

Loretta Jean Gragg, Executive Director

Purpose: The Ninety-Nines are women pilots united to foster a better understanding of aviation. The group participates in flying competitions and maintains a resource library with a display area dedicated to the preservation of women's achievements in aviation. It also bestows the Amelia Earhart Research Scholar Grant to a specialized, professional scholar and develops aviation programs and courses for schools.

Professional Women Photographers

c/o Photographics Unlimited
17 17th Street, Number 14
New York, NY 10011
(212)255-9678

Mariette Allen, Chairperson

Purpose: This group of professional women photographers conducts educational and artistic activities to stimulate public interest in, support for, and appreciation of photographic art (particularly members' works). The group maintains a speakers' bureau and conducts group shows and projects.

Society of Women Engineers

345 East 47th Street, Room 305
New York, NY 10017
(212)705-7855

B.J. Harrod, Acting Executive Director

Purpose: The Society of Women Engineers supplies information on the achievements of women engineers and the opportunities available to them. It also assists women engineers in preparing to return to active work following temporary retirement (including pregnancy and child rearing). The group offers scholarships, awards, and career guidance.

Religious Organizations

B'nai B'rith Women (BBW)

1828 L Street Northwest, Suite 250
Washington, DC 20036
(202)857-1380

Elaine K. Binder, Executive Director

Purpose: This Jewish women's group engages in activities that support Jewish women and their families through educational projects, caregiving for the elderly, youth projects, and philanthropy (giving large gifts of money).

Buddhist Churches of America

Federation of Buddhist Women's Associations
1710 Octavia Street
San Francisco, CA 94109
(415)776-5600

Seikan Fukuma, Executive Director

Purpose: This group is composed of women members of Buddhist churches of the Jodo Shinshu faith. They promote American Buddhism through educational programs, community service, and recreational programs.

Episcopal Women's Caucus

P.O. Box 5172
Laurel, MD 20726

Purpose: This group is a network for lay (nonclergy) and ordained men and women concerned with the full ministry of all women and minorities in the Episcopal Church.

International Lutheran Women's Missionary League

3558 South Jefferson Avenue
St. Louis, MO 63118-3810
(314)268-1531

Shirley Meckfessel, Office Manager

Purpose: This league is for women's groups within the congregations of the Lutheran Church-Missouri Synod in the United States and Canada. The International Lutheran Women's Missionary league offers missionary education, inspiration, and service to others, including raising funds for the missions. Missionaries are people of a religious faith who leave their own country to feed, educate, and teach the poor people of another country about religion.

Mary's Pence

P.O. Box 29078
Chicago, IL 60629-9078
(312)783-3177

Maureen Gallagher, Contact

Purpose: This Roman Catholic women's organization collects and distributes funds for "alternative" ministries such as women's shelters, legal services, housing, economic development, education and literacy programs, and centers for creative theology (the study of God and religion).

North American Council for Muslim Women

902 McMillen Court
Great Falls, VA 22066
(703) 759-7339

Sharifa Alkhateeb, President

Purpose: The North American Council for Muslim Women is a multinational Muslim women's group that works to solve the social, economic, and development problems of Muslim women, their children, and their communities. The council sponsors education about the Koran (the holy book for followers of Islam), lobbies government on issues affecting the group's membership, and provides leadership training and development.

Presbyterian Women

100 Witherspoon Street
Louisville, KY 40202
(502)569-5365

Gladys Strachan, Executive Director

Purpose: The group provides a forum for Presbyterian women to examine issues involving justice, peace, freedom, world hunger, apartheid (segregation or political and economic discrimination based purely on race), child abandonment, rape, divorce, and displaced women. The group also offers economic justice consultations, organizes overseas study seminars and leadership training events, and conducts local, regional, and national workshops for women.

Woman's National Auxiliary Convention of Free Will Baptists
P.O. Box 1088
1134 Murfreesboro Road
Nashville, TN 37202
(615)361-1010

Mary R. Wisehart, Executive
Secretary-Treasurer

Purpose: This group provides opportunities for women to fulfill their role in the family, church, and community, and assists young people in making a commitment to Christianity. The group contributes to the needs of missions, maintains a store of supplies for missionaries, and provides loans to qualified Christian students attending the Free Will Baptist College in Nashville.

African Methodist Episcopal Church
Women's Missionary Society
1134 11th Street Northwest
Washington, DC 20001
(202)371-8886

Delores L. Kennedy Williams, President

Purpose: The Women's Missionary Society sponsors retreats, leadership training programs, international exchanges, missionaries, and educational programs for religious leaders. It also operates an information bureau, organizes charitable activities, and offers children's competitions, awards, and services.

World Federation of Methodist Women, North America Area
623 San Fernando Avenue
Berkeley, CA 94707
(415)526-5536

Sylvia Faulk, President

Purpose: Members of the federation are women from the various Methodist denominations in the United States, Canada, and the Caribbean. Their goal is to end discrimination worldwide and to pass legislation to end child abuse. The group supports literacy programs and training on food production, malnutrition, hygiene, and family planning.

Young Women of the Church of Jesus Christ of Latter-Day Saints
76 North Main
Salt Lake City, UT 84150
(801)240-211

Ardeth G. Kapp, President

Purpose: This group seeks to strengthen the spiritual life of young women from the ages of twelve to eighteen through Christian values and experiences. The group conducts training, sponsors service projects, and bestows a special achievement medal.

Science/Technology Organizations

American Association for the Advancement of Science (AAAS)
National Network of Women in Science (NWIS)

Office of Opportunities in Science

1333 H Street Northwest
Washington, DC 20005
(202)326-6670

Shirley Malcolm, Program Head

Purpose: This group provides and promotes full access to career information and education for women and minority students, including Native American, Asian American, African American, Mexican American, and Puerto Rican women, in science and engineering.

National Science Foundation
Targeted Programs for Women/Girls
4201 Wilson Boulevard
Arlington, VA 22230
(703)306-1234

Purpose: The National Science Foundation, an independent agency that is part of the Executive Branch of the U.S. government, is concerned primarily with supporting research and education in the sciences and engineering. Targeted Programs for Women/Girls explores ways to make science and technology programs more accessible to women and girls.

Women and Mathematics Education
Mount Holyoke College
302 Shattuck Hall
South Hadley, MA 01075
(413)538-2608

Charlene Morrow, Executive Director

Purpose: Members of this group are individuals who are concerned with promoting the mathematical education of girls and women. The group serves as a clearinghouse for ideas and resources and gives an annual award to an educator who promotes mathematical education of women.

Social/Health Organizations

Alcoholism Center for Women
1147 South Alvarado Street
Los Angeles, CA 90006
(213)381-8500

Brenda L. Underhill, Executive Director

Purpose: This recovery facility works with women alcoholics, especially those considered at high risk for a return to drinking. High-risk women include those who are adult daughters of alcoholics, survivors of incest or battering, and lesbians.

Big Brothers/Big Sisters of America
230 North 13th Street
Philadelphia, PA 19107
(215)567-7000

Thomas M. McKenna, Executive Director

Purpose: Big Brothers/Big Sisters operates local One-to-One Programs that match children from single parent homes with adult volunteers who serve as mentors and role models. Mentors are people already established in a profession who help those just entering.

Disabled Womyn's Educational Project
P.O. Box 8773
Madison, WI 53708-8773
(608)256-8883

Catherine Odette, Executive Officer

Purpose: The project's focus is helping lesbians (female homosexuals) who have physical disabilities. The project supports legislation that is sensitive to members' needs, operates a reference library, and maintains a speakers' bureau.

Federation of Feminist Women's Health Centers

1680 Vine Street, Suite 1105
Los Angeles, CA 90028-8837
(213)957-4062

Carol Downer, Executive Director

Purpose: Members of this group work to ensure that interested women and men receive birth control information. They also educate women about the normal functions of their bodies and work to improve the quality of women's health care.

Girl Scouts of the U.S.A.

830 Third Avenue
New York, NY 10022
(212)940-7500

Mary Rose Main, Executive Director

Purpose: Girl Scouts strives to meet the special needs of girls and to help them develop into happy, resourceful individuals willing to share their abilities as citizens in their homes, their communities, the country, and the world. The Girl Scouts also provides girls with opportunities to expand personal interests, learn new skills, and explore career possibilities.

The Global Fund for Women

2480 Sand Hill Road, Suite 100
Menlo Park, CA 94052-0420
(415)854-0420

Virginia Wright, Assistant to the President

Purpose: The fund is a nonprofit institution that provides money to start, strengthen, and link groups that are committed to women's well-being internationally and to "work for their full participation in society."

International Mother's Peace Day Committee

P.O. Box 102
West Liberty, WV 26074
(304)336-7159

Jeanne V. Schramm, Chairperson

Purpose: This committee seeks to unite mothers and others worldwide to promote the establishment of the first Sunday in June as International Mother's Peace Day. The committee stages letter writing campaigns and peace demonstrations to help achieve their goal.

Ladies Against Women

48 Shattuck, Suite 70
Berkeley, CA 94704
(510)841-6500

Mrs. T. "Bill" Banks,
    Lady Chair-Man

Purpose: Ladies Against Women supports the return of American society to what they term "the good old days." Specifically, members want a return to male authority figures and for women to be treated like "ladies." The group maintains a speakers' bureau and a library with material about traditional male and female roles and relationships.

Mothers Against Drunk Driving (MADD)

511 East John Carpenter Freeway,
    Number 700
Irving, TX 75062
(214)744-6233

Dean Wilkerson, Executive Director

Purpose: MADD is made up of concerned volunteers who encourage citizen participation in working towards reform of the drunk driving problem in the United States. MADD acts as the voice of victims of drunk driving accidents, supports law enforcement programs, and sponsors Project Prom/Graduation, which offers drinkers rides home on prom night.

National Abortion Rights Action League (NARAL)

1101 14th Street Northwest,
 Fifth Floor
Washington, DC 20005
(202)408-4600

Kate Michelman, Executive Director

Purpose: The league's goal is to sustain a pro-choice political constituency in order to maintain the right to legal abortion for all women. Members coordinate grassroots (local) activities, lobby and advise the U.S. Congress, and testify in court cases and at hearings.

National Clearinghouse for the Defense of Battered Women

125 South Ninth Street, Suite 302
Philadelphia, PA 19107
(215)351-0010

Sue Osthoff, Director

Purpose: The clearinghouse aids battered women who have assaulted or killed their abusers in order to protect themselves and/or their children. The clearinghouse offers lawyers, advocates, and expert witnesses.

National Clearinghouse on Marital and Date Rape

2325 Oak Street
Berkeley, CA 94708
(415)524-1582

Laura X., Contact

Purpose: Members of this group provide women with education about rape and rape-prevention training. They also advocate fair legal and societal treatment of rape victims. The group's goal is to make intimate relationships safe and equal for both partners.

National Congress of Neighborhood Women

249 Manhattan Avenue
Brooklyn, NY 11211
(718)388-6666
Jan Peterson, Executive Officer

Purpose: This group works for neighborhood revitalization (to clean up and restore an area) by sharing ideas and experiences of members, who are low- and moderate-income women from diverse ethnic and racial backgrounds.

National Displaced Homemakers Network

1625 K Street Northwest
Washington, DC 20006
(202)628-6767

Jill Miller, Executive Director

Purpose: The network offers assistance to women whose traditional homemaker/mother role has ended abruptly due to divorce, spouse's job loss, or death of a spouse. Among the services offered

Pro-life demonstrators work to end abortion.

are information about job training, education, and other forms of government assistance.

National Right-to-Life Committee

419 Seventh Street Northwest,
   Suite 500
Washington, DC 20004
(202)626-8800

J.C. Wilke, President

Purpose: This pro-life organization opposes abortion, euthanasia (mercy killings), and infanticide (the killing of living children because of birth defects). The committee supports abortion alternative programs that involve counseling and adoption, provides ongoing public education programs, and lobbies the U.S. Congress on abortion issues. It also encourages passage and ratification of a constitutional amendment to protect all human life.

National Society, Daughters of the American Revolution (DAR)

1776 D Street Northwest
Washington, DC 20006-5392
(202)628-1776

Eldred M. Yochim,
   President General

Purpose: The society conducts historical, educational, and patriotic activities and maintains a genealogical/ historical research library, an Americana (early American history and art) museum, and documentary collections of items written before 1830. The society, which is involved in education, initiated American History Month (February) and Constitution Week. Members are women who are descendants of American Revolutionary War (1775–81) patriots.

National Woman's Christian Temperance Union (WCTU)
1730 Chicago Avenue
Evanston, IL 60201
(708)864-1396

Rachel B. Kelly, President

Focus: The union's membership is nonpartisan, interdenominational Christian women dedicated to educating America's youth about what the group believes are the harmful effects of alcohol, narcotic drugs, and tobacco on the human body and American society. Members of the group promote total abstinence through teaching the relationship of alcohol to the mental, moral, social, spiritual, and physical well-being of the individual and the nation. The union sponsors essay, poster, and speech contests.

National Women's Hall of Fame
76 Fall Street
Seneca Falls, NY 13148
(315)568-8060

Nancy Woodhull, President

Purpose: The hall honors "those women citizens of the United States whose contributions to the arts, athletics, business, education, government, the humanities, philanthropy, and science, have been of greatest value for the development of their country." The hall's staff plan special exhibits, annual essay and poster contests, and an annual induction of honorees.

National Women's History Project
7738 Bell Road
Windsor, CA 95492
(707)838-0478

Molly McGregor, Director

Purpose: The National Women's History Project publishes an annual resource catalog that promotes education on the history of women, especially history with a multicultural focus. The project also sponsors National Women's History Month in March, maintains an archive, and holds workshops and educational training sessions for teachers.

Older Women's League (OWL)
666 11th Street Northwest, Suite 700
Washington, DC 20001
(202)783-6686

Purpose: The league focuses on issues important to middle-aged and older women, including access to health care insurance, support for family caregivers, reform of social security, reform of jobs and pensions for older women, and effects of budget cuts on women. The league operates a speakers' bureau and prepares educational materials.

Reproductive Rights National Network

17 Murray Street, Fifth Floor
New York, NY 10007
(212)267-8891

Vienna Carroll, Director

Purpose: The Reproductive Rights National Network advocates reproductive freedom, including the right to an abortion, adequate and safe birth control methods, child care, the right to live openly as a homosexual, freedom from sterilization abuse and reproductive hazards on the job, and an end to population control policies. The group lobbies Congress, develops media messages, and offers referral services on a national level.

Society for the Study of Breast Disease

Sammons Tower
3409 Worth
Dallas, TX 75246
(214)821-2962

George N. Peters, Secretary

Purpose: The society serves as a forum for members to discuss research findings, trends, treatments, and other medical data. Members are physicians and nurses who are engaged in the fields of obstetrics and gynecology, surgery, radiology, family practice, and medical and radiation oncology (the use of X rays to fight cancer).

Stop Equal Rights Amendment

c/o Eagle Forum
Box 18
Alton, IL 62002

Stop ERA leader Phyllis Schlafly speaking to a group of her supporters

(618)462-5415

Phyllis Schlafly, Chairperson

Purpose: This group, also known as "Stop ERA," seeks to expose what it sees as the ERA's hidden agenda: gay rights and abortion. The group is still active even though the ERA was defeated because it fears a renewal of support for ERA passage.

United Nations Development Fund for Women

304 East 45th Street, Sixth Floor
New York, NY 10017

Members of the Women's International League for Peace and Freedom don't believe that women or men should serve in the military.

(212)906-6400

Sharon Capeling-Alakija, Director

Purpose: This independent fund provides money to educational programs in developing countries, including training in child care, food preservation, energy resource development, and skill building in small business management. It was founded by the United Nations General Assembly following the International Women's Year in 1975.

Women's International League for Peace and Freedom

1213 Race Street
Philadelphia, PA 19107
(215)563-7110

Purpose: Members of this league support equal rights for women but believe that neither men nor women should participate in the military. Members are women activists who oppose militarism (the build-up and threatened use of armies in political conflict).

Young Women's Christian Association of the United States of America (YWCA-USA)
726 Broadway
New York, NY 10003
(212)614-2700

Gwendolyn Calvert Baker,
Executive Director

Purpose: The YWCA offers girls and women chances to participate in organized sports, recreation, health education, service projects, clubs and classes, and counseling. The group's goal is to make contributions to peace, justice, freedom, and dignity for all people. The YWCA maintains recreational/class facilities, summer camps, and shelters throughout the United States.

Sports Organizations

National Association for Girls and Women in Sport
1900 Association Drive
Reston, VA 22091
(703)476-3450

Purpose: The goal of the association is to support and foster the development of quality sports programs that enrich the lives of women and girls. Members are teachers, coaches, athletic trainers, officials, athletic administrators, and students.

12

Social Concerns

"When you cease to make a contribution you begin to die."

—Eleanor Roosevelt, First Lady and social activist

Women barred throughout history from participating fully in society have found other ways to leave their mark on those around them. In almost every society, women have been denied the right to vote, to own property, to hold public office, or to become educated. Nevertheless, throughout history women have always managed to influence their worlds. In most cases, this influence was positive, as women directed their attention mainly to improving the social conditions of the time.

Modern women have also been involved in a huge variety of causes, including recycling, protecting the environment, animal rights, toxic waste monitoring, child care, toy and clothing safety, political prisoners, and reproductive rights. The causes are many, and so are the women involved. Space limitations dictate that this chapter discuss only some of the major initiatives (movements) started by women from many different places and in many different times. For the purposes of this discussion, the social concerns of women can be grouped loosely into several major categories. Among them are the concern for:

- children
- disadvantaged people
- those in need of reproductive information
- those working in unsafe or unfair conditions
- those living among violence

Children

Many women, perhaps because of their close connection with childbirth and raising families, have been concerned throughout history with the well-being of the children in their society. Some of these women and their causes are detailed below:

Candy Lightner and Mothers Against Drunk Driving (MADD)

In 1995, drunk drivers in the United States killed more than 16,500 people and injured another one million. These statistics are staggering, and have been high for many years as drivers who drink continue to evade stiff legal penalties. Although drunk drivers continue to injure and kill thousands of people each year, the situation is better than in the past.

As a result of one drunk driver, one mother decided to fight for stricter laws. That mother was Candy Lightner, a real estate agent who lived in California with her twin daughters and son. In 1980, her thirteen-year-old daughter Cari was killed in a hit-and-run accident with a drunk driver who had had four previous DWI convictions. (DWI means "driving while under the influence" of liquor or drugs.)

Even as she mourned her daughter, Lightner was learning just how little the legal system seemed to care about the circumstances behind Cari's death. "Death caused by drunk drivers is our only socially acceptable form of homicide," Lightner has said. In response, she formed Mothers Against Drunk Driving or MADD. This lobbying group has changed America's attitude about drunk driving and like the Temperance movement of the 1800s has once again made alcohol a political issue in the United States.

MADD's membership is composed of mothers and other relatives whose children have been killed or maimed by drunk drivers. Their goal is to enforce the penalties already on the books and, if necessary, to enact stiffer penalties to curb the incidence of drunk driving. MADD now has 3.2 million members nationwide and operates through a national headquarters in Texas. It has 430 local groups throughout the United States.

Since 1980, Lightner and her organization have convinced Congress to raise the national drinking age from eighteen to twenty-one (teens were involved in 1 out of every 5 fatal accidents involving liquor). In addition to education and political lobbying, the group sponsors special projects such as Operation Prom/Graduation and Campaign Safe & Sober, which offer free rides home to drinkers on prom night or New Year's Eve.

The mission of MADD is to stop drunk driving and support victims of this violent crime. MADD's agenda includes:

- laws that make it illegal for underage (under 21 years old) persons to drive with any alcohol in their bloodstreams

- lowering the amount of alcohol that can legally be present in the blood of drivers

- greater use of sobriety checkpoints to catch drunk drivers and to act as a warning to other drivers

- mandatory alcohol testing of all drivers involved in accidents resulting in death or injury

- mandatory imprisonment of drivers convicted of more than one drunk driving offense

- license plate/vehicle confiscation for repeat offenders

MADD helps victims and families of victims with a number of programs. These include court watching, media/press events, candlelight vigils, telephone help lines, and rating the states by reporting on how each one is progressing in the fight against drunk driving.

Lightner herself has been honored many times for her work. She has served on the Presidential Commission on Drunk and Drugged Driving, is a member of the National Highway Safety Advisory Council, was named to *Good Housekeeping*'s Most Admired Woman's Poll in 1986, and was honored by *Time* magazine as one of Seven Who Succeeded in 1985. Although Lightner has since left MADD, she continues her work as a social activist. In 1992 she founded Americans Against Crime, a support and lobbying group.

Candy Lightner founded MADD after her daughter was killed by a drunk driver.

Peggy Charren and Action for Children's Television (ACT)

In 1968, Peggy Charren started Action for Children's Television or ACT to challenge the entertainment industry about the poor quality and lack of programming directed toward children. Charren and her early supporters were especially concerned about the amount and type of violence they saw in cartoons and about the heavy advertising that occurred during children's prime-time viewing hours (after school and Saturday mornings).

Charren's grassroots (local) organization eventually grew into a nation-

Child Labor Laws and "Mother" Jones

During the Industrial Revolution (from the mid-1700s to the mid-1800s), cities grew as farmers left the countryside to work for better pay in the many factories that were starting up in England and the United States. With the farmers came their wives and children and, in many cases, they all became factory workers. Conditions in the factories depended upon the owners. Enlightened owners knew that fair pay, reasonable hours and work load, and good lighting and ventilation (air flow) meant that their workers were happier, healthier, and more productive. Unenlightened owners, on the other hand, thought that children could be paid less and that sick laborers could be easily replaced by those healthy people flooding the cities in search of work.

Many factory owners, especially those who ran textile (fabric) mills, used children in their factories, since children were ideally suited to some jobs. Because children's hands and fingers are smaller than adults', they were better able to untangle threads on sewing and weaving machines. Since they were shorter and weighed less, children could work inside or on top of machines. Best of all, because they were children, they could be paid a fraction of what an adult man earned.

Like adults however, children were expected to put in fourteen- and sixteen-hour days and work six days a week. They received little or no education and were prone to develop respiratory and bone diseases from the poor conditions in the factories. When they became too sick to work, they were let go. In the early 1800s, about 40 percent of the mill workers in New England were children between the ages of seven and sixteen. There were early laws against the use of child labor, but these laws were weak and mostly unenforced.

It was these weak child labor laws that ignited reformers like "Mother" Jones to take action. Mary Harris "Mother" Jones (1830–1930) was one of the most famous labor organizers in American history. Born in Ireland, she later came to the United States and worked as a dressmaker. In 1867, she lost her husband and four children to a yellow fever epidemic. After the loss of her

al organization and a powerful lobbying group. Its goal was to end the violence and commercialism of children's programming and increase the educational and cultural offerings designed for children.

ACT faced four huge obstacles while trying to change the type of children's programming being offered. The obstacles included:

- The U.S. broadcasting industry feared that it would lose money if they were

family, Jones dedicated the next fifty years of her life to improving the working conditions of those around her. She was particularly active in trying to improve the life of mine workers and their families.

Jones felt special pity for the child laborers she encountered during her work. On one occasion, she helped a group of child workers who were on strike for better working conditions. Together, Jones and the children marched from their mill in Kensington, Pennsylvania, to the home of President Theodore Roosevelt in Oyster Bay, New York. Once there, Jones confronted the president, demanding that he look at the children's hands, which had become crippled from operating the mill looms.

In part, because of efforts like those of Jones, the Owens-Keating Child Labor Law was passed in 1916. The law limited the age at which children could be put to work, and limited the hours per day they could work. Today, thanks in large part to agitators like Jones, strict laws govern the age at which children can begin to work and the minimum wage they can be paid.

forced to broadcast more educational or cultural programs because it was assumed these types of shows would not attract advertisers.

- The First Amendment of the U.S. Constitution prevents any type of government interference in free speech.

- The advertising and toy industry liked the current format because it made a great deal of money for them by using specific toys as the main characters

Television shows such as The Mighty Morphin Power Rangers *sparked many women concerned with children and television violence to start activist groups.*

of cartoons. Toy advertisers and sellers profited because the programs helped sell more toys.

- Few Hollywood writers had been encouraged to develop quality children's shows, so the talent available to write new programs was limited.

During its twenty-two-year battle to improve children's programming, ACT used many tools, including:

Window on the World: Morphin Mania

In 1995, much of the concern about violence in children's television programming focused on a show called *The Mighty Morphin Power Rangers*. The show revolves around teenagers who are able to transform themselves into warriors and fight a variety of evil beings in a virtual world.

The concept sounds far-fetched, but the worries of parents were very real. They believed that their children were exposed to a steady diet of TV violence and that the *Power Rangers* typified the worst of the mindlessly violent plotlines. One Canadian mother decided to fight back.

Kathryn Flannery lived in Waterloo, Ontario, and was the mother of two preschoolers (aged two and four). After seeing the show in 1994, she prohibited her children to watch it. She also took her concerns to Canwest Global, the network that aired the program in her area, but she received no response.

Flannery's next move was to consult Patricia Herdman, another Ontario resident who had recently founded the Coalition for Responsible Television. On Herdman's advice, Flannery complained to the Canadian Radio-Television and Telecommunications Commission, the federal broadcast regulator. Her complaint contained a petition with the names of fifty-five neighbors, teachers, and parents. All asked that the show be withdrawn.

Flannery soon learned that her petition had been passed along to the Canadian Broadcast Standards Council, which decided that the show was excessively violent and censored it. The censoring came despite the fact that *The Mighty Morphin Power Rangers* was a commercial success. The show was broadcast to thirty countries and had spawned a whole range of moneymaking spinoff products. This example shows how one woman's concern resulted in a popular TV show being edited to a shorter length, and the extra time being made up in public service announcements about positive behavior.

- programs that educated parents and teachers about the negative effects of heavy television watching on children
- campaigns to improve the diet of children, prompted mainly by the overwhelming amount of junk food and heavily sugared cereal advertisements that aired during children's programs
- comparisons with the fine programming, like the award-winning *Sesame Street, Mr. Rogers' Neighborhood,* and *The Electric Company,* that was

coming out of the Children's Television Network and being aired on public television stations

- surveys, petitions, and studies that indicated parents would support advertisers who backed quality television programming for children

In 1990, the U.S. Congress finally passed the Children's Television Act. This federal mandate (an order that comes from the federal government) was the first of its kind in the forty-five-year history of television broadcasting. The act required local television stations to provide a set amount of quality educational programming for children. In addition, it limited the number of minutes per hour that could be devoted to advertising on children's programs. Today, that ratio is fourteen minutes advertising time for every hour of children's programs (contrast that to adult programs, where the ratio of advertising time to programming is eight minutes per hour).

ACT was disbanded in 1992 after its primary goal, the passage of the federal legislation, had been achieved. However, Charren remains active and vocal about the need for quality children's programs. She is the nation's foremost consultant on children's television programming, and her concerns now extend to the material to which children are exposed in movies, video games, and on the Internet.

Tipper Gore and Record Warning Labels

It was 1985, and rock and roll was firmly entrenched in American society.

Tipper Gore, wife of then-senator Al Gore of Tennessee, was the mother of teenagers. One day she listened to the lyrics of a song on one of her daughter's albums. Gore was shocked at the sexually explicit words and themes she was hearing. She turned her outrage into action and cofounded the Parents Music Research Group, later renamed the Parents Music Research Center or PMRC. Later she wrote a book titled *Raising PG Kids in an X-rated Society.*

The PMRC's primary goal is for record companies to develop a rating system that evaluates the lyrics of rock songs. The proposed ratings system is similar to that used by the Motion Picture Association of America (G = general audience, PG = parental guidance suggested, etc.). The rating system would help control the sale of inappropriate material to children.

Gore and other PMRC members also started a public campaign that demanded that record executives be more responsible in their musical offerings. She berated them for glamorizing sex and violence in material that was meant to become popular with teenagers and younger children.

In the mid-1980s, Gore's advocacy of the warning labels seemed like censorship. But by 1995, her warnings about the negative impact of sexual and violent lyrics seemed like a prediction come true. Many social scientists believe that hearing the explicit lyrics has desensitized (numbed) children to violence in general and, in particular, sexual violence against women. Today, thanks in part to Gore's efforts, record companies are more sensitive to how they package their offerings. Although a rating system has not been established for recordings as of the mid-1990s, warning labels are used on many tapes and albums that have inappropriate lyrics for children.

Disadvantaged People

Among the disadvantaged are the mentally ill, the economically poor, the illiterate (those unable to read and write well), the handicapped, foreigners unfamiliar with American society, and the homeless. Here are several initiatives started by women who responded to the needs of the disadvantaged.

Dorothea Dix and the Mentally Ill

Throughout history, mentally ill people have been regarded as evil by the rest of society. Many civilizations throughout the world view the mentally ill as being possessed by evil spirits or acting out the work of the devil. Before the mid-1800s, American society treated mentally ill people like criminals. These people were locked up in prisonlike facilities and often bound, gagged, and drugged to control their behavior.

In 1820, a teacher named Dorothea Dix (1802–1887) established a school for girls in 1820 in Boston, Massachusetts. Around 1840, a friend asked Dix to teach a Sunday school class to the women prisoners in a nearby jail. There Dix found

Dorothea Dix became an advocate for the mentally ill.

many mentally ill women who had been arrested and jailed alongside common criminals. Her experience in the prison inspired her to investigate and then campaign for the improvement of the living conditions in prisons, poor houses, and hospitals.

After two years of visiting these places, Dix was ready to publicly make her case. In 1843, she testified before the Massachusetts state legislature about the inhuman conditions she had found in hospitals caring for the mentally ill.

Dix then took her investigative work to other states, where she discovered similar conditions. She found that the men-

Window on the World: India

Phoolan Devi is an Indian peasant girl who revolted against the strict caste (social class) rule that is still observed in India. Indian social classes range from the Brahmins, the top caste, to the Untouchables, the lowest caste. People cannot marry outside their caste and, for the most part, socialize only with members of their own caste.

In 1979, an early marriage arranged by Devi's father ended badly. Instead of returning to her family's care, she became an outlaw. Devi actually had few options, since her caste and her father dictated how she would spend her life. Devi, however, chose to disregard these societal rules and showed her contempt for the caste system by staging a series of raids against people of higher castes.

Nicknamed the "beautiful bandit," Devi waged war against the different castes until 1983, when she surrendered to Indian authorities. After serving eleven years in prison, she emerged to organize a group to help other lower caste Indian women deal with their situation.

---

tally ill who were also poor were penned up like animals. For each state she visited, Dix prepared a report like the one she had delivered to the Massachusetts legislature. Each set of state legislators, moved by her eloquence, her facts, and the newspaper publicity that followed her, passed laws and set aside money for hospital and prison reform.

Because of Dix's pioneering work, institutions for the mentally ill and destitute (poor) were established in twenty U.S. states and in Canada. Her influence extended to Europe as well. Dix's U.S. activities were read about, and social reformers took to heart her book, *Prisons and Prison Discipline*. As a result, European prisons and almshouses were drastically reformed.

During the U.S. Civil War (1861–65), Dix served as superintendent of women nurses for the Union (Northern) Army. Following the war, she resumed her efforts to found new, progressive mental hospitals, and she succeeded. When Dix began her work in 1841, there were 13 mental institutions in the United States. When she died in 1887, there were 123. Dix's willingness to look at the mentally ill in a new light encouraged others to do so, and by the 1900s, the mentally ill were the subject of a new branch of medicine called psychiatry.

Jane Addams and Hull House

By the early 1800s, the immigrants traveling to America were no longer primarily from England. Instead they came from Germany, Scandinavia, and Ireland. Many of these new immigrants did not speak English, and fewer still understood the workings of American society. The situation for these immigrants improved largely through the efforts of Jane Addams (1860–1935), founder of Hull House. In 1899, Addams purchased the Hull mansion in Chicago, Illinois, with the idea of turning it into a settlement house, a privately funded institution to help poor and immigrant people find a place in American society. The services offered by Hull House included child care, medical attention, and classes in English, job training, sewing, and citizenship. Hull House also provided cultural programs like concerts and lectures and offered meeting space for clubs and labor-union groups.

Hull House, while it was not the first settlement house, became the most famous. By 1910 there were four hundred settlement houses in eastern and midwestern U.S. cities with large immigrant populations. Because of Addams and her supporters, American society was challenged to look at the poor and the newcomers in a new way. This new view led to a new profession called social work. The settlement house workers (or social workers as they would later be called) concerned themselves with every aspect of their clients' lives, from sanitation to housing and work conditions, to protection of children and immigrant workers' rights. The experience of Addams and Hull House led to a number of reforms, many of which

Social activist Jane Addams

became laws to protect the disadvantaged of American society.

Reproductive Information

Reproductive information refers to education about sexual organs and their function, pregnancy, birth control, and maternal care, which is health care given to pregnant women. Throughout history, the whole reproductive cycle remained a mystery to most women. Cultural ceremonies and religious rites explained some of the changes women noticed in their bodies, but for the most part no scientific or medical information was available to them.

Window on the World: Bulgaria

Dimitrina Petrova, a philosopher and a member of the Bulgarian Parliament, helped to write the country's new constitution when it overthrew its Communist dictators after the fall of the Soviet Union. Petrova, who is also fluent in several languages, is an advocate for the Gypsies, an oppressed ethnic group in her country. She is the founder of the Human Rights Project, an organization dedicated to winning full civil and legal rights for the Gypsy minority. Historically, the nomadic Gypsies have been a persecuted group throughout eastern Europe, where they have been regarded as a superstitious and dishonest sect.

In fact, in many societies, even through the beginning of the 1900s, reproductive information was controlled by law as well as by custom. Laws prevented women from learning about birth control devices from their most likely source: their doctors. Other laws, like U.S. Post Office regulations, prevented people from delivering information about birth control and venereal (sexually transmitted) diseases through the mail.

Margaret Sanger and Birth Control

Margaret Sanger (1883–1966) was an educated woman of middle-class background. However, she became America's pioneer of birth control for poor and working women. Before she challenged the system, little was known or understood about birth control and more often it was illegal.

It was Sanger's firsthand experiences as a public health nurse that led her to question why poor women had so many pregnancies, such poor maternal care, such high mother and infant death rates, and so many cases of untreated venereal disease. Sanger sought to help these women by publishing an article about venereal disease. However, the U.S. Post Office prevented the distribution of the article by using the Comstock Laws of 1873. These laws prevented "obscene" material from being sent through the mail. Just as Sanger was about to be arrested on charges of obscenity, she left for Europe. She spent her year-long, self-imposed exile studying and learning about birth control methods.

In Holland, Sanger studied with Dr. Havelock Ellis and met other social activists like Maria Stopes and Aletta Jacobs. Since information about birth control devices was more openly shared in Europe, Sanger was able to learn about the workings of diaphragms (a rubber circle that fits over the cervix to prevent sperm from entering the uterus), condoms, and spermicidal douches.

When Sanger returned home, she was determined to share her knowledge of birth control methods with the people she believed most needed it. She chose a poor Jewish-Italian neighborhood called

Brownsville in Brooklyn, New York, and opened her birth control clinic in 1916. Assisting Sanger were her sister, Ethel Byrne, who was a registered nurse, and Fania Mindell, a translator. At the clinic, Sanger and her associates gave out information and instructions in how to use the diaphragm and how to watch for symptoms of venereal disease.

Within ten days, Sanger and her helpers were arrested on charges of creating a public nuisance. When the three women were sentenced to do thirty days of labor in a work house, Byrne staged a ten-day hunger strike. Her goal was to call public attention to the idea of a woman's choice to become a mother or not, or as Sanger called it, "voluntary motherhood." Byrne was eventually pardoned by the governor and released. Although the charges against Sanger had not been dropped, she was also released, and she and Byrne immediately reopened the clinic.

A judge later heard Sanger's case and decided that while she could not distribute condoms and diaphragms, doctors could. Indirectly, Sanger had paved the way for the intimate relationship that now exists between gynecologists (a doctor who specializes in the diseases and physical makeup of women) and their patients. This reliance on doctors as an avenue of information is one that Sanger used throughout her long career as a birth control advocate.

Sanger's efforts to distribute reproductive information continued throughout her life. Her writings include a 1914 pamphlet called *Family Limitations* and

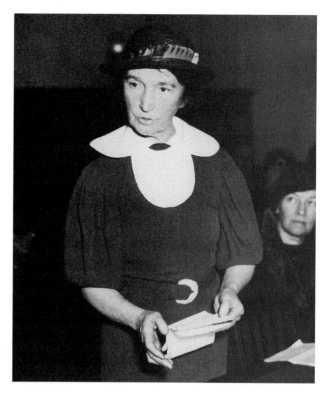

Birth control advocate Margaret Sanger testifying before a Senate committee in 1934

many books, including *What Every Mother Should Know* (1917) and *My Fight for Birth Control* (1931). In 1921, Sanger founded the American Birth Control League. The organization eventually evolved into Planned Parenthood, one of the nation's largest distributors of low-cost reproductive information. Sanger had accomplished her goal: to give women access to birth control devices. She had also established a nationwide system of advice centers where women could learn about the devices and methods that would help them in their quest to ensure "voluntary motherhood."

Window on the World: Thailand

Chantawipa (Noi) Apisuk is a feminist living in Bangkok, Thailand. Her cause is the end of prostitution (selling sex for money), an industry that employs some seven hundred thousand people in Thailand. In Bangkok's biggest red light (prostitution) district, Noi founded Education Means Production of Women Engaged in Recreation (EMPOWER). This group focuses on bettering the life and livelihood of prostitutes, some of whom are barely teenagers and many of whom have families to support and no other means of earning a living.

One of the reasons for the high number of prostitutes in Thailand is that farm girls who have little education and no job skills migrate to the city. Desperate, they turn to prostitution to support themselves. Noi's organization offers a glimmer of hope by running schools to provide the education these women need to qualify for different jobs. EMPOWER is currently engaged in educating prostitutes and the general Thai public about AIDS and the danger of unprotected sex.

Unfair/Unsafe Working Conditions

Throughout much of history, rich people have hired poorer people to work for them. The poorer people might be house servants, farm workers, factory hands, or tutors. These working people often faced unfair or unsafe working conditions. For instance, employees might be paid a low wage, or might be exposed to toxic chemicals. If they threatened to leave, their employer could easily find another worker.

In the early 1820s, American farm girls began to leave their family homes and journey to New England mill towns where they could earn as much as $3.00 a week. At the time, this was considered a fair and even generous wage. Part of the salary went for the girl's room and board, which the mill owner supplied. For several years, all went well. The girls were happy with the money, most of which was sent home to help their fathers or to pay for their brothers' education.

Then economic conditions changed. Mill owners earned less on their goods, so they paid the mill girls a lower salary. After a time, the girls objected. A series of small strikes in the 1830s led to a strike by fifteen hundred workers in 1836. The mill girls were demanding higher wages and shorter working hours (they were working between twelve and fourteen hours each day). The strike ended abruptly when the owners cut off the workers' food supply and turned them out of their company-owned boardinghouses.

Sarah Bagley helped "factory girls" such as these receive better working conditions.

Sarah Bagley and the Lowell Mill Girls

In response to the mill owners' unfair treatment, workers in many industries began to organize themselves into associations that were ancestors of the modern labor unions. Workers believed that they had more power speaking as a group than as individuals. Many of these first labor organizers were women from the mills. Sarah Bagley, a weaver in a Lowell, Massachusetts, mill, was elected president of the Female Labor Reform Association in 1844. She rallied the mill workers through newspaper articles, speeches, and demonstrations. When mill owners wanted the workers to speed up their rate of production by tending to four looms instead of three, Bagley and her association members refused. Unfortunately, Bagley's strikes failed to end the mill owners' unfair demands, but her courageous actions did focus much public attention on the plight of the "factory girls."

The efforts of Bagley and others like her resulted in an 1874 law that mandated (officially required) a ten-hour working day and other labor reforms. Those efforts also showed the power of collective (group) action, a lesson that other union organizers were quick to learn.

Dolores Huerta leads a rally of the United Farm Workers.

The involvement of women in labor issues has continued to this day. With Cesar Chavez, Dolores Huerta founded the organization that would become the United Farm Workers in 1962. The United Farm Workers brought to public attention the poor wages and backbreaking work done by migrant workers (farm workers who travel from one area to another in search of work). The organization is most famous for the boycott (refusal to use or buy a product) they launched against grape growers, an economic tool that won better working conditions for grape pickers. In the 1970s, the movie *Norma Rae* focused attention on the struggle of textile workers to win a fair wage. Actress Sally Field played the union organizer in the film.

Violence

America's history is one of violent confrontation, with weapons often used to settle disputes or as a scare tactic. Although violence has always been present in the United States, it seems to have increased in the 1980s and 1990s. Violent crime captures headlines daily, and record-setting murder rates, gang violence on the streets and in schools, car-jackings, and workplace assaults have increased citizens' fears. As a result, women have taken the lead in trying to curb the incidence of violence so that all American citizens can feel safe.

Women's Peace Party

The Women's Peace Party was founded in 1915 in response to World War I (1914–18) then raging in Europe. Jeannette Rankin, the first congresswoman and a U.S. representative from Montana, was a member of the Women's Peace Party. In 1917 she voted against the United States's going to war, but she was outvoted by other congressional representatives and America entered anyway. Other members of the party included Jane Addams, founder of Hull House; Charlotte Perkins Gilman, author of *Women and Economics;* Florence Kelley of the National Consumer's League; and Carrie Chapman Catt, a leader of the Women's Suffrage movement.

U.S. congresswoman Jeannette Rankin was a member of the Women's Peace Party, which called for an end to war.

The antiviolence tradition continues to be a cornerstone of women's social concerns. Later peace groups have included the Women's International League for Peace and Freedom, Women Strike for Peace, and Women Against Military Madness.

Clementine Barfield and Save Our Sons and Daughters (SOSAD)

Save Our Sons and Daughters or SOSAD was founded in 1987, a year when the city of Detroit, Michigan, experienced what seemed to be an explosion in youth violence and killing. That year

alone, forty-three young people under the age of seventeen were killed, and another three hundred were wounded. The violence was connected to drug use, drug sales, and gang wars. In many ways, Detroit is typical of older U.S. cities: many people without jobs, a shrinking number of taxpayers because people and businesses have moved out, and increases in violence and crime.

SOSAD's founders were two women who had been personally touched by youth violence. Clementine Barfield had lost her sixteen-year-old son to a bullet fired by an alleged drug dealer in

Window on the World: World Pacifism

In 1990, thirty-year-old Eva Michels was the director of Peace Outreach, Action Reconciliation, in Germany. Michels explained the group's focus during a 1990 Celebration of Conscience in Bryn Mawr, Pennsylvania: "The issues I work on focus around the new alignments in Europe and the severe questions needing answers. We must connect ecology and economics with the peace movement."

The event in Bryn Mawr marked the fiftieth anniversary of the United States's legalization of conscientious objector status. A conscientious objector is a person who refuses to serve in military combat situations even if she or he is drafted into the armed services. The person objects to the violence of war based on deep religious or philosophical beliefs.

The Bryn Mawr gathering drew pacifists (people who don't believe in war) from the United States, Germany, the former Soviet Union, the Czech Republic, Colombia, El Salvador, Israel, and Thailand.

the 1990s, SOSAD's members include children, parents, educators, and community leaders who seek an end to the killing of young people in Detroit. Their tools are crisis intervention (telephone hotlines whose counselors can calm angry people) and violence prevention programs. Members also act as court watchers who attend criminal trials to offer support to victims' families.

Early in its existence, SOSAD members developed a nine-point plan to address youth violence in Detroit. The plan called for:

- An increase in police foot patrols in Detroit neighborhoods.
- Expansion of the court-watching program.
- Support for then-mayor Coleman Young's "get tough" approach to youth crime.
- Amnesty (a general pardon) for youths who turned in handguns to authorities.
- Strict enforcement of handgun ordinances.
- Youth drug rehabilitation programs in every police precinct.
- Training in nonviolent problem resolution in Detroit public schools.
- Youth participation in neighborhood rehabilitation projects.
- Public demonstrations of support for SOSAD's goals.

According to Barfield, "[Adults] have not shown them [children]. We have sat back and let drugs and guns take over

1986, and Lula Mae Wimbush had lost a niece to gunfire that erupted at a slumber party the same year. When Barfield and Wimbush announced their organization, the parents of other victims joined. In

our neighborhoods. It's time we declared war . . . and took our neighborhoods back. It's time we took our children back."

Although SOSAD is a local Detroit group, similar groups have been formed throughout the country. The grassroots (local) efforts of women like Barfield and Wimbush have focused national attention on what social scientists are now calling an "epidemic of teen violence." This increased public attention has led to more funding for community policing programs and violence prevention classes in schools.

Linda Lantieri and the Resolving Conflict Creatively Program (RCCP)

Linda Lantieri is the national director of the Resolving Conflict Creatively Program (RCCP), which she cofounded in 1994 in New York City. Lantieri believes that violence is preventable, and her focus is getting that message to school-age children. RCCP tries to minimize misunderstandings by educating children about the values and beliefs of various ethnic groups. The program also offers alternatives to violence and teaches creative conflict resolution skills to students, teachers, parents, and administrators.

In the 1993–94 school year, RCCP reached 120,000 students in 5 public school districts, including those in New York City; New Orleans, Louisiana; Anchorage, Alaska; and districts in Southern California and New Jersey. RCCP is now the largest school-based program of its kind in the United States.

Founder of SOSAD Clementine Barfield holds the program from her son's funeral service.

Among the maxims that RCCP teaches are:

- it is always better to listen first and then talk
- there are always choices for how to deal with a situation
- there is never just one solution (be creative in finding a way out)
- there are more ways to behave than just passively or aggressively

"The world yearns for a new way of fighting, one in which people can be strong without being mean," Lantieri says. "Conflict is part of life, and we

Peace Pilgrim Hikes Across America

A woman who named herself "Peace Pilgrim" is featured on the cover of the 1996 *Women Who Dare* calendar because, at age 45, this woman left her traditional life behind (including her name) and adopted a new name and costume that reflected what would be her message for the rest of her life. The front of her shirt read "Peace Pilgrim." The back read "25,000 miles on foot for peace."

Peace Pilgrim was on her seventh trip across America, on foot, when she was killed after being hit by a car. Before she died, however, this woman's journey and her message had won her hundreds of friends. Thousands of people heard her message of peace, which shows how much one dedicated woman can accomplish.

wouldn't want to eliminate it even if we could. But we urgently need to find ways to end the violence between diverse groups of people that causes so much unnecessary pain and suffering. . . . Our children deserve a future in which their right to safety is reclaimed and their cultural diversity is celebrated."

Sarah Brady and Handgun Control, Inc.

Handgun Control, Inc., is a public citizen's lobby that works for legisla-tive controls and government regula-tions on the manufacturing, importation, sale, transfer, and civilian possession of handguns. The group was started by Sarah Brady after her husband, Jim Brady, a press secretary for then-president Ronald Reagan, was seriously wounded in 1981 by a man who had recently pur-chased a handgun. Although the assas-sin was shooting at Reagan, whom he wounded slightly, Jim Brady was hit in the head by one of the bullets. The wound left him permanently unable to walk or speak clearly.

Jim Brady was injured by a men-tally troubled young man who purchased a handgun for $33 at a pawnshop. The shooter, John Hinckley, had a record of psychiatric hospitalizations. Never-theless, he was able to select a gun, lie on a registration form, purchase the gun, and walk out—a ten minute trans-action. When Sarah Brady finally under-stood how easy it was to purchase weapons in the United States, she made it her business to challenge the status quo (the way things are). Brady founded Handgun Control, Inc., and began lob-bying the U.S. Congress to pass gun control legislation.

Brady and her supporters were fac-ing a huge battle, however. The right to bear arms was written in the U.S. Bill of Rights and strongly supported by the National Rifle Association (NRA), one of the most powerful lobbying groups on Capitol Hill. Brady's proposed leg-islation did not ban the sale of weapons, but it did impose a waiting period

Working to End Violence

Erin Donovan is director of Teens, Crime and the Community, an organization funded by the National Crime Prevention Council. Donovan's group runs a program that teaches children how to make their neighborhoods safe.

Kim Reed is legal counsel for Enough Is Enough, Inc. This group uses a "white ribbon" campaign to educate children about guns, violence, conflict resolution, peer mediation, self-respect, and confidence. (Conflict resolution is a tool for creatively solving problems. Peer mediation is the use of trained young people who encourage a nonviolent solution between two arguing people or groups.)

Children who go through the program receive a white ribbon upon graduation. Part of the graduation ceremony requires them to sign a pledge that they will use words, not guns, to solve their problems. The group uses former gang members and other volunteers to reach students in the Washington, D.C., public schools.

Nancy Gannon is director of Education, Straight Talk About Risks Program at the Center to Prevent Handgun Violence. The organization was founded by Sarah and Jim Brady (see text). Its mission is to teach schoolchildren the skills they need to solve their problems nonviolently. The group tries to make children and adults aware of the fact that murders, suicides, and unintentional shootings can easily occur in homes where there are handguns.

between when a purchase request was made and when permission for the purchase was granted. Brady knew that police statistics showed that most crimes were committed in the heat of anger. If a waiting period could give someone time to calm down, Brady reasoned that fewer crimes would be committed. Her legislation also proposed that owners and their weapons be registered on a national data base.

In 1991, ten years after Jim Brady was shot, the House Judiciary Committee voted 23 to 11 to support the so-called Brady Bill. This bill imposed a mandatory five-day waiting period on handgun purchases. From this House committee, the bill went to a full vote in the U.S. House of Representatives and then the U.S. Senate. In 1993, the Brady Bill was passed into law. Among its many provisions, it called for:

- a five-day waiting period between requesting and receiving permission to purchase a handgun

- a check to see if the purchaser had a criminal background

Window on the World: Egypt

Huda Sh'arawi (1882-1947) founded the women's movement in Egypt and is recognized throughout the Arab world as an early leader in the struggle for women's rights. Like other upper-class Egyptian girls of her time, Sh'arawi was educated at home by a tutor. She was taught French and Turkish, the "civilized languages" of the time, and other lady-like subjects. But she also listened in on her brother's sessions and learned to read Arabic. Thereafter she was a self-taught woman who read every Arabic text she could find from philosophy to economics to political tracts.

In 1910, Sh'arawi opened a school for girls. Unlike the vocational schools of the time, which taught girls job-related skills like midwifery, Sh'arawi's school offered a general education. After World War I ended in 1918, the Egyptians began their struggle for freedom from British rule. Women who were concerned about the issue met at Sh'arawi's home. With their encouragement, Sh'arawi wrote a letter to Lady Burnett, the wife of the British high commissioner of Egypt. The letter said, in part:

"What do you think, Madam, of your government giving itself the right to impose curfews in a time of peace (here in Egypt) and to banish persons who have committed no crime except to want to live freely in their own country? What can you say about your own soldiers who roam the quiet streets of Egypt with revolvers and machine guns, firing at unarmed people if those people's voices are raised to ask for justice and liberty?

"Do all these deeds, Madam, result from Britain's efforts to serve justice and humanity?"

Sh'arawi's letter was followed by a petition signed by 350 women. The British did not begin to loosen their reins on Egyptian freedom until about 1923. By then, Sh'arawi and other Egyptian women had formed the first women's association in the country. After attending the International Conference of Women in Rome as Egypt's delegate, she returned home to question the customs under which she had been raised. She shed her veil (women in Egypt always appeared veiled when in public) and never again wore it.

In 1924 she established the Women's Union and a magazine designed to raise awareness of the need for increased freedom for women in this Arabic and largely Muslim society. Throughout her life, Sh'arawi continued to set up schools, promote Arabic as the official language of Egypt, and encourage women artists and intellectuals. She founded the All-Arab Federation of Women, which became a model for other pan-Arabic organizations.

- $200 million to upgrade the computer data bases that would supply this information

During her nearly fifteen-year battle to pass the Brady Bill, Brady helped redefine the "right to bear arms," the right guaranteed in the U.S. Constitution. With her eloquence and facts, Brady won over many law enforcement organizations as well as the American Medical Association. When asked about her stamina during the fight to pass the bill, Brady says, "I think it's ridiculous that we as a society don't do something about the violence."

Mother's Peace Day

Julia Ward Howe (1819-1910), a composer and peace advocate, wrote the stirring song *The Battle Hymn of the Republic.* The song became the standard of the Union (Northern) army during the U.S. Civil War (1861–65). Howe, who believed that her song would spur on the Union in its righteous cause (the end of slavery), went back to actively working for peace after the war.

In 1872, Howe suggested that the United States set aside an annual "Mothers' Peace Day," a day dedicated to peace. For several years, she held an annual Mother's Day meeting in Boston. Support for her idea grew, and in 1907, Anna Jarvis campaigned for a nationwide observance of "Mother's Day." The holiday received national recognition on May 9, 1914, when U. S. President Woodrow Wilson recommended that Congress and the federal agencies celebrate the day. In 1915, Wilson officially declared Mother's Day a national day of observance.

13

Education

To Educate or Not to Educate

The goal of an educator is to produce an adult who will play a certain role in society, a role that society has decided is important to it. Until fairly recent times, the goal of educators of girls—when girls were educated at all—had been to produce wives, mothers, and homemakers. Their education centered around what they needed to know to run a home.

This failure to provide girls with an education equal to that of boys stemmed from the belief that women were the intellectually inferior sex—that they basically were not as smart as boys.

Though girls received little intellectual training until recently, the question of their need for education has sparked debate through the centuries. The friends of girls' education have been few, the enemies many. The arguments against educating girls have been based on twisted notions of girls' immorality (their tendency to do wrong), their virtue (their tendency to do good), their fragile bodies, or their feeble minds. It was long thought that

"The father of very intellectual aspect, his falcon eye softened by affection as he looked down on his fair child ... he said: I shall not have Maria brought too forward. If she knows too much, she will never find a husband; superior women hardly ever can."

—Margaret Fuller in The Great Lawsuit: Man Versus Men; Woman Versus Women

343

women were actually biologically incapable of learning math. It has even been argued that if a girl were allowed to go to college, she would never be able to bear children.

Education in the Western Tradition

Ancient Egypt, Greece, and Rome were influential in shaping many of the ideas about female education in Western cultures. In some ancient societies, after a child was born it was laid on the ground. If the father intended to educate his child, he immediately picked it up. But if he did not intend to educate it, the child was carried away and exposed, or left out in the open without shelter. It was usually the unhappy fate of daughters to be exposed.

The Greek Model

The Greek thinker Plato, who lived in the fourth century B.C., is considered one of the earliest supporters of women's education. However, even Plato believed that women had "weaker natures" than men. He declared in his *Republic* that "all the pursuits of men are the pursuits of women also, but in all of them a woman is inferior to a man."

If educated at all, Greek girls received only a very basic training in reading and writing. It was thought that there was little need to educate girls: because their judgment was said to be weak, they would always be subject to the guardianship of males.

Greek girls were first taught by their mothers to sew and spin thread or yarn. Then women came under the care of their husbands, who taught their wives how to manage the men's households. It was considered proper for women to stay in the house most of the time.

Girls from wealthy Greek families were more fortunate when it came to education. A famous school for privileged (wealthier) girls was organized by the Greek poet Sappho in her home. Her curriculum emphasized music, poetry, and dancing, and the development of feminine charms to please men.

The Roman Model

The Roman Empire was established in 27 B.C. and lasted until A.D. 476. The Romans adopted the Greek belief in female inferiority. However, because Roman society valued family life more than the Greeks did, women's position in it was also more valued. As a result, it was not unusual for upper-class Roman women to be educated.

But they were educated to make them better mothers to their sons, who were expected to take part in civic life as adults. Though tutors were hired to educate the sons of the wealthy, daughters were usually allowed to sit in on these classes. Schools were even available to the poorer classes.

The Christian Tradition

After the fall of the Roman Empire in A.D. 476, Christian attitudes about educating women gained influence. In the early days of the church, women had been allowed to preach and were taught along with men. Then came the writings of the church father Paul, who commanded women to keep silent in the churches. If a woman wished to learn anything, he affirmed, she should ask her husband. Childbearing and obedience should be her roles.

So it came about that from the sixth century to the eleventh century the only women who received any education were women who entered the convent. These girls studied reading, writing, and singing—for religious purposes—and a little grammar and arithmetic. Some girls studied drawing and painting so they could copy and illuminate (illustrate) religious manuscripts. Some of these manuscripts, decorated with brilliant colors and precious metals, are considered rare works of art. Often girls attending the convent acquired some medical knowledge, in part to protect their modesty by avoiding male doctors. Students and teachers spoke Latin in the convents long after the society outside had abandoned it for the common languages of the people.

The convent was the major source of education for girls until the twelfth century. (There is no record of any formal education for girls outside the church before that time.) Then, convent education declined with the rise of universities, which were all-male institutions. These men began to express their disapproval of teaching women to read and write unless they planned to become nuns. Even so, a few women are known to have taught law, philosophy, rhetoric, and medicine at Italian universities into the thirteenth century.

Education Becomes Secular

As education moved out of the hands of the church after the twelfth century, European noble families began to provide tutors for their boys and sometimes for their girls. Boys received a more religious training, while girls concentrated on social and literary skills.

Girls studied music, dancing, and games like chess and checkers. They also learned astrology and some medicine and surgery. For the most part, however, the main goal of education for girls was to make sure they remained pure until marriage and knew how to conduct themselves in society. Although middle-class women sometimes had tutors and the convents were open to them, the main emphasis of girls' education was on household duties.

Among the poor there was little interest in men's education and even less in women's education. Simple survival was the main aim of the poverty stricken at a time when famines, plagues, and wars were common.

Education in the Late Middle Ages

The Middle Ages lasted from about 500 to 1500. During part of that time, a

Window on the World: China

China is the country that occupies most of the landmass in eastern Asia. It is the world's most populous country, with 1.2 billion people in 1994. The Chinese civilization is one of the most ancient in the world.

Traditionally, women have not been highly valued in China. Girls are taught early to listen and submit to the opinions of men in all matters, even to men (or boys) younger than themselves. This has been true throughout most of China's history.

The reform movement to educate Chinese women began in 1842. Its purpose (like the purpose of education in the Western world) was to make women better mothers for the benefit of their sons. Missionaries opened China's first girls' schools in 1844 and 1873, but the Chinese government did not open a school for girls until 1907. The girls' schools produced many of China's leading women activists, teaching them military tactics in physical education class. These educational opportunities benefitted only a handful of women, however.

The Communist Party of China, a political party founded in 1921, pledged to support the complete freedom of women. Since then, however, China has faced invasion by other countries, civil wars, and other disruptive events. This has caused universities to shut down and high school education to suffer. Because of a lack of money and qualified teachers, colleges are small and only the most highly qualified students are permitted to attend. Women must score higher on entrance examinations than men to be considered for admission.

series of religious wars known as the Crusades was being fought. Fighting ability became the most highly prized quality in men, leaving the ladies of the houses free to study economics (money management) and whatever other subjects that might interest them. While staying behind to manage their family estates, some ladies acquired property rights and even political power. Because power during the Middle Ages rose out of owning land, this unusual situation created a small number of very influential women.

To entertain themselves, these women sponsored singers called troubadours and required them to sing stories about courtly love (a code of behavior that requires a man to declare his devotion to a lady). The ladies acted as literary patrons, supporting the songwriting efforts of the troubadours with money or gifts. They also made suggestions about what these musicians should sing about. This was one of the very few times in history that women would find themselves empowered in the educational process.

Chinese university professor Xiao Lu (an alias she uses because she fears government punishment) wrote about this policy:

"One must ask why it is that while the government officially promotes sexual equality it chooses to adopt such a blatantly discriminatory practice. The explanations given by administrators are: 1) it is less economical to train women than men and, 2) women are not suitable for certain work. It is pointed out that women after graduation will get married and have children; even under the current policy of one child per family this will mean that a woman will need at least one maternity leave. Then, since the care of children is still the major responsibility of women, she will have to spend time at home even with the provision of nurseries and child care facilities.... All of this means that the return on her college education is likely to be less than that of her male counterpart. Furthermore, it is still widely believed that while girls do better than boys in elementary and middle schools and therefore tend to pass college entrance exams in larger numbers, after they reach their sophomore year they tend to become concerned with marriage and family and consequently will not do as well."

China is slowly taking steps to insure literacy among its female population. In 1991, females made up 46 percent of the enrollment in primary school, 43 percent of the enrollment in secondary school, and 33 percent of full-time enrollment in universities and equivalent institutions. Still, about one-third of China's total population was illiterate, and nearly one-half of the illiterate population was female.

Education in the Renaissance

The period from about the fourteenth through the sixteenth centuries is known as the Renaissance. The Renaissance was one of the great ages in the history of the Western world, a time when knowledge and learning flourished. But the social and political changes of the time sent women back to their traditional role in the home. Although they could participate to some extent in cultural activities, the activities were devised by and for men.

Some Renaissance noblewomen were allowed to study literature. This study was regarded favorably unless a woman made too great a show of her abilities. Male scholars warned women to limit themselves to studying Latin, Greek, and Roman writers and the writings of the Christian church fathers. A knowledge of arithmetic, geometry, and public speaking was prized in men, but these were not considered suitable areas of study for women. The emphasis throughout the period was on development of the qualities of modesty, patience, humility, and obedience—those qualities that would allow women to remain contented and passive at home.

Education and the Reformation

During the sixteenth century, a movement known as the Reformation started in England and Western Europe. It aimed to reform some practices of the Roman Catholic Church. The movement resulted in the establishment of Protestant churches.

Protestants had their own ideas about educating girls. In the Netherlands and Germany, where the Protestant movement began, separate girls' schools were built. This was the first step toward the idea of universal education. However, the concept of education for all would not be widely accepted for another three hundred years.

Education in Early America

The majority of settlers who came to North America in the seventeenth century were Europeans, mainly from England. They brought with them English ideas about education and European ideas about the inferiority of women. The man of the house had the final say in the rearing and education of children. In fact, since he was far more likely to be able to read and write than his wife, the father was most likely to do the teaching. Few fathers saw any value in giving a daughter more than a very basic education. Her destiny,

after all, was to be a wife and mother, and (it was thought) not much schooling was needed for that.

Later, informal classes might be taught by housewives in "dame schools" or by clergymen in their spare time. Making sure children could read the Bible was the primary purpose of these classes.

In 1647 Massachusetts passed a law providing for grammar schools when a town's population reached one hundred families or households. These schools prepared male students for entrance to Harvard University in Cambridge, Massachusetts, which had been founded in 1636 to educate ministers. Daughters from wealthy families were the only girls who had access to any formal schooling.

It was not that girls lacked the desire to learn. In the 1700s, a girl wrote to her brother, who had been sent to school in England: "I find you have got the start of me learning very much, for you write better already than I expect to do as long as I live." Women regretted not having been better educated. In 1778, Abigail Adams, the wife of future U.S. president John Adams, wrote to her husband complaining about "the trifling narrow contracted education of the females of my own country."

By the time the American Revolution began in 1775, a person who could sign his or her own name was called literate. While 80 percent of men in New England (the most educationally advanced colonies) could sign their name, only 40 to 45 percent of women could.

Timeline: Historic Moments in Women's Education

1787   Benjamin Rush creates the Young Ladies Academy in Philadelphia. As future mothers, his students would be able to teach their sons "the principles of liberty and government."

1792   Sarah Pierce opens the Litchfield Female Academy in her Connecticut home. It wins a widespread reputation for the quality of its educational offerings.

1821   Emma Willard opens the Troy Female Seminary for girls in New York.

1823   Catherine Beecher founds the Hartford Female Academy in Connecticut. It was designed as an alternative to factory work for women in the eastern states.

1824   The first public high school for girls is founded in Worcester, Massachusetts.

1831   The Huntsville Female Seminary opens in Alabama and becomes one of the United States's most prestigious schools.

1833   Prudence Campbell opens the Canterbury Female Boarding School, a teacher-training school for African American girls, in Connecticut.

Education After the Revolution

After the American Revolution (1775–81), books and magazines began recommending that young girls receive an education equal to that of boys, and few objections were raised to this idea. It was thought that an educated mother was necessary for the rearing of sons who could run the newly formed country. So, the old Roman idea of education for girls to make them well-trained mothers for patriot sons was revived. Still, the education of most children of the time was very limited.

Children in the early nineteenth century attended public primary (elementary) schools, also known as common schools, usually one-room schoolhouses with girls seated on one side and boys on the other. There both boys and girls learned to read, write, and do simple arithmetic.

At first more boys than girls attended. But as publicly supported education expanded, girls were almost always included along with boys. The education offered by these schools was very basic, since they only went up to the eighth grade.

When the federal government began collecting statistics on school enrollment in the last half of the nineteenth century, it was found that about one-half of all American children

In rural America, many students attended classes in one-room schoolhouses like the one pictured here.

between the ages of five and nineteen were enrolled in some type of school. Enrollment rates for boys and girls were about the same.

Education in High Schools

Massachusetts was the first state to experiment with high school education for girls as well as boys. In the early nineteenth century, separate facilities were built. Smaller communities that could not afford separate schools for boys and girls built high schools with separate entrances and classrooms. Eventually, these "mixed" schools became "mixed classrooms." Critics argued that it was wrong to educate boys and girls together because they were destined to take different paths in life. Others declared that the presence of girls in the classroom would make boys more polite. But it was simple economics that settled the matter of mixed classrooms—separate facilities cost more money.

Education in the South

The idea of common schools attended by both boys and girls was slower to catch on in the American South. At first young girls were taught at home, mainly by their mothers. However, by the 1850s increasing numbers of women were attending academies—usually sponsored by churches—that were intended to educate young women to meet their responsibilities as future mothers. In the North female academies quickly evolved to include the training of future teachers. This was not so in the South, where, because of the absence of common schools, female teachers were not needed.

Southern laws prohibited teaching slaves to read and write and more than 90 percent could not do so. Slave girls who worked in the houses on large Southern plantations were sometimes able to learn to read and write by listening to the lessons given to the daughters of the house. Some slaves whose masters permitted them to learn even ran secret "midnight schools," where in the middle of the night and at great risk of being discovered and punished they taught their fellow slaves what they had learned.

Education in the Wild West

Because the American West was settled later than the East and South, there was less prejudice there against equal educational opportunities for girls. But settlers lived so far apart that for a long time there were no schools at all. Children were taught the basics—reading, writing, and arithmetic—by pioneer women in their homes. As late as the 1860s, fewer than one-half the children in Oregon had received any formal schooling whatsoever. Education was not made compulsory (meaning that everyone had to attend) in California until 1874.

When there were enough children in an area, families worked together to build one-room schoolhouses, which also served as churches on Sunday. Boys and girls of all ages were taught in the same room by one teacher. Teachers, who were mostly male, were not paid well, and trained teachers willing to endure the rough living conditions were difficult to find. Often teachers lived with their students' families, moving from one home to another throughout the school year so the expense of their food and lodging was shared.

Educational Attainment

The U.S. government first began collecting school statistics in 1869–70. That year, only about 2 out of every 100 seventeen-year-olds received a high school diploma. Over the next forty years this ratio increased to 9 out of every 100 seventeen-year-olds. At first high school graduation was an uncommon occurrence throughout the country, but since statistics have been kept, the graduation rate has always been higher for females than males.

As late as 1940, it was common for people to attend school only through the eighth grade. That year more than one-half of the entire U.S. population had no more than an eighth-grade education.

Window on the World: India

India, a nation in southern Asia, had a population of 919,000 in 1994—that's more people than any other country except China.

India's constitution, enacted in 1950, prohibits discrimination against women. (This is a constitutional provision for equality that has still not been passed in the United States.) The reality of equality in India, however, has not been attained. India faces vast problems, including scarce food and land, disputes among its many different religious groups, and great economic differences among the country's castes (classes) of people.

Membership in an Indian caste depends upon the family into which a person is born. Different castes place different restrictions on women. India's upper castes are more restrictive, which means the women in those castes lead more secluded lives.

India was controlled by the British from 1757 to 1947. Schools for girls were not established in India until 1820. Western missionaries and philanthropists opened the first girls' schools to promote Western religions, and girls of the lower castes were the first to enroll. Fearful of the influence of Western religions on the country's female population, some Indian groups then opened girls' schools and girls from higher castes enrolled. The Indian government finally began contributing to girls' education in 1854. By 1882, there were 127,000 girls enrolled in school, a very small fraction of the population.

For the most part, higher education (college and university) enrollment was limited to the wealthy through the early twentieth century. Statistics show that in 1869–70, sixty-three thousand students were attending higher education institutions throughout the country. This represented only about 1 percent of the entire population aged eighteen to twenty-four. About 21 percent of these students (around thirteen thousand) were female. Today, more than fourteen million students in the United States attend higher education institutions. Women make up more than one-half that number.

Women Go to College

The acceptance of equal education for girls stopped short at the college or university level. Although colleges for young men dated back to the founding of Harvard in 1636, there was no institution that allowed young women to enter before the 1830s. In 1833, Oberlin College in Ohio was the first to open its doors to women and racial minorities. Antioch College in Ohio began enrolling both men and women in 1852. Female students did so well academically at Oberlin and Antioch that the pressure was on

The curricula in India's early girls' schools, as in the United States, was geared toward the female role as mother and homemaker. Schools were strictly sex-segregated and were at first staffed by European female teachers. As more Indian women acquired an education, more female Indian teachers staffed the girls' schools.

Female education in India has not kept pace with males. In 1907, only 3.6 percent of school-age females were enrolled in school, compared to 23.1 percent of school-age males. In 1991, 66.3 percent of the female population was illiterate, compared to 38.2 percent of the male population. In rural India (the area outside the cities), about 60 percent of boys and girls enter primary school. Five years later, only 35 percent of the boys will still be enrolled, and only 16 percent of girls. Rural illiteracy rates are double the urban (inside the cities) illiteracy rates.

In the book *Sisterhood Is Global,* Political scientist Devaki Jain wrote about the situation of Indian women: "Half as literate as men, the women cluster in monotonous [boring], low-paid occupations. Every trend-statistic indicates further deterioration [worsening]: more women 'seeking work,' more women among the destitute [poor].... An average Indian woman's day is one long stretch of toiling for survival."

to admit them to other institutions. State universities, especially in the West, soon began to include women students.

However, many of the new state universities that were open to women did not provide the same challenging education that the best men's colleges did. And even the private coeducational colleges did not treat women as full equals. Mary Sharp College, which had opened in Winchester, Tennessee, in 1851, was the first women's college to require that students learn Greek and Latin, offering a full four-year program with a degree of difficulty approaching that of the best men's colleges. Elmira College in New York followed in 1855.

The Seven Sisters

The real breakthrough in higher education for women came with the opening of Vassar College in 1865. Vassar was the first of the distinguished women's colleges that would become known as the "Seven Sisters." Businessman Matthew Vassar proposed to build a hospital in Poughkeepsie, New York, as a memorial to his own accomplishments.

Timeline: More Historic Moments in Women's Education

1833 Oberlin College in Ohio admits its first women and minority students. That same year the Michigan legislature provides funding for a state university and sets aside places for women. However, none are actually allowed to attend until 1870.

1837 Mount Holyoke Female Seminary is founded by Mary Lyon in South Hadley, Massachusetts. Its purpose is to provide low-cost teacher training to girls from all economic classes. It achieves collegiate standing in the 1880s.

1840 Georgia Female College in Macon, Georgia, grants the first full bachelor's degrees to women.

1850 The Female Medical College of Pennsylvania (now the Medical College of Pennsylvania) is founded in Philadelphia. In 1889, Susan La Flesche Picotte graduates from the school and becomes the first Native American woman to earn a medical degree.

1851 Mary Sharp College, the first women's college to require classical languages and a full four-year course for women, is founded in Winchester, Tennessee.

1852 Antioch College in Ohio opens its doors to men and women. Catherine Beecher organizes the American Women's Education Association, whose purpose is to establish women's schools.

1855 Elmira College is founded in New York. It is the United States's second college for women to require classical languages and a full four-year course load. It is the first such college to survive to the present time.

1862 The Morrill Land Grant Act of 1862 permits the building of state colleges. All of them admit women. Mary Jane Patterson, the first African American woman to graduate from college, receives a degree from Oberlin College.

1865 Vassar College, the first college for women with a substantial endowment and well-equipped campus, is opened.

1872 The first African American lawyer, Charlotte B. Ray, graduates from Howard University Law School.

1873 Susan Blow opens the nation's first kindergarten that is part of a public school system.

A friend suggested that a fully endowed (funded) college for women was a better idea. Many of the young women who came to Vassar were not prepared for the difficulty of the curriculum there, so a preparatory department was established, offering high school level classes. The same was true of students seeking to enter Wellesley College when it opened ten years later in Wellesley, Massachusetts. Smith College also opened in 1875 in Northampton, Massachusetts. Mount Holyoke Female Seminary, which had been established in 1837 in South Hadley, Massachusetts, became a quality women's college in 1888.

Bryn Mawr College, established in Bryn Mawr, Pennsylvania, in 1880, was the brainchild of Martha Carey Thomas. In 1877, Thomas became one of the first women to graduate from Cornell University and later became the first woman president of Bryn Mawr. Bryn Mawr differed from the other women's colleges in many respects. The first three of the seven sisters had all-female faculties; Thomas hired a mostly male faculty (one of her first hires was future U.S. president Woodrow Wilson). No high school level courses were offered at Bryn Mawr, and entrance requirements were strict. Students wore caps and gowns to class, as was the custom of the time for male students. This type of clothing is now worn by high school and college students only at graduation ceremonies.

Meanwhile, many of the quality men's schools were still refusing to admit

Women at Oberlin College

Although Oberlin College in Ohio was the first college in the country to admit women and blacks, it could not be said that it gave women a college education equal to what men were given. Oberlin's literature referred to men as the "leading sex" while women were referred to as "the female appendage." The presence of women, said Oberlin's founders, provided men with a social outlet. Women were admitted to the college's "female department" and were given separate college degrees.

Lucy Stone, later a well-known speaker for the American Anti-Slavery Society, attended Oberlin. She wrote: "Oberlin's attitude was that women's high calling was to be mothers of the race." She said female students were "washing the men's clothes, caring for their rooms, serving them at table, listening to their orations [speeches], but themselves remaining silent in public assemblages [gatherings]." Stone objected to the fact that Oberlin women were required to take debating classes, in which they learned how to argue an issue, but they were not allowed to debate in public.

women. Finally, Harvard and Columbia Universities agreed to affiliate themselves with Radcliffe (Cambridge, Massachusetts) and Barnard (New York City) Colleges. The Seven Sisters, as they are still known—Vassar, Wellesley, Smith, Bryn Mawr, Mount Holyoke, Radcliffe, and Barnard—were profoundly influential. The fortunate few women who were able to attend (Smith College had opened with only fourteen students) suffered ridicule and sometimes hostility from their own families for entering the doors of higher education.

By 1870, 1 percent of college-age Americans attended college; 21 percent of these were women. By 1910, 5 percent of college-age Americans attended and 40 percent of them were women.

By 1890, more than 125 women's colleges existed. Within twenty years, about 15 percent of the nation's colleges were women-only and another 58 percent were coeducational. In 1897, the U.S. Commissioner of Education noted that in spite of doubts about the ability of women to be educated, "it has become an historical fact that women have made rapid strides, and captured a greater number of honors in proportion to their numbers than men." Ten years after the admission of women into the University of Chicago, 56 percent of the initiates (new members) into the honor society Phi Beta Kappa were women. Wherever women were given the opportunity, they proved themselves more than capable.

Does Education Make a Woman "Unwomanly"?

Many who opposed higher education for women believed that women's natures made them ideal as the moral center of the home and the rearers of children. These same critics felt the intellectual strain of learning Greek or mathematics at the college level would make women unfeminine.

In 1873, Edward Clarke of the Harvard Medical School published *Sex in Education; or, A Fair Chance for the Girls.* He stated that even though he believed women were mentally capable of doing college work, their health and ability to have children would be destroyed in the process. Blood that should be flowing to their reproductive organs would instead be directed to their brains, he warned. He described highly intelligent young women who either died or were disabled as a result of their academic successes at college. His book caused many women to doubt themselves and their fitness for college.

Adding to the argument against educating women was the discovery at the end of the nineteenth century that college-educated women married later than noncollege-educated women. Sometimes they did not marry at all. Many college-educated women who did marry did so at a later age and produced fewer children than their uneducated counterparts. Thus, women's education was seen to have had a bad influence. While one of the main reasons for opening colleges to women had been to make them better wives and mothers, now many women were choosing not to become wives and mothers at all!

Women in Medical School

Although the battle for equal higher education for women was mostly won by the twentieth century, the idea of women in medical schools still met with

Timeline: More Historic Moments in Women's Education

1875 Wellesley and Smith Colleges for women are founded in Massachusetts.

1881 Spelman, a pioneer black women's college, opens in Atlanta, Georgia. Originally named the Atlanta Baptist Female Seminary, it is renamed in 1884 to honor Laura Spelman Rockefeller, a major donor.

1882 The Association of Collegiate Alumnae is founded for women college graduates. It and other similar groups unite in 1922 as the American Association of University Women.

1885 Bryn Mawr College for Women is founded in Pennsylvania.

1889 Barnard, the first coordinate college (a woman's school affiliated with a men's university), is founded at Columbia University in New York City.

1894 Radcliffe, a coordinate college, is founded at Harvard University in Cambridge, Massachusetts.

1898 Washington College of Law, a co-educational institution, is founded in Washington, D.C., by Ellen Spencer Mussey and Emma Gillett. Both women had been refused admission by established law schools.

1902 Fannie Farmer opens a cooking school in Boston, Massachusetts, for the education of homemakers, not chefs.

1918 The U.S. Commission on the Reorganization of Secondary Education recommends that students be prepared for the world of work. Vocational education classes are added to high school curricula across the nation.

1921 Martha Carey Thomas opens the Bryn Mawr Summer School for Women to educate female blue-collar workers.

great opposition. Added to the general feeling that practicing medicine was for men only was the belief that only men were blessed with the necessary scientific ability. Another argument against medicine as a career for women was that it was incompatible with female modesty. Some said that a really feminine woman would not (or should not) be able to function in the presence of pain and blood.

In the second half of the nineteenth century, a number of popular novels appeared that depicted the conflict between a young woman's "mistaken" desire for medical education and her "true" vocation as a wife and mother. In these novels, the young woman repents, abandons her medical studies, and finds true fulfillment by marrying the hero, usually a doctor.

Higher Education Degrees Conferred: 1870–1990

Year	Bachelor's (B.A./B.S.)		Master's (M.A./M.S.)		Doctor's	
	Male	Female	Male	Female	Male	Female
1869–70	7,993	1,378	0	0	0	0
1879–80	10,411	2,485	868	11	51	3
1889–90	12,857	2,682	821	194	147	2
1899–1900	22,173	5,237	1,280	303	359	23
1909–10	28,762	8,437	1,555	558	399	44
1919–20	31,980	16,642	2,985	1,294	522	93
1929–30	73,615	48,869	8,295	6,044	1,946	353
1939–40	109,546	76,954	16,508	10,223	2,861	429
1949–50	328,841	103,217	41,220	16,963	5,804	616
1959–60	254,063	138,377	50,898	23,537	8,801	1,028
1969–70	451,097	341,220	125,624	82,667	25,890	4,022
1979–80	473,611	455,806	150,749	147,332	22,943	9,672
1989–90	491,488	558,169	153,643	170,201	24,731	13,867

Source: "120 Years of American Education: A Statistical Portrait," U.S. Department of Education, National Center for Education Statistics, January 1993.

Unlike these fictional heroines, Elizabeth Blackwell (1821–1910) and her sister were the first women to earn American medical degrees. Blackwell worked as a teacher before being urged to apply to medical school by a dying friend who regretted not being treated by a woman doctor. In 1849, the only school that would accept Blackwell (in Geneva, New York) granted her this country's first medical degree awarded to a woman. Blackwell had medical degrees from both American and French colleges when she was automatically placed on the British Medical Register in 1859. The next year the British Medical Association ruled that holders of foreign degrees could not practice medicine in England.

The first female medical student at Harvard University withdrew from the school after male students staged a protest when they heard that she planned to attend a lecture. Johns Hopkins Medical School in Baltimore, Maryland, did

Female medical students in 1900 dissect cadavers during anatomy class.

not admit women until 1893, when Mary Hovey increased her promise of a $60,000 gift to $306,000 if they would do so.

Opposition to women in medical school was not limited to America. In England, female medical students seeking to enter an anatomy class were blocked by male students, who threw mud at them. In France, a female intern was burned in effigy by classmates (that is, a dummy representing her was set on fire). A Spanish medical student had stones thrown at her in class. In Russia, medical school classes were opened to women in 1872 because of an extreme shortage of doctors. Still, the conditions for females

were so hard that twelve members of the first group of ninety students died (two from suicide and two from a lung disease called tuberculosis), and only twenty-five graduated.

Women medical students persisted in spite of all the obstacles put in their way. By 1910, there were more than seven thousand woman physicians in the United States. Overseas, by the beginning of World War I in 1914, France had six hundred women doctors, while Germany and Great Britain had around five hundred each. Russia had the most women doctors in Europe—fifteen hundred, or 10 percent of the country's total medical profession. It is interesting to note that

The Industrial Revolution and Education

The term "industrial revolution" is used to describe changes that result from the introduction of new technologies. The Industrial Revolution that began in England in the mid-1700s and spread over the next 150 years to the United States and elsewhere had profound effects on education in the United States.

First, many people moved from the country to the city to work in the factories that were built to take advantage of new laborsaving machinery. Then, many more people came from other countries to work in the new American factories. These people were called immigrants, and they tended to settle in cities where they had relatives. A concentration of large numbers of people in a small area made the building of new schools practical. At the same time, new printing methods made textbooks cheaper to produce.

The new schools, however, faced a different situation from the early schools. Earlier, English-speaking colonists gathered in small communities and were taught to read using the Bible. During the Industrial Revolution, schools were built in neighborhoods where people spoke many different languages and practiced different religions. Educators believed that people needed to learn a common language so they could live, learn, and work together.

New kinds of textbooks were created, such as Noah Webster's *Speller,* which aimed to simplify and standardize a spelling system so that everyone spelled the same words the same way. Other new textbooks taught patriotism instead of religion as a way to unify the country.

During this period, more and more young women entered the rapidly expanding teaching profession. In Massachusetts, for example, the number of female teachers increased 156 percent between the 1830s and the 1880s. Part of the reason for this shift was the Civil War (1861–65). Before the war, most teachers were men. Those same men became soldiers during the war, leaving their teaching jobs vacant. Women stepped forward to fill them and have been teaching ever since. Unfortunately, these early female teachers were paid less than half of what male teachers were paid.

---

unlike in the United States, the medical profession is not highly regarded in Russia, where women now represent about 70 percent of doctors.

In 1994, a historic event was reported by the news media. For the first time in American history, women outnumbered men among first-year medical students at 18 of the country's 126 medical schools. Yale School of Medicine led the field, with women numbering 56 percent of its 1994 entering class.

Women as Teachers

When the idea of educating girls along with boys became popular after the American Revolution, an array of "female academies" opened. The academies admitted any girl whose family could afford tuition. In 1821, when Emma Willard opened her famous seminary (school) for girls in Troy, New York, the purpose of girls' education was expanded to include training as teachers. This addition to the curriculum was to insure that young women could earn a living in the "unlucky" event they did not marry. Willard emphasized that her school would give girls a different type of training from what men received because of what she believed to be "the absurdity of sending ladies to colleges."

An early observer of the American scene, Harriet Martineau (1802–1876) discussed the teaching profession in her book *Society in America* (published by Saunders & Otley in 1837). Teaching was difficult, and teachers were held in low regard and poorly paid:

Women continue to hold the majority of lower-paying elementary and high school teaching jobs.

Teaching and training young children is, to a few, a very few, a delightful employment.... Let philanthropists [people who donate to charity] inquire into the proportion [numbers] of governesses [teachers] among the inmates of lunatic asylums.... The most accomplished governesses in the United States may obtain 600 dollars a year in the families of Southern planters; provided they will promise to teach everything. In the north they are paid less; and in neither case, is there a possibility of making provision [saving money] for sickness and old age.

Education, Income, and Gender

Usually, the more highly educated a person is, the more that person can earn. During the 1980s, the income for women with less than four years of high school increased by 17 percent over the 1970s, and the income for women with a high school diploma rose by 27 percent. Incomes for women with four years of college rose by an astounding 45 percent.

Today, despite these large increases for women, salaries for men continue to be significantly higher than salaries for women with equal levels of education. For example, men with four years of college earn a salary that is an average of *86 percent* higher than the salary of women with an equivalent education. The salary for males with four years of high school is *nearly double* that of women with a similar level of education.

As educational opportunities opened up for women in the latter part of the nineteenth century, normal schools, usually offering a two-year program, were opened for the training of teachers. Until the 1920s, only single women could teach in public schools. Most people agreed that women, whether trained as teachers or not, belonged at home.

By 1989, women represented 83.7 percent of elementary school teachers and 49.7 percent of secondary school teachers. It is interesting to note that women represented less than 30 percent of college professors, the highest-paid group of teachers.

Education in Modern America

Today, nearly 100 percent of American children attend school. The focus of education has changed since the days when it was considered necessary only to be able to read the Bible. It is expected that all children will graduate from high school and be able to read, write, and have a basic knowledge of history, mathematics, science, and the workings of the country's political system.

Before 1918, high schools offered college preparatory classes to the fortunate few who would receive higher education. Students were required to take classes such as Latin, Greek, advanced mathematics, and philosophy. By 1918, it had become obvious that most students did not go on to college. About this time, more vocational education courses were added to the curriculum. These courses were intended to prepare students for the world of work.

The world of work was very much sex-segregated, with men holding most of the higher-paying jobs and females clustered in the lower-paying jobs. High school boys began to take classes that would lead to highly paid jobs, while girls concentrated on typing, home economics, and sewing. As the years went by, it became easier for girls to avoid classes like math and science because more and more electives (courses of choice rather than required courses) were added to the curriculum. Even as late as the 1960s, when girls were asked what they wanted to be when they grew up, they tended to answer one of only four careers: teacher, secretary, nurse, or mother.

This situation has been gradually changing in recent years. Girls are being encouraged to take more math and science courses that can lead to better-paying careers, and more male-dominated careers are opening up for women.

Current Problems, Solutions, and Trends

Issues concerning women's education that have arisen since the 1970s include:

- sexual stereotyping in textbooks and curricula

- sexual harassment at school

- lack of funding for programs and scholarships for women athletes

- debates over the relative merits of single-sex and coeducational schools

- gender disparities in widely used scholastic aptitude tests and

- debates over the value of women's history programs

Sexual Stereotyping in Textbooks and Curricula

Sexual stereotypes about females have blurred the accuracy of textbooks and

Illiteracy in Selected Countries: c. 1990

This table show the percentage of the female adult population who are illiterate in selected countries. Figures are for the latest available year.

Country	Illiterate Females
Argentina	6.4%
Brazil	23.4%
Chile	9.2%
China	48.9%
Colombia	16.1%
El Salvador	33.2%
India	74.3%
Paraguay	15.2%

Source: Selected from *The Economist Book of Vital World Statistics: A Complete Guide to the World in Figures,* The Economist Books Ltd., London, 1990, pp. 210-11.

curricula for years. A stereotype is a fixed and unchanging idea about something.

Around the 1970s, in part because of a revitalized women's movement, people began to pay more attention to the treatment of girls in school texts. They found that male-centered stories far outnumbered female-centered stories. When girls appeared in stories, they were shown as weak, whiny, and selfish, and always needing someone's help. In illustrations, women were invariably shown wearing aprons and holding dishtowels. If they

Timeline: More Historic Moments in Women's Education

1969 San Diego University in California establishes the first women's studies bachelor's degree program.

1972 U.S. Congress passes Title IX, which is federal legislation that makes sex discrimination illegal in schools receiving federal funds. The first annual Berkshire Conference on the History of Women is held in the Berkshire Mountains in western Massachusetts.

1974 The U.S. Congress passes the Women's Educational Equity Act, which is federal legislation that strengthens Title IX.

1979 The National Women's Studies Association holds its first meeting.

1992 The American Association of University Women publishes its report titled *How Schools Shortchange Girls.* The report documents why girls' school performance and self-esteem decline as they approach adolescence.

1995 Shannon Faulkner becomes the first female to attend the Citadel, a male-only military school. She, along with more than twenty-four male recruits, dropped out after a week of harassment from fellow students.

had a career, it was most likely that of a teacher or nurse. In mathematics textbooks, problems showed girls at the store buying materials for sewing or cooking. Meanwhile, boys were shown doing woodwork, sailing, climbing mountains, and going to the moon.

These kinds of textbooks received much negative publicity. People believed that the stories had a harmful effect on girls' self-esteem. Low self-esteem is a problem because it can keep girls from living up to their full abilities. Since the 1970s, textbook publishers have become much more sensitive to the ways in which girls and women are portrayed. This sen-

sitivity has extended to rethinking how African Americans and other ethnic and racial groups are discussed in textbooks as well.

Sexual Harassment at School

Surveys conducted in recent years show large numbers of students, both boys and girls, reporting the experience of sexual harassment at school. Sexual harassment refers to sexual behavior that is unwanted and unwelcome to the victim.

Sexual harassment can have a serious effect on a child's self-esteem. It can negatively affect his or her entire education. Some students who have experienced sexual harassment report that they no longer want to attend school. Partly as a result of the survey findings, many schools have adopted official sexual harassment policies that are communicated to all students and are enforced when a student or teacher does not conform to them.

Lack of Funding for Programs and Scholarships for Women Athletes

The issue of funding for programs and scholarships for women has focused in recent years on athletics. Surveys have shown that women's participation in college athletics lags behind men's, and so does women's share of the money colleges spend on athletic scholarships. Before 1972, high school gym classes were sex-segregated, and girls were offered far fewer athletic programs than boys.

In 1972, the U.S. Congress passed an amendment to the Civil Rights Act known as Title IX. This law makes it illegal to practice sex discrimination in schools that receive federal government money. The law was intended to make schools treat girls as well as they treat boys in a number of areas, such as sports programs. Title IX was strengthened in 1974 by the passage of the Women's Educational Equity Act.

Usually, when a lawsuit is filed under Title IX, it involves athletics. Schools have been forced by Title IX to provide better athletic programs for girls. In spite of Title IX, however, studies show that very few schools provide equal funding for boys' and girls' athletic programs.

Single-Sex vs. Coeducational Schools

An early argument in favor of sex-segregated schools was made by Edward Clarke in his influential book *Sex in Education* (1873). Because he believed that being educated with boys would overwork a woman's brain to the point that she could not bear children, Clarke suggested that coeducation be replaced with less-demanding schools for girls.

Today, people have different opinions about whether girls should be educated separately from boys. Some say that single-sex classes are beneficial because boys demand more attention in the classroom, leaving the teacher with less time to devote to girls. People who have observed elementary school students have noticed that on the playground, the boys take over the playground area and equipment, leaving only a small area for the girls. This can make girls feel like they are invisible.

Separate Math and Science Classes?

In 1992, when a Teen Talk Barbie doll appeared on the market and stated "Math class is tough," her statement was greeted by many with dismay. She seemed to be saying that teenage girls could not do well at math. Many people believe that girls face great obstacles when it comes to math, science, and computer classes. By the time they reach high school, large numbers of girls have absorbed the message that these classes

Female college students at Mills College in Oakland, California, protest the admission of men to the all-women's school.

are too hard for them or that boys do not like girls who excel in them. Often they do not participate in class, and some even drop out. However, it is important that girls learn these skills because they will need them to succeed in the world of work.

Some people suggest that girls may feel more comfortable participating in sex-segregated math, science, and computer classes. Some even go so far as to say that girls should attend all-girls' high schools. However, other observers favor completely coeducational classes because it is important for boys and girls to learn to get along together.

Gender Disparities in Aptitude Tests

Gender disparities (sex differences) between boys' and girls' scores on aptitude tests have been the subject of much discussion and study in recent years. It was noticed that by the time girls graduated from high school, their scores on tests like the Scholastic Aptitude Test (SAT) had fallen below the scores of boys. This happened even though girls' scores are equal to or better than boys' scores on almost all aptitude tests in the early grades. These lower test scores create a problem because many colleges use the SAT scores of high school students when deciding whom to admit and whom to

SAT Scores: 1987 and 1994

This table shows Scholastic Aptitude Test (SAT) scores of high school boys and girls in 1987 and 1994. Note that since 1987, all girls improved their math and verbal scores. This is shown under National Averages. Black girls improved their test scores more than any other group. A perfect score is 800 points in each part of the test.

Race/ethnic group	1987				1994			
	Verbal		Mathematics		Verbal		Mathematics	
	Boys	Girls	Boys	Girls	Boys	Girls	Boys	Girls
American Indian	396	391	452	413	397	395	459	425
Asian American	408	403	543	498	417	414	557	514
Black	354	349	391	367	348	354	399	381
Mexican American	387	373	449	402	375	368	448	410
Puerto Rican	366	355	423	380	371	365	432	395
Other Hispanic	393	382	459	408	389	379	462	414
White	452	442	514	466	445	441	519	475
Other	415	396	485	428	426	424	505	459
National averages	435	425	500	453	425	421	501	460

Source: "Gender Gap Continues to Close in S.A.T.'s," *New York Times,* August 25, 1994, p. A8Y. Primary source: College Board.

award scholarships and honors programs. The question is, what happens during the years between elementary school and high school to make girls' scores fall below boys' scores?

Gender disparities in aptitude test scores are most dramatic on mathematics and science tests. However, since 1972, boys have scored higher than girls on *both* the verbal and the mathematics parts of the SAT.

The causes of the gap in test scores are not completely understood. One possible answer was suggested in the magazine *Education* (Volume 114, Number 3, Spring 1994). After studying a group of students taking the SAT, the observers concluded that one reason for the difference in boys' and girls' scores was the fact that the SAT is a timed test. When test-takers were allowed to use as much time as they needed, girls' scores increased greatly, but boys' did not change. Boys still received higher scores, but the gender disparity between scores became much narrower.

What Is the Value of Women's History Programs?

History is the story of the past. History as it has always been studied in the Western world has been written mainly by men. Its subject matter has been the public deeds of Western white men. Women, who have led mostly private lives, have been largely ignored.

Beginning in the 1960s, some people began suggesting that there was value in approaching the study of history from another point of view. They suggested that a field of study that left out one-half of the world's population was a misleading history and that women's lives were worth studying and remembering. Some historians suggested that in order to know where we are going, we needed a complete understanding of where we *all* have been.

Universities began to create and offer women's studies courses. Critics of these courses maintain that they are not scholarly, that they are just fads, that women have had such a small impact on history that they are not worthy of devoting course time and effort. Some critics also say that the effort to emphasize women (or minorities) leads to a neglect of important male historical figures.

Despite criticism such as this, today women's studies courses are a regular offering at a growing number of U.S. colleges. Institutes for the study of women and women's issues have been established at Stanford University, Wellesley College, and the University of Minnesota; a new one is planned at the University of Michigan. Another trend is the growth in the number of courses on black and Third World women at colleges and universities.

14

Science and Exploration

"Perhaps ... unconsciously I was responding to a call of the woman in me—woman, preserver of the race—to mitigate [end] suffering and save life."

—American physician
Bertha Van Hoosen

Women scientists and healers were fairly common in ancient Europe. But, when formal medical schools and licensing programs were established during the eighteenth century, women began to be barred from pursuing careers in science and medicine. It is interesting to note that while the eighteenth century marks the beginning of a period of scientific discovery in Europe known as the "Age of Enlightenment," it was an enlightenment restricted mostly to men.

Similarly, when the Industrial Revolution of the 1700s and 1800s found men actively engaged in invention, business, and government, women—because of custom and lack of education—were once again kept from entering these occupations.

Women have long left the comforts of home to visit foreign lands. Usually, however, most of these women went as wives and mothers accompanying their husbands who were looking for better hunting grounds or more fertile soil for farming. As a result, few of the names of these earliest female explorers have

Timeline: Women Scientists Through the Ages

400 Hypatia, one of the most famous of the ancient scholars, lived in Alexandria, Egypt, and practiced as a professor of mathematics, an astronomer, and a philosopher.

1566 French astronomer Marie de Coste Blanche publishes *The Nature of the Sun and Earth.*

1643 Italian scientist Evangelista Torricelli makes the first barometer (an instrument that measures changes in air pressure), thereby producing the first vacuum known to science.

1678 Italian noblewoman Elena Cornaro becomes Europe's first female doctor of philosophy.

1740 French physicist Emilie du Chatelet publishes *The Institutions of Physics.*

1745 Italian astronomer and natural philosopher Laura Maria Caterina Bassi begins lecturing on experimental physics at the University of Bologna.

1748 Italian mathematician and professor Maria Agnesi writes a textbook on algebra that becomes the standard for students in many European countries.

1766 Anna Manzolini, an Italian anatomy professor, makes wax models of internal organs to help her students learn about the human body.

1828 Caroline Herschel, a German astronomer, is awarded the Gold Medal

been recorded. Later trip records, however, like those to the Americas, the Middle East, and Africa, did include the names and undertakings of the European women who ventured there.

Some of the better-known women scientists, researchers, doctors, inventors, and explorers who blazed new trails and opened doors for other women are celebrated in this chapter.

Women in Science

The contributions of women to the sciences range from discovering stars to documenting the plant life of faraway lands to creating medicines to combat cancer and other life-threatening diseases. The fact that only a fraction of the scientific discoveries made by women can be included here is a testament to the richness and the scope of women's accomplishments.

In reading this chapter you will find that many scientists have worked in several areas during their careers. However, for purposes of organization, this section is divided by the branches of science: earth sciences, physical sciences, life sciences, behavioral sciences, and applied sciences (such as engineering).

of the Astronomical Society. She is later made an honorary member for her discovery of three nebulae (a thinly spread mass of interstellar gas and dust) and eighteen comets.

1847 American astronomer and teacher Maria Mitchell discovers the comet that would bear her name. In 1848 she becomes the first woman elected to the American Academy of Arts and Sciences.

1882 Eleanor Ormerod of Great Britain is appointed consulting entomologist (a person who studies insects) to the Royal Agricultural Society of England for her work in identifying insects harmful to crops.

1898 Hertha Ayrton becomes the first women to be named a full member of the Institute of Electrical Engineers in England.

1903 Polish-French physicist Marie Curie becomes the first woman to win a Nobel Prize in chemistry, for her research on radiation.

1907 Austrian physicist Lise Meitner begins the work that leads to the discovery of how atoms are split. A pacifist, she later refuses to help make the atom bomb.

1911 Marie Curie and two male colleagues win the Nobel Prize for physics for their discovery of the elements radium and polonium.

Earth Sciences

Earth science is the study of the physical components of Earth—its water, land, and air—and the processes that influence them. Like the other fields of science, earth science is subdivided into many branches. Some of these include ecology, geology, oceanography, and meteorology.

Ecology is the study of how humans impact Earth's environment. American Joan B. Berkowitz is a physical chemist who has become an expert on hazardous waste. She has testified before the U.S. Congress and the U.S. Environmental Protection Agency often consults with her when making policy decisions on environmental management. Geraldine V. Cox is an American biologist whose speciality is environmental science. She has focused on developing policies for the safe conduct of the chemical industry. Kenyan environmentalist Wangari Maathai is known for her efforts to fight the deforestation of her African country. Deforestation results from cutting down trees without planting new ones.

Geology is the study of Earth and its physical makeup. In 1893, Florence Bascom, one the most famous of the American geologists, became the first woman

Timeline: Women Scientists Through the Ages

1923 Evelyn Cheesman launches her career as one of Britain's most famous entomologists. Over thirty years of expeditions, she brings back more than forty thousand species of insects for study.

1926 American psychoanalyst Karen Horney attacks Sigmund Freud's claim that women are unhappy and dissatisfied because they were not born men.

1930 Naturalist Caroline Dorman becomes the first woman employed by the U.S. Forestry Service and plays an important role in establishing the 600,000-acre Kisatchie National Forest in Louisiana.

1931 American astronomer Annie Jump Cannon becomes the first recipient of the Henry Draper Gold Medal from the National Academy of Sciences. She classifies more than 400,000 stars in her lifetime.

1934 American anthropologist Ruth Benedict introduces the idea of "patterns of culture," which states that cultures have personalities just as people do.

1935 French chemist Irene Joliot-Curie is cowinner of the Nobel Prize for chemistry for her work in the synthesis (making) of new radioactive elements.

1930s British archeologist Kathleen Kenyon helps excavate (unearth) the walls of Jericho in the Middle East, King Solomon's mines in Africa, and a Roman amphitheater in London.

1951 British crystallographer Rosalind Franklin takes X-ray photographs of the molecular structure of DNA protein, pro-

to receive a doctoral degree in geology from Johns Hopkins University. She was also the first to be elected a fellow (member) of the Geological Society of America. Her special area of study was the crystalline (composed of or resembling crystals) rock formations in the mid-Atlantic states. In 1896, Bascom published a study on ancient volcanic rocks. She was also the first woman to work for the U.S. Geological Survey.

Adriana C. Ocampo is an American planetary geologist who is involved in designing systems for spacecraft for missions to Mars and Jupiter. Her specialty is developing the remote sensing instruments that gather data about these other planets.

A paleontologist is a geologist who uses fossils to learn about the history of life. (Fossils are pieces of ancient plants or animals usually found in rock formations.) Julia Anna Gardner was an American paleontologist who studied the mollusks (animals such as snails or clams that live in the water and have a hard outer shell)

viding an important clue in its chemical construction.

1961 In Africa, British anthropologists Mary and Louis S. B. Leakey discover the skeleton of a previously unknown human ancestor.

1962 American marine biologist Rachel Carson publishes *Silent Spring,* which alerts the public to the dangers of pesticides (bug killers) and sparks the environmental movement.

1964 Dorothy Crowfoot Hodgkin wins the Nobel Prize for chemistry for her use of X-ray techniques to reveal structures of important biochemical substances, such as vitamins.

1967 American physicist Marguerite M. Rogers receives the Society of Women Engineers Achievement Award for her work in air-launched tactical (military) weapons.

1972 British economist Barbara Ward Jackson publishes *Only One Earth: The Care and Maintenance of a Small Planet,* a book about how to share Earth's resources.

1993 Susan E. Leeman receives the Excellence in Science Award from Eli Lilly and Company for being one of the founding members of the science of neuroendocrinology (a combined study of the immune, endocrine, and nervous systems).

1995 American bacteriologist Monica K. Borucki and her colleague report finding spores of bacteria that are 25 to 40 million years old.

she found in many different layers of Earth's crust. Today, her pioneering work helps petroleum geologists locate deposits of oil so they know where to drill. Tilly Edinger, a German-born American, studied fossil remains to learn more about the brain of ancient humans. She helped found the science of paleoneurology. (Neurology is the study of the nervous system.)

Scientists who concentrate their study on Earth's surface are called geographers. A geographer is interested in Earth's continents, climates, life forms, and resources. British mathematician, astronomer, and geographer Mary Somerville published *Physical Geography* in 1848, and it became a standard text for geography students in Europe.

Physical Sciences

Physical science is any of the sciences, such as physics, chemistry, and astronomy, that analyze the nature and properties of energy and matter. Chemistry is the study of matter at its most basic level, that of atoms and molecules.

Creative Thinking in Science: Rachel Carson

American environmentalist Rachel Carson was born in 1907 and grew up on a 65-acre farm in Springdale, Pennsylvania. She began college as an English major because of her love of writing. But a biology requirement changed her life, and in 1928, she earned a college degree in biology. She then spent a summer studying at the Marine Biological Laboratory in Woods Hole, Massachusetts, where she saw the ocean for the first time. Carson went on to earn a master's degree in marine biology from Johns Hopkins University in Baltimore, Maryland, in 1932.

Carson took a position writing brochures about aquatic biology (sea life) for the U.S. Fish and Wildlife Service, becoming the first woman hired as a scientist by this agency. But when her writing proved too poetic for her science-minded supervisor, she began to sell her articles to magazines. Carson published her first book, *Under the Sea-Wind,* in 1941. The book explores how life forms along the coastal floor of the Atlantic Ocean are inter-related. Next came *The Sea Around Us.* Published in 1950, this book discusses how nature reuses everything produced on the planet (for example, fallen leaves rot and become fertilizer for the spring crops). It won the National Book Award.

Carson's next major work, *Silent Spring* was published in 1962. It is credited with sounding the alarm that led to the ecology movement. Today we know the dangers of the overuse of pesticides (bug killers) and fertilizers, and we take recycling of cans, bottles, and newspapers for granted. In the 1960s, this was not the case.

The mysterious deaths of birds on a friend's property sparked Carson's scientific interest in a pesticide called DDT. After the state had sprayed the area with the pesticides to control the mosquito population, Carson's friend noticed that the birds began dying. Carson believed that the DDT use and the bird deaths were related.

In *Silent Spring,* Carson made her claim public, stating that DDT was making peo-

The most famous woman chemist of all time was Marie Curie, who was born in Poland and worked in France. In 1903, she and her colleagues won a Nobel Prize for physics for their efforts in expanding the knowledge of radioactivity. Curie won the Nobel Prize again in 1911, this time for chemistry, and became one of only a very few people to ever repeat the honor. Her second award was for the discovery of the radioactive elements radium and polonium. Curie's daughter, Irene Joliot-Curie, was also a renowned scientist. In 1935, Joliot-Curie

ple and animals sick. The many pesticides used were poisoning the air, earth, and water. "If we keep using these chemicals," she wrote, "spring might someday come silently with no birds left to sing, and no people left to hear them." Like her other books, *Silent Spring* became a bestseller. But Carson had taken on two huge opponents: the U.S. Agricultural Department and the pesticide industry. They claimed DDT was safe and that Carson was wrong.

Then President John F. Kennedy formed a special panel of the nation's top scientists to conduct research and find out who was right. The panel supported Carson. As a result, the *environmental-ecology movement* spread worldwide, with people in many nations concerned about living in harmony with nature. In the United States, the Environmental Protection Agency and many state and local laws protect the environment from the overuse of pesticides and fertilizers and many other potentially harmful substances.

and a colleague were awarded a Nobel Prize in chemistry for recognition of their synthesis (making) of new radioactive elements.

Another famous chemist was Englishwoman Dorothy Crowfoot Hodgkin, who received the 1964 Nobel Prize for chemistry for her use of X-ray technology to determine the structures of important biochemical (the chemical composition of a particular living system) substances. Some of Hodgkin's discoveries included the deciphering of the structure of vitamin B^{12} and penicillin.

Marie Curie

the hormone that regulates the amount of sugar in the blood. The disease can be fatal if left untreated. In 1947, Cori became the third woman to be awarded a Nobel Prize. She won in the category of physiology or medicine. Another famous biochemist was American Florence B. Seibert, whose work on the study of bacteria made blood transfusions safe and common. She was inducted into the Women's Hall of Fame in 1990.

Chemist Katherine Burr Blodgett was the first woman scientist hired by General Electric (GE). In 1935, she registered a patent (a legal and exclusive right to produce, use, and sell what one has invented) on an invention that led to a film used to coat nonreflecting (nonglare) glass. Chemist Gertrude Belle Elion received the 1988 Nobel Prize in chemistry for her research, which led to the development of drugs used to treat cancer and diseases of the kidney, joints, and immune system. One of Elion's most famous discoveries was AZT, the drug most often used to treat AIDS patients. In 1991, she won the National Medal of Science and became the first woman elected to the National Inventors Hall of Fame.

Marguerite Davis, an American chemist, studied vitamins A and B and contributed significantly to our understanding of human nutrition. American Mary Engle Penington discovered methods for better preserving fresh food, including the best ways to slaughter animals, freeze vegetables and fruits, and keep milk from spoiling.

In the 1920s, American biochemist Gerty T. Cori and her husband were doing basic research on how the body uses and stores sugar. Their work had a profound effect on how we understand the disease diabetes. Diabetes is a disorder in which the body doesn't produce enough insulin,

Marie M. Daly became the first African American woman to earn a doctorate in chemistry when she graduated from Columbia University in 1948. Since then, she has devoted her life to studying the effects of substance abuse on the human body. American biochemist Elizabeth Miller and her husband devoted their lives to studying how chemicals, called carcinogens, could interact with the human body to cause the development of cancer. Elizabeth F. Neufeld, a French-born American biochemist, has done research on various genetic diseases. Her work opened the way for prenatal (before birth) diagnosis of life-threatening fetal (a developing baby is called a fetus) disorders.

American atmospheric chemist Susan Soloman has done much important research on the ozone layer, which protects life on Earth from the harmful radiation of the Sun. Florence W. Van Straten, an American physicist and meteorologist (weather scientist), has studied ways to "seed" clouds to produce rain in dry areas. Indian atmospheric chemist Sulochana Gadgil has contributed much to scientists' understanding of monsoon (heavy rain) conditions. Hungarian-born American physical chemist Maria Telkes was responsible for creating the heating system installed in the first U.S. solar-heated home in 1948.

Italian-born American chemist Guiliana Cavaglieri Tesoro is an expert in polymers, the large molecules used to make plastics. Her accomplishments include an antistatic chemical for synthetic (man-made) fibers, flame resistant material, and permanent press coating.

Physics, another branch of physical science, is the study of matter and energy. Many physicists are also astronomers, scientists who concentrate their study on space and celestial (related to the sky) bodies. Astrophysicists, for instance, are scientists who study the size, temperature, mass, and shape of distant bodies such as stars and planets. However, some physicists choose to concentrate on learning more about the properties of Earth.

Dutch physicist Tettje Clasina Clay-Jolles did research on cosmic rays and ultraviolet radiation in the 1920s. Vera Cooper, an American astronomer, shook the scientific world with her proof that up to 90 percent of the universe is made of matter we cannot see. Today she is one of only seventy-five women who are members of the prestigious National Academy of Sciences.

English-born American astronomer Cecilia Payne-Gaposchkin discovered that hydrogen (a gaseous element) is the most abundant substance in the universe, a discovery that is now the basis for analyzing the universe. In 1967, Irish astronomer Jocelyn Bell Burnell discovered pulsars, stars that emit regular radio waves. English-born American astrophysicist E. Margaret Burbidge is best known for her studies of quasars and for taking the first accurate measures of galactic masses. Indonesian-Dutch astronomer Joan George Erardus Gijsbert Voute identified and described more than eleven thousand binary star systems during her career. Binary stars are a pair of stars that revolve around a common center of gravity. Russian astronomer Alla G. Massevitch created the charts that kept track of her country's *Sputnik* satellites in space.

Female Network Helps Women Scientist

The American Association of University Women (AAUW) was founded in 1881 to provide support for education and research, the keys to achieving equity for women of all ages, races, and creeds. In a recent fund-raising letter by Anne L. Bryant, its executive director, she relates an anecdote about how the AAUW helped one female scientist change the course of history.

"The year was 1919. Europe had been ravaged by World War I [1914-18]. And radium was far too expensive for a scientist of modest means to afford for experiments. Even one as famous as Madame Marie Curie.

"As a result, Madame Curie's ground-breaking research had reached a virtual standstill. That's when the American Association of University Women (AAUW) came to her rescue.

"AAUW members from Maine to California helped raise an astonishing $156,413, enabling Madame Curie to purchase one gram of radium and continue her experiments. [These] experiments helped her create the field of nuclear chemistry and forever changed the course of science.

"Madame Curie received the Nobel Prize for her work. But despite her dramatic success in the laboratory, she could not find a way to tear down the barriers that blocked her admittance to the revered French Academie des Sciences.

"Her problem? Madame Curie was a woman. Even after Marie Curie won an incredible second Nobel Prize, the all-male Academie would not admit her to their exclusive club. Today, more than 70 years later, the Academie still has only three women members."

Bryant's letter goes on to explain that female scientists continue to be seen as exceptions to the rule in our male-dominated society: "We must still fight to get the same education a man does. And ultimately, the same degree of recognition, be it in the classroom or the workplace." Today the AAUW continues to support teachers and researchers such as Curie through grants and special programs.

German-Polish American physicist Maria Goeppert-Mayer and her colleagues developed the "shell theory" of how the particles in the nucleus of an atom are arranged. Her early research was used to create the bombs that helped the Allies (the United States, England, and Russia) win World War II (1939–45). She received the 1963 Nobel Prize for physics.

In 1957 Chinese-born American physicist Chien-Shiung Wu and her colleague published a scientific paper that challenged a basic law of nuclear physics and forever changed the way in which scientists view atoms. In 1975, Wu became the first woman president of the American Physical Society. She received the National Medal of Science in 1976.

American Helen T. Edwards, who specializes in particle physics, looks for ways to break up atoms so she can learn more about how protons (a stable positively charged subatomic particle) and antiprotons work. This type of research is valuable in creating huge amounts of energy. American biophysicist Edith H. Quimby helped develop ways to use X-rays, radium, and radioactive isotopes (similar species of atoms of a chemical element) to diagnose and treat diseases such as cancer.

Mathematics is also a branch of physical science. Marjorie Lee Brown became one of the first African Americans to earn a doctoral degree in mathematics when she graduated from the University of Michigan in 1949. She was a topologist, a mathematician who studies the surface and shapes of objects. Sometimes topologists specialize further and become cartologists or map-makers. Marie Tharp is an American cartographer and geologist who has helped map the ocean floor.

American Cathleen Synge Morawetz has created mathematical models to help us better understand optics and acoustics (how we see and hear things). Karen

Uhlenbeck, an American, has won awards for her work in geometry and partial differential equations.

Statistics is a branch of mathematics. American statistician Gertrude Mary Cox was instrumental in developing ways for the biological sciences to gather and interpret data. Once the statistics were analyzed, scientists could notice trends and predict future behavior of certain types of crops and diseases. Another type of statistics involves the study of epidemics (a rapid spread of disease) to learn what populations may be affected in the future. This is called epidemiology. Eleanor Josephine Macdonald, an American epidemiologist, was the first to study cancer cases. Before her, epidemiologists had concentrated only on communicable (contagious) diseases. Her work has resulted in early detection programs for cancer and other noncommunicable diseases throughout the United States.

Life Sciences

Branches of science such as anthropology, biology, or medicine are collectively known as life sciences. These sciences deal with living organisms and their organization, life processes, and relationships to each other and their environment. The life science of anthropology is the study of a people's culture. Some anthropologists study current cultures, while others become paleoanthropologists and concentrate on ancient cultures.

In 1925, American anthropologist and explorer Delia Akeley became the

American anthropologist Margaret Mead

scope. Bacteria may sometimes cause disease in living organisms. American bacteriologist Anna W. Williams helped save thousands of lives with her diphtheria antitoxin she developed in 1894. Diphtheria, a contagious disease causing a high fever and difficulty breathing, was often fatal during the 1800s. Rebecca Craighill Lancefield, another American bacteriologist, created a system for identifying the streptococcus bacterium, which causes various diseases in humans. American Evelyn Maisel Witkin studies bacterial mutation (changes in the genes or chromosomes of living things) to learn more about how cells repair damage. Her work has helped those suffering from radiation poisoning. And American limnologist Ruth Patrick pioneered methods for studying freshwater ecosystems. (A limnologist studies the system's plant and animal life at the microscopic level to learn about the impact of pollution.)

A Chinese-born American molecular biologist of note is Flossie Wong-Staal. She has been part of the AIDS research effort from the beginning. AIDS is a fatal disease that attacks and breaks down the body's immune system, thus making it more susceptible to infections and other diseases. Wong-Staal worked in the lab that first identified the AIDS virus and has since devoted her career to finding both a vaccine and a cure for AIDS. In 1990 she became the head of the AIDS laboratory at the University of California in San Diego. Helene Doris Gayle is another American AIDS researcher. A pediatrician (children's doctor) and

first white woman to cross the African continent, and she was one of the first Westerners to study the Pygmy tribes of Zaire. Three years later, American anthropologist Margaret Mead published *Coming of Age in Samoa,* which supported the idea that behavior is learned rather than inherited genetically.

Biology is the life science that studies the origin, history, characteristics, and habits of plant and animal life. Like many other branches of science, biology has its own subdivisions.

A bacteriologist is a scientist who studies bacteria, life forms so tiny that they can only be seen through a micro-

Creative Thinking in Science: Lynn Margulis

American biologist Lynn Margulis has challenged conventional thinking in the scientific world several times. The first time came in the early 1960s, when she publicly disagreed with Charles Darwin's claim that random (occasional or accidental) mutations (changes in the genes or chromosomes of living things) were responsible for many evolutionary changes. Margulis believed that a few random mutations could not possibly explain the complex and continuing changes she was seeing in the ancient fossil and plant samples she was studying.

The results of her research brought Margulis to believe that it was the merging (mixing) of species that created evolutionary changes. For example, she believed that the food available to an insect could have had an impact on how and why that insect species changed. This idea was called the hypothesis of symbiotic organisms or symbiogenesis. Symbiosis is a relationship in which two life forms rely one another for some vital nutrient or for protection. For years, scientists resisted Margulis's hypothesis because it did not fit the traditional Darwinian model used. Then, in 1991, Margulis published *Symbiosis in Cell Evolution,* a book that convinced many in the scientific community of her controversial theory and is now considered a classic in modern biology.

As a result of her original thinking, Margulis was invited to join the National Academy of Sciences (the principal science organization in the United States) and was awarded a Guggenheim grant to continue her research.

Based on her observations, Margulis next challenged conventional science when she developed the Gaia hypothesis in conjunction with her colleague, James E. Lovelock, a British atmospheric chemist. Margulis had become interested in the interaction she observed between changes in air temperature, soil conditions, and the oceans. Carrying the idea of symbiosis one step further, she and Lovelock based the Gaia hypothesis on the idea that Earth has the ability to regulate itself, to maintain an ecological balance despite human interference. The colleagues believe that all parts of nature are interconnected so that they can provide the right conditions that make life possible. The also believe that the natural systems of Earth are so closely interconnected that a change in one will create a change in all.

Today most of Margulis's research money comes from the National Aeronautics and Space Administration (NASA). With its mission of exploring other planets, NASA is interested in theories on how plant life originates and how other planets' ecosystems may work.

epidemiologist, she has traveled to Asia and Africa to study the disease and try to develop a large-scale strategy to fight it.

Microbiology is the branch of life science that deals with microorganisms. Hattie Alexander is a microbiologist who developed a serum to combat influenzal meningitis. This disease causes the membranes enclosing the brain and spinal cord to swell. Before Alexander's serum, the disease was nearly 100 percent fatal in young children. Elizabeth H. Blackburn, an Australian-born American molecular biologist, helped discover DNA and cell division. American Maxine Singer is a DNA researcher who contributed to establishing guidelines for genetics research. Jewel Plummer Cobb is an African American cell biologist who studied melanin, the pigment that adds color to human cells. Janet D. Rowley, an American cytogeneticist, studies leukemia cells and developed new tools for diagnosing this type of cancer. (Cytogenticists specialize in the branch of biology that deals with the formation, structure, and function of cells.)

Zoology is the study of animals and animal life. American zoologist Libbie Henrietta Hyman gained international fame in 1940 when the first volume of her six-volume set called *The Invertebrates* was published. The books set up the classification system for invertebrates (animals without a backbone).

Some zoologists focus their study on a particular type of animal. Entomologists, for instance, study insects. In 1675, German entomologist and illustrator Maria Sibylla Merian published the first of six volumes documenting the life cycles of European insect and plant species.

Other zoologists become naturalists, scientists who study animals in their natural surrounding. English naturalist Miriam Rothschild, for instance, became an expert on fleas and other parasites. Ornithologists study birds. Florence Merriam Bailey was an American ornithologist known for her field trips to American mountain ranges during the late 1800s. She documented the bird life from the Adirondacks in New York to the Rockies in Colorado. American Margaret Morse Nice studied the birds of her native Oklahoma to learn more about their territorial instincts.

British researcher Jane Goodall specializes in ethology, the scientific study of animals in their natural habitats. Goodall is credited with making the first recorded observations of chimpanzees eating meat and making and using tools. Toolmaking was previously thought to be an exclusively human trait.

Another well-known naturalist and ethologist is Joy Adamson, an Austrian scientist who chose to live in Kenya so she could study African wild animals. Her special interest was in lions. She began a national animal orphanage in Nairobi to care for the offspring left when hunters and poachers killed mature animals. The story of her special relationship with the female lioness Elsa is told in the film *Born Free*. In 1985, zoologist Dian Fossey was murdered in Rwanda,

Jane Goodall with a poster to save chimpanzees

Africa, probably by poachers who objected to her outspoken protection of endangered animals, especially gorillas. Her story is told in the film *Gorillas in the Mist* starring Sigourney Weaver.

Medicine is another type of life science. Some doctors specialize in research, while others practice medicine. One branch of specialization is anatomy. An anatomist examines the structure of plants and animals through dissection and microscope study. American Florence Rena Sabin studied the anatomy of newborn infants to learn more about the central nervous system. She is also known for her study of the lymphatic system (a network of vessels that is part of the immune system) and the often-fatal disease tuberculosis. In 1925, Sabin was elected to the National Academy of Sciences in recognition of her work with cells, blood, the immune system, and embryos. American anatomist Mildred Trotter contributed immensely to our knowledge of bones, both as tissue and as a site of mineral mass in the body.

A geneticist studies human and animal genes to learn more about how characteristics are passed from generation to generation. American geneticist Ruth Sager has studied the makeup of cells to determine how to prevent some harmful characteristics from being passed on from parent to offspring. German geneticist Charlotte Auerbach is known for her work in chemical mutagenesis, which is the use of chemicals to create mutations (changes in the genes or chromosomes) in living creatures. The mutants are necessary because scientists learn much about normal growth from them.

A pathologist studies how substances harm living tissue. American pathologist Alice Hamilton did much to publicize the harmful effects of lead (a metallic element) in dishes, drinking water, and water pipes. American Harriet Hardy studied occupational diseases and exposed the harmful effects of asbestos and other fibers. Asbestos is now considered a carcinogen (a cancer-causing substance). American Maud Slye spent her life studying generations of rats to learn about how cancer was inherited.

A virologist studies how viruses act on the human body. Dorothy Millicent Horstmann, an American virologist, played a major, but often unacknowledged, role in developing the polio vaccine in the 1940s. Before polio vaccinations were considered feasible, Horstmann conducted groundbreaking animal studies proving that the polio virus reaches the nervous system through the blood stream.

A pharmacologist studies and produces medicines. In the early 1960s, American pharmacologist Frances Oldham Kelsey helped alert the public to the dangers of thalidomide, a sedative that could cause birth defects in the unborn children of pregnant mothers who used the drug. African American pharmacologist Dolores Cooper Shockley was the first black woman to earn a doctorate in pharmacology. Her work has been in the area of stress, hormones, pain killers, and nutrition.

Among those notable women practicing medicine is Myra A. Logan, an African American physician believed to be the first woman to perform open heart surgery in 1943. Another African American, Irene D. Long, is the chief of the Occupational Medicine and Environmental Health Office at the National Aerospace Agency. Past practitioners include Katharine Scott Bishop, who was an anesthesiologist (the doctor who administers the sleeping drug during surgery).

Creative Thinking in Science: Christiane Nüsslein-Volhard

Christiane Nüsslein-Volhard is a geneticist (a scientist who studies the principles of heredity) at the Max Planck Institute in Tübingen, Germany. Nüsslein-Volhard is best known for her studies of the fruitfly, which she used to explore the early stages of embryonic growth (the beginning stages of an organism's development). More recently, however, Nüsslein-Volhard has changed species and begun to examine the zebra fish. To those familiar with scientific research, Nüsslein-Volhard's switch was astonishing. Most scientists research a single species, building their entire career on continuing insights they gain from years of such concentrated study.

But Nüsslein-Volhard was intensely curious about how a single cell (an egg) can develop into a complex, multicelled creature. The fruitfly, an invertebrate (an animal without a backbone), gave her some of these answers. But she wanted to learn how a vertebrate (an animal with a backbone) conducted the same process. She chose the zebra fish because the embryos are transparent and because they develop outside the mother's body instead of in a womb where changes could not be observed.

After clearing the fruitflies from her laboratory, Nüsslein-Volhard had seven-thousand aquariums built. Today, Nüsslein-Volhard and her staff are busy creating mutant zebra fish so they can study how genes change. Mutants are animals or plants who have characteristics they did not inherit from their parents, but they pass the characteristics along to their offspring. Eventually Nüsslein-Volhard hopes to understand the basic patterns of development of the zebra fish, as she now understands the basic development of the fruitfly. For her fruitfly research, Nüsslein-Volhard and her colleague were awarded the Nobel Prize for medicine in 1995.

Bishop also studied the effect of vitamin E on pregnant women. African American May Edward Chinn battled both sexual and racial prejudice to practice medicine in New York City during the 1930s. She performed major surgery in her patients' homes when no hospital would allow her on staff.

A marine biologist studies the plants and animals that live under the sea. One famous marine biologist is Eugenie Clark, an American who has made a lifelong study of deep-sea sharks. She has gone undersea in the small Russian research submarine called *Mir*, discovered 11 new species of fish, and has ridden a whale shark. Her nickname is "Shark Lady." Clark is also known for her engaging writing style, which makes ocean discoveries interesting for a nonscientific audience.

Spanish-born marine biologist Angeles Alvarino has identified 22 new species of ocean plant life. American marine biologist Rita R. Colwell has developed methods for harvesting medical and industrial products from the sea. American Sylvia A. Earle was one of the first marine biologists to use scuba gear to explore the ocean's depths. She is the former chief scientist of the National Oceanic and Atmospheric Administration and continues to work in oceanography. An oceanographer is a scientist who specializes in studying the ocean and its life. In 1990 American oceanographer Kathleen Crane and her team discovered hot vents in the floors of a Russian lake and suggested this was the site of a widening crack in the Asian landmass.

Behavioral Sciences

Behavioral science is a broad term that describes the study of living people, their actions, their feelings, and their lifestyles. Psychology, for instance, is the study of human emotions and mental health. Psychiatry is the study of human emotions from a medical point of view. In 1932, Melanie Klein, an Austrian psychoanalyst (a doctor who treats mental disorders by exploring the patient's past experiences), helped found the field of child psychology. Patricia S. Cowings is an African American psychophysiologist, a person who studies how emotions affect the body. She conducted research for the National Aeronautics and Space Administration (NASA), which is interested in learning how long space flights affect astronauts' bodies and minds. Cowings relied on biofeedback (a process that puts people in touch with their physical reactions so they can learn to control them) to help her collect data.

A public health scientist is concerned with the well-being of a community of people. Physician Sara Josephine Baker was the first woman to win a doctoral degree in public health. In 1902, Baker ran the newly created division of child hygiene in New York City and helped significantly reduce the infant mortality (baby death) rate.

Nutritionists apply the principles of biology to human eating habits. African American nutritionist Cecile Hoover Edwards has made a career of studying the nutritional needs of disadvantaged people. She has managed programs for and studies on the nutritional needs of pregnant women and preschool children. Nutritionist Gladys Anderson Emerson helped establish the minimum daily requirements for the U.S. Department of Agriculture. These requirements set guidelines for how many servings of each food group people need to remain healthy. These requirements are spelled out on nearly every food product sold in the United States today.

Applied Sciences

Applied sciences put principles of science to practical uses. Computer science, for instance, is an applied science. A computer scientist of note was Grace Hopper, an admiral in the U.S. Navy. Hopper was one of the first to recognize the potential of computers back in the early 1960s, when the smallest computer was the size of a room. In part because of Hopper's efforts, today's computers are small, found nearly everywhere, and are easy to use. She began to write computer programs in English rather than in mathematical code and to use computers to write some of their own programs. In 1984, Hopper was inducted into the Engineering and Science Hall of Fame.

Engineering is the use of scientific and mathematical principles to design and build structures, machines, and systems. It is another example of an applied science. American engineer Thelma Estrin specialized in using computers to measure the brain's electrical signals. Her work helped create internal brain maps and discover the site of epileptic (seizure) cells. Aerospace engineer Yvonne Claeys Brill was born in Canada but now lives in the United States. While working for the National Aeronautics and Space Administration (NASA), she developed new rocket propulsion systems for communications satellites. American engineer Barbara Crawford Johnson designed the backup entry guidance systems for the Apollo space missions. American aeronautical engineer Sheila E. Widnall has added to the knowledge of wind currents and how they affect aircraft flight. She became the first woman to be named secretary of the U.S. Air Force. Anoth-

Computer scientist and rear admiral Grace Hopper helped to revolutionize the computer field.

er aeronautical engineer is Christine Darden, who is looking for ways to reduce the sonic boom that results when a plane breaks the sound barrier. (The sonic boom is the shock wave caused by an aircraft traveling faster than the speed of sound, sometimes causing damage to structures on the ground and often heard as a loud explosive boom.)

Aerospace engineering is just one of the areas in which women engineers work. Engineer Jessie G. Cambra helped design California's transportation systems. Roberta Nichols, a research engineer with the Ford Motor Company, is internationally known for her innovative work in alternate fuel vehicles. American electrical engineer Irene Carswell Peden lived in Antarctica to study how radio- and electromagnetic waves travel through Earth. American industrial engineer Lillian Gilbreth and her husband, Frank, pioneered motion-study techniques—methods to minimize wasted time and energy and increase productivity in industry.

Women in Medicine

Women are no strangers to the medical field. Throughout history, women have been physicians, nurses, physical therapists, and pharmacists. They may have been known by other names (healers, herbalists, and, in some cases, witches), but their function was still the same: to care for the ill and wounded. Women in prehistoric villages in Africa, in medieval castles in Europe, and in colonial towns in North America all sought out or grew plants that could be used in medicines. Many became very skilled in diagnosing and treating diseases such as inflammations (swelling), boils (sores), fevers, and tumors. Not surprisingly, many women healers throughout history have concentrated on issues related to women's and children's health.

Midwifery

Since the beginning of time, women have helped each other bear and care for their children. This process is called midwifery. In ancient times, the midwife most often was an older woman who had borne children herself and who had some basic knowledge of herbal medicines. However, women in ancient times had little idea of anatomy (human physical makeup). As a result, the maternal death rate (death of the mother during childbirth) was incredibly high.

However, by the time of the Roman Empire (27 B.C. to around A.D. 460), confidence in midwives had increased. Julius Caesar himself is said to have been brought into the world by a midwife who sliced open his mother's abdomen to deliver him. The midwife stitched up Caesar's mother and today his name is associated with a common method of delivery, the Cesarean section (or C-section).

As medical and scientific knowledge increased, so did the skills of the midwife. By the 1200s, nurse-midwives were respected in most medieval European towns. In England, 37 women surgeons were licensed in London by an Act of Parliament. While these women could practice all sorts of medicine, many concentrated on childbirth and the special needs of women. They were, in fact, the first gynecologists (doctors who specialize in women's health and diseases).

Several Italian women are among the most famous of these early midwives. Trotula practiced medicine and taught at the medical school at Salerno, near Naples, in A.D. 1100. In 1390, Italian physician Dorotea Bocchi earned her

Timeline: Women Healers Throughout History

1601 French healer Louise Bourgeois becomes midwife to Marie de' Medici, Queen of France.

1671 English midwife Jane Sharp publishes *The Midwives' Book on the Whole Art of Midwifery,* which becomes the standard childbirth text for midwives.

1754 Dorothee Leporin becomes Germany's first female doctor.

1815 Regina von Siebold becomes one of Europe's first gynecologists.

1919 American physician Bertha Van Hoosen becomes the first professor and first head of the obstetrics (the branch of medicine concerned with pregnancy and childbirth) department at the coeducational (admitting both sexes) institution of Loyola College in Chicago.

1925 American nurse Mary Breckenridge founds the Frontier Nursing Service, which delivers medical care on horseback to families in the mountains of southeastern Kentucky.

1969 Elisabeth Kübler-Ross publishes *On Death and Dying,* which revolutionizes how dying patients are treated by medical and psychological caregivers.

medical degree from the University of Bologna. Italian professor Costanza Calenda lectured on medicine at the University of Naples in Italy in 1423. French healer Catherine Lemersne was certified and licensed as a midwife in Lille, France, in 1460.

But the fate of the midwife soon changed for three reasons. The first was the growth of universities throughout Europe. While the spread of knowledge was beneficial, the universities admitted only men. Therefore, it was only men who were formally instructed in the medical arts. The second reason was the growth of towns and with them the political governments that ran them. These governments liked to collect fees through taxes and licenses. Licenses were used to grant official permission to practice a trade. Since the city governments (run by men) chose to grant licenses only to male doctors, the female midwives soon found themselves out of jobs. The third reason was the influence of the Catholic Church. At that time, the church fathers considered women less intelligent and less pure than men. This poor opinion soon caused a full-scale witch hysteria. Many of the women healers were reclassified as witches and persecuted by priests and other church leaders.

By the 1600s, women had been effectively shut out of the formal medical practice in Europe. As always, though, they found other ways to exercise their

St. Hildegard of Bingen

Because Hildegard of Bingen was a woman of many gifts, it is difficult to categorize her. She was born in Germany in 1098 and lived during the Middle Ages. She gained fame during her life as a healer and as a saint.

Since her childhood, Hildegard had experienced visions in which God and the saints visited her. Both the Roman Catholic Church and the local population came to regard her as a prophet (inspired by God). At an early age, she was sent to a convent (a religious home and school) where she learned to read and study music and medicine. She became a nun and eventually became the leader of her convent community.

Unlike most women of her time, Hildegard was educated, and she published a five-volume set of writings, the last three of which covered medical subjects. She took a holistic view of health. This mean that she believed that a healthy lifestyle would help prevent sickness. Many other physicians of the day, however, preferred to concentrate on medicines and procedures for healing people once they became ill.

In her medical writings, Hildegard takes a sympathetic view of women. At the time, women were considered less holy than men. Hildegard disagreed. Both her medical advice and her kinder attitude toward women eventually influenced other church scholars and physicians of her time.

skills and abilities. Many became specialists in herbal medicines. Others published their scientific knowledge in pamphlets and books. The first of these published works was *Concerning the Disorders of Women,* written by the Italian physician Trotula. The text of a later book by Louise Bourgeois of France was stolen by several male authors who set themselves up as authorities on childbirth.

Midwives regained their popularity in the 1960s and 1970s when some women started to object to the impersonal, male-dominated medical nature of their childbirth experience. These women wanted other nurturing women nearby as they went through labor. Today, midwifery is a branch of nursing.

Women Denied Admission to Medical College

Until the mid-1800s, women students were not admitted to medical colleges in the United States and most

European countries. Medicine was considered too indecent and gory a profession for women. However, English-born Elizabeth Blackwell disagreed. In 1849, she became the first woman to earn a medical degree from a U.S. college. The next year in Philadelphia, Pennsylvania, the Quakers (a religious group) founded the Female Medical College of Pennsylvania, now called the Woman's College of Pennsylvania.

Conditions in England were equally oppressive to women. In 1854, English nurse Florence Nightingale revolutionized the profession of nursing. An upper-class woman, Nightingale traveled to the Crimean Peninsula (between Turkey and Russia) to nurse injured British soldiers. At first, the medical establishment scoffed. However, her success in saving lives soon changed their attitudes. Soon Nightingale was asked to supervise the army's hospitals. She did so, instituting rules on cleanliness, routine, and nutrition that did much to ease the suffering of the wounded. An American nurse raised in the Nightingale tradition included Dorothea Dix, who became the superintendent of nurses for the Union (North) during the American Civil War (1861–65).

During the Civil War, women proved that they could take on the jobs that became available when men took to soldiering. The New England Hospital for Women and Children opened in 1862 with an all-female staff. In 1872, Linda Richards became the first nurse to graduate from the hospital's professional nursing program, the first such program in the United States.

Elizabeth Blackwell became the first American woman to receive a medical degree.

In 1866, Lucy Hobbs became the first woman to earn a D.D.S. (dental) degree from an American school. After the war, Clara Barton traveled to Europe where she learned of a Swiss relief organization. Barton returned to the United States and, in 1881, founded a similar organization, the American Red Cross.

European women were also proving that they could handle the stresses of the medical professions. In 1870, Elizabeth Garrett Anderson attended medical school in Paris, France, and became the first British female physician in modern times.

Women were often encouraged to become nurses instead of doctors.

In 1882, Aletta Jacobs, Holland's first female physician, opened the world's first birth control clinic in Amsterdam.

Nursing soon became an honorable profession for upper-class young women. In 1910, American nurse Frances Elisabeth Crowell became the executive secretary for the Association of Tuberculosis Clinics in New York City, an experience that led her to promote the public health movement. In 1911, American physician Alice Hamilton published a report on lead poisoning among factory workers that was the first study of occupational health (work-related) diseases.

Nevertheless, women were still not entirely accepted by the male political or medical establishments. In 1917, after they were banned from the military, American female physicians formed their own all-female medical force, which provided professional services to the wounded and sick during World War I (1914–18).

Women continued to challenge established medical practice in other fields, too, especially in the area of family planning. In 1918, British paleobotanist (a person who studies ancient plants) Marie Stopes published *Wise Parenthood,* a handbook on contraceptive

Helen Brooke Taussig

Helen Brooke Taussig may be credited with saving the lives of thousands of children through an operation she pioneered. Taussig, a pediatric cardiologist (a children's heart doctor), was born in 1898 in Massachusetts. She studied medicine at Boston University after Harvard University refused to admit her because she was a woman. Taussig later transferred to Johns Hopkins University in Baltimore, Maryland, where she received her medical degree in 1927. After graduation, she remained at Johns Hopkins, which is both a medical school and a teaching hospital.

Early in her studies, Taussig realized that she wanted to specialize in diseases of the heart. She was named head of the hospital's new pediatric cardiology clinic in 1930. Because of a hearing loss, Taussig learned to rely on all her senses when diagnosing a child's condition. She could hear little through a stethoscope, so she used her eyes and hands to help her examine a child.

Taussig's special interest became "blue babies," children who turned blue from a lack of oxygen. This condition was caused by a defect in the heart, which pumps oxygen-rich blood through the body. During the mid-1940s, Taussig worked with another doctor, Alfred Blalock, to develop an operation that rerouted some of the body's blood vessels. This rerouting allowed oxygen-rich blood to reach all parts of the body. In addition to saving thousands of babies, the operation also had a great influence on many other cardiac procedures done at the time.

Taussig's other great contribution to medicine came in the 1960s, when she helped determine that a rise in birth defects was caused by a sleeping pill that pregnant women took called Thalidomide. As a result, the pill was eventually withdrawn from the marketplace. Taussig helped lead the fight to ensure that better testing would be done on drugs before they were released for public use.

methods. It was the first step in her campaign to educate women about birth control. Stopes inspired and offered advice to Margaret Sanger, the public health nurse who publicized birth control methods in the United States. (For more on Margaret Sanger, see Chapter 12, "Social Concerns of Women.")

Today, the practice of medicine is open to women in industrialized countries. Medical schools and research facilities routinely admit and hire women. Statistics still show, however, that women doctors are clustered in the lower-paying medical professions such as family practice and pediatrics.

Women Explorers and Discoverers

Throughout history, women have been traveling to strange lands and making discoveries about the people, customs, and landscape they have found. For the most part, however, women traveled with men instead of setting off on their own. In ancient Rome, for instance, a woman might accompany her husband if he were assigned as magistrate to some distant outpost of the Roman Empire. During the Crusades (1000–1300), women traveled with the Christian armies to the Middle East in their quest to recapture the Holy Land (what is now the country of Israel). These women went as wives, nurses, cooks, seamstresses, and laundresses.

One class of people traveled consistently throughout the Middle Ages and the Renaissance. These were the royal families of the kingdoms in Europe. Since marriage was a way to gain more land and riches, many brides found themselves traveling long distances to meet their grooms. Catherine of Aragon, for instance, was a Spanish princess who married King Henry VIII of England. Princesses were brought up to expect a foreign marriage, even though it meant that they may never see their homeland again.

Other classes of women also knew that they were destined to travel. Among them were the millions of European immigrants who traveled to the "New World" beginning in the 1600s. Once landed, many of these women continued to push westward, taking the Oregon and other trails to yet another frontier.

Victorian Women Travelers

In the mid-1800s, England experienced a startling phenomenon. Women were leaving home to journey to distant lands and then returning home to write about their adventures. This traveling phenomenon is noteworthy for several reasons.

One reason these British women travelers were significant was because they lived during the Victorian Era. This was the time when Queen Victoria ruled England (from 1837 to 1901, one of the longest reigns in British history). Victoria's influence was far-reaching. She believed women should be stay-at-home mothers and that education mattered little. As a result, girls during this period received little education, had few legal rights, and were guided by a strict code of conduct. Women dressed in heavy, uncomfortable clothing, did not speak in public, and were concerned only with family, servants, and church.

But this effort to create meek, obedient girls—to dampen any spark of curiosity and creativity in women—sometimes backfired. Some parents believed their daughters deserved some education, and these girls, a small minority, were taught by tutors. Other parents believed they needed to protect their daughters against the harsh world. When these parents died, they often left their money and houses to their daughters, so they would be provided for.

Timeline: Women on the Move

c. 1390 Margery Kempe, an English housewife, makes a pilgrimage (holy journey) to the Middle East. Her writings are one of the first autobiographies in the English language.

1814 British noblewoman Hester Stanhope settles on Mount Lebanon and becomes famous throughout the Middle East as the "Queen of the Arabs."

1856 British author Isabella Bird Bishop publishes *The Englishwoman in America,* which details her trip alone to Hawaii. She later traveled to Japan, Korea, Persia (modern-day Iran), Tibet, and the Rocky Mountains.

1858 American journalist and suffragist Julia Archibald Holmes wears bloomers, moccasins, and a hat to complete her ascent to the top of Pike's Peak in Colorado.

1873 British noblewoman Anne Blunt begins her travels in the Middle East, which eventually include trips to Turkey, Algiers, Egypt, the Sinai peninsula, Iraq, and Saudi Arabia.

1877 British Egyptologist Amelia Edwards writes *A Thousand Miles up the Nile* about her travels in Africa.

1879 British botanical painter Marianne North exhibits the paintings she made during trips to Turkey, Syria, Egypt, Canada, the United States, Brazil, Jamaica, Borneo, Java, Sarawak, Sri Lanka (Ceylon), India, Australia, the Seychelles, Chile, and South Africa.

1881 British travel writer Constance Gordon-Cumming publishes *At Home in Fiji.* Her other travels take her to Sri Lanka (Ceylon), Hawaii, China, Japan, New Zealand, and Austria.

1889 American newspaper reporter Nellie Bly travels around the world in 72 days.

1906 American adventurer Fanny Bullock Workman climbs Pinnacle Peak in the Nun Kun Range in the Himalayas.

1908 American archaeologist Annie Smith Peck climbs Mount Huascaran in Peru, estimated at 24,000 feet to be the tallest peak in the Americas.

1912 Alexandra David-Neel, a French travel writer, becomes the first woman to interview the Dalai Lama, the spiritual leader of the Buddhist religion.

1912 American climber Dora Keen becomes the first known person to scale Mount Blackburn, a 16,390-foot peak in Alaska.

1913 British anthropologist Daisy Bates travels to Australia where she lives among and writes about the Aborigines (native people).

Timeline: More Women on the Move

1914 British explorer Gertrude Bell works with Lawrence of Arabia to incite the Arabs to overthrow their Turkish rulers and side with the Allies (Great Britain, France, Russia, United States) during World War I (1914–18).

1917 American Osa Johnson begins her career as one of the first wildlife photographers.

1926 American business executive and photographer Louise Arner Boyd organizes a polar bear hunting excursion to the Arctic. She later becomes the acknowledged authority on the east coast of Greenland.

1926 British writer Vita Sackville-West travels to Persia (now Iran) with her husband, who works at the British Embassy in Tehran. Her journeys also take her to India and Egypt, providing her with more material for her now famous travel diaries.

1927 American pilot Louise Thaden flies her plane to 20,000 feet, higher than any woman had gone. She later sets an endurance record and wins a number of races.

1930 British pilot Amy Johnson becomes the first woman to fly solo from England to Australia.

1932 American flier Amelia Earhart flies solo across the Atlantic Ocean.

1936 Beryl Markham of Kenya flies from London to New England (against the wind) to show that two-way commercial plane service is practical.

1961 Irish cyclist Dervla Murphy rides overland to India. Other bicycle trips take her to England, Spain, Germany, Tibet, Nepal, the Andes, and Northern Ireland.

1963 Russian cosmonaut (astronaut) Valentina Tereshkova becomes the first woman to travel in space. She orbits Earth forty-nine times in three days in the craft *Vostok 6*.

1976 British sailor Clare Francis becomes the fastest solo yachtswoman (sailor) to cross the Atlantic Ocean.

1977 New Zealand sailor Naomi James becomes the first woman to sail solo around the world.

1983 Astrophysicist Sally Ride becomes the first U.S. woman astronaut in space.

1986 American pilot Jeana Yeager and her colleague fly the airplane *Voyager* around the world without refueling. Their trip takes nine days.

1992 Astronaut Mae Jemison becomes the first African American woman to travel in space.

1995 American adventurer Suellen Finatri completes a 4,500 mile solo trip on horseback from Michigan to Alaska.

For the most part, Victorian women travelers came from the middle- or upper-class and had slightly unusual upbringings. They had education and money, two advantages denied many of their contemporaries (women living at the same time).

One such woman traveler was Mary Kingsley, who was born in Cambridge, England, in 1862. While Kingsley did not have a tutor, she did have free run of the family library. She spent many hours there, studying history, geography, and literature. During her studies, she learned of the many foreign lands that made up the British Empire. These countries included India, Australia, Egypt, and parts of Africa.

When Kingsley's parents died in 1892, she set off for Africa on behalf of the British Museum. Like the other European females of her day, Kingsley wore long, heavy skirts, several petticoats, and a tightly laced corset around her middle. How she could breathe, let alone catch trains, seems like a mystery to modern women. But she did catch trains, ships, and caravans.

When Kingsley made a second voyage to Africa in 1894 she went as a trader. Before leaving England she purchased a huge quantity of cloth. She then traveled for 11 months, trading throughout West Africa. Other adventures took her to Mount Cameroon, which she climbed (at 13,000 feet tall, it is the highest peak in West Africa). She wrote of her adventures in a book titled *Travels in West Africa* and published many articles on African tribes and customs.

Kingsley journeyed to South Africa in 1899 as a journalist and nurse to cover the Boer War. The war was between the Dutch settlers (called Boers) and the invading English. In 1900, while still in South Africa, she died of typhus. Kingsley had indeed seen much of the British Empire by the time of her death.

Modern Explorers

Today, women travel the globe, alone, in pairs, and in groups. Women war correspondents cover battles in the Middle East and eastern Europe. Women join safaris in Africa, mountain climbing expeditions in Nepal, and trips into the Amazon rain forest. Women tourists have seen the Aswan Dam in Egypt, the step pyramids of Mexico, and the savannahs of South Africa. As never before in history, the world today is open to women explorers, adventurers, and discoverers.

Not only is the world now open to modern women explorers, but so is space. In 1992, Mae Jemison became the first African American woman to fly in outer space.

Jemison was born in Alabama in 1956. She grew up in Chicago, where her love of science and space was fed by trips to the Chicago Museum of Science and Industry. In 1973, Jemison entered Stanford University in California, where she studied chemical engineering and African American studies. While a student, she also pursued her love of dance and archae-

Far From Home: Nellie Bly

American newspaper woman Nellie Bly loved a challenge. She wrote for a New York newspaper, *World,* at a time when women did not become journalists. Once hired, she became one of the first of what we now call "investigative reporters." Many times she selected her topics herself.

At one time during her career, Bly went undercover to a mental hospital and exposed the horrible conditions there. Her story helped spark reform in how mentally ill patients were treated and how the hospitals were run. She also had herself arrested for theft so she could experience firsthand what it was like to be a woman in prison. What she found and reported helped change how female inmates were housed. Bly exposed the substandard working conditions in New York sweatshops (garment factories) and even tackled bribery (paying money for political favors) in government circles.

Her greatest feat, however, was traveling around the world in 72 days. Bly's goal was to beat the 80 days it took fictional traveler Phineas Fogg in Jules Verne's *Around the World in 80 Days.* Bly's trip was remarkable because she was traveling at a time when women did not venture far from their homes alone.

Bly's next big adventure came during World War I (1914–18). She traveled to Europe to cover the war along the Eastern Front, between Germany and Russia. She became a war correspondent at a time when female newspaper reporters (still a rare breed) were assigned to write about home, family, and fashion issues.

Nellie Bly's path of adventure took great personal and moral courage. She was exposed to physical danger throughout her life, and she was often criticized by the very society she was helping to change. However, her willingness to do what had not been done before, to go where others had not gone, helped other women challenge the traditional roles they held.

ology (the scientific recovery and study of the remains of past human activities).

Next Jemison went to Cornell University in New York City to study medicine. As a medical student, she joined others who traveled to places of great human need, such as Cuba (in the Caribbean Sea off the coast of Florida), Kenya (in Africa), and Thailand (in southeast Asia). In Thailand she worked in a camp for Cambodian refugees. After graduating with her medical degree, Jemison joined the Peace Corps, which took her to Sierra Leone and Liberia, both in Africa.

When she returned home in 1985, Jemison set up a medical practice in Los Angeles, California. But she also continued to study and take engineering courses at night school. She soon applied to NASA for a slot in the astronaut training program. In 1987, she was accepted, and after a year of training, Jemison was made an astronaut in August 1988.

It was another five years, however, before Jemison was scheduled for her first mission. For eight days in September 1992, she flew as a mission specialist aboard the space shuttle *Endeavor.* Her work included using biofeedback (the use of monitoring devices to gain some control over involuntary bodily functions) to quiet motion sickness, the effects of space on human calcium levels, and the effect of weightlessness on biological development in organisms.

As of the mid-1990s, Jemison was heading her own technology development company, a job that kept her in touch with learning and exploration. Jemison's love of new experiences continues unabated. In the early 1990s she appeared in an episode of the television program *Star Trek: The Next Generation.*

Women Inventors

Women have invented devices and processes since the beginning of time. For instance, archaeologists routinely unearth devices for making open-fire cooking easier and safer. Many ancient civilizations used iron hooks and trivets (a three-legged metal stand for holding a pot) to keep faces and hands away from cooking fires. Women have been clever at devising ways to tend their infants, as well. Their inventions have ranged from child carriers to tethers (ropes) to keep their children confined in a safe area.

When it comes to processes, women have again concentrated their energy in the area of the home arts. They pioneered ways of preserving fruits and vegetables so that their families could enjoy them during the winter months. Drying, salting, canning, and pickling are just some of these "kitchen-type" processes.

Women inventors are also well represented in the areas of clothing and home improvements. Their creations include more comfortable clothing for women and many domestic appliances such as toasters, vacuums, and stoves. Sometimes a historical event will stimulate the creativity of inventors. The Industrial Revolution, the Civil War, and the urbanization of America were three periods that saw a great deal of patent activity. (Patents are grants made by a government that assures an inventor the exclusive right to manufacture, use, and sell an invention for a certain period of time.)

Inventions spurred by the Industrial Revolution (1700s to mid-1800s) included patents for better locomotive parts, cast iron stoves, and building products that used iron supports, railings, elevators, and light fixtures. The greatest flowering of American women inventors came in the latter part of the 1800s, however,

Timeline: Women Who Created Useful Products

1715 Sybilla Masters invents a new way to clean and cure the Indian corn growing in several American colonies. (Because women are not allowed to receive a patent, her husband receives a patent on the process from the English government.)

1809 Mary Kies invents a process for weaving straw with silk or thread (useful in bonnet making), becoming the first woman to receive a U.S. patent.

1812 Tabitha Babbit patents a circular saw.

1821 Sophia Woodhouse receives a patent for her "new and useful improvement in the manufacture of grass bonnets and hats."

1841 Elizabeth Adams invents a pregnancy corset (to support the weight of the woman's abdomen).

1871 Martha J. Coston patents a holder for the material used in pyrotechnic night signals (a system of color-coded flares that allowed armies to communicate over long distances).

1876 Emily E. Tassey improves the equipment used to raise sunken vessels (her later patents are for dredging [digging] machines and for methods of propelling ships).

1877 Mary Nolan invents a fireproof building material shaped in interlocking bricks. She calls the material "Noleum."

1882 Adeline D. T. Whitney invents alphabet blocks.

1883 Nancy M. Fitch patents a kiln (oven) for firing (baking) pottery.

1884 Harriet W. R. Strong invents a hook and eye to fasten garment openings.

1886 Josephine Cochran patents her dish washing machine.

1887 Maria Allen invents the first disposable diaper.

1893 Sara Tyson Rorer invents Jell-O™ by adding sugar to gelatin.

when they patented everything from an ore (a mineral) refining process (Carrie Everson in 1886) to Anna Breadin's "noiseless school desk" in 1889.

The American Civil War (1861–65) did much to encourage creative thinking from inventors, both in the North and South. In 1863, Clarissa Britain patented an improvement in ambulances. Since the number and severity of wounds had increased with the introduction of the rifle, whose bullets shattered bones, the ambulances were necessary to carry the wounded from the battlefields. In 1864, Mary Jane Montgomery patented an "improved war-vessel," made of steel

1899 Letitia Geer takes out a patent on her "medical syringe" (a needle for administering shots).

1900 Florence Parpart invents a street cleaner .

1906 Minnie Agnes Phelps patents a "combined toaster and warming oven."

1914 Mary P. Jacobs creates a brassiere.

1918 Marjorie True Gregg patents a pant-like garment that is quickly adopted by women farm workers during World War I (1914–18).

1928 Marjorie Joyner patents a permanent waving machine for African American women's hair.

1938 Lillian L. Greneker patents a display mannequin.

1941 Hedy Kiesler Markey (known in Hollywood as "Hedy Lamar") files for a patent on a secret communication device to aid in the Allied (Great Britain, Russia, United States) effort during World War II (1939–41).

1951 Marion Donovan patents a disposable diaper that begins the modern diaper industry.

1957 Bette Nesmith Graham patents Liquid Paper™, a typewriter correction fluid.

1969 Ann Moore invents the "Snugli," the first modern baby-carrier.

1975 Ruth Siems and her research team invent an instant stuffing mix.

1987 Lila M. Beauchamp is issued a patent for antiviral compounds (drugs to treat viruses).

1988 Susan Daluge takes out a patent for her invention of "antibacterial compounds."

1993 Patricia Bianconi and her colleague invent a diamond or diamond-like film from a polyacetylene plastic.

that discouraged barnacles (hard-shelled animals) from attaching themselves to the portion of the ship that was underwater. Yet another war-inspired invention was Sarah Mossman's 1865 soldier's cap, which was used by Union forces. One of the big problems the Northerners encountered during their fighting in the South was the heat and the insects. Mossman's cap had a flap that hung over the back of the soldiers' neck to protect them from both irritants.

The urbanization of American came during the late 1800s, when the steady wages offered by the factories drew families to the cities. Farmers left their land

and immigrants from around the world flocked to America's major cities. They worked in the automotive, steel, and clothing plants. Even with steady wages, many of them remained fairly poor and had to live in small apartments. With so many people squeezed into several tiny rooms, space was valued. The space crunch led to another wealth of inventions. They included Julia Blanche French's 1874 patent for a bed frame, which she later improved to include drawers and a safe. In 1885, Sarah E. Goode patented a folding cabinet bed, becoming the first known African American woman to win a patent. In 1902, Adeloe Nadeau patented a combined rocking chair-cradle for crowded apartments.

In modern times, as women have been allowed the same education and work experience as men, their range of inventions has grown. Today, women inventors are known for their medicines, software programs, spacecraft, and contributions to genetic engineering.

15

Jobs and Money

"The story of women's work ... is a story of constant changes or shiftings of work and workshop, accompanied by long hours, low wages, insanitary conditions, over-work, and the want on the part of the woman of training, skill, and vital interest in her work."

—Helen L. Sumner, author of Volume IX of the report History of Women in Industry in the United States

Throughout the twentieth century, women have become increasingly absorbed into the American workforce, an arena previously dominated by men. Although poor women have always worked, by the 1970s, nearly all single women and one-half of married women were also in the workforce.

Today as never before in history, women hold top positions in high-income fields, from film, television, and music, to sports, literature, business, and politics. Their names are known every-where: Demi Moore, Oprah Winfrey, Madonna, Jackie Joyner-Kersee, Steffi Graf, Toni Morrison, Carol Moseley-Braun, and many others.

All have achieved prosperity and fame through talent, hard work, and determination, and many serve as role models for younger women. But what about the average woman or girl, whose name may never be in the national spotlight? Can she still attain a degree of prosperity and comfort? The answer depends on a variety of factors, but perhaps most importantly on the girl's education and outlook.

Timeline: Women's Work

1740 At age 17 Eliza Lucas Pinckney is left in charge of several of her father's plantations in the Carolina colonies. Her experiments with new crops such as indigo (blue dye) are a major contribution to the colonies' economy.

1834 The Lowell mill girls (textile workers) in Massachusetts go on strike.

1844 The Lowell Female Labor Reform Association is organized, making it one of the first labor unions.

1845 Complaints by the Lowell mill girls lead the Massachusetts legislature to order the first government investigation of U.S. labor conditions. The investigating committee takes no action other than to recommend that the mill owners learn "less love for money, and a more ardent love for social happiness."

1869 The Knights of Labor is formed "to secure to the toilers a proper share of the wealth that they create." Women are accepted as members, and some rise to national leadership positions.

1870 More than 14 percent of the American female population over age 16 are "breadwinners."

1873 E. Remington & Sons license their invention, the typewriter, opening up a new kind of employment for women.

1889 Jane Addams founds Hull House in Chicago. Among the services it offers to poor immigrant (foreign-born) women are child care, English classes, vocational skills classes, living quarters for working women, and meeting rooms for labor unions.

1892 Illinois becomes the first state to limit the number of hours per day women could be required to work. (This limit is ten.) By 1917, thirty-nine states adopt laws protecting working women, and eight set minimum wages for women.

1900 American women over age 16 make up 20.6 percent of the labor force.

1903 The National Women's Trade Union League is formed. It organizes New York City's garment workers.

1908 By upholding a court case called *Muller* v. *Oregon,* the U.S. Supreme Court affirms the state's right to pass laws regulating the number of hours women can work. Muller claimed that his female laundry workers should be able to work as many hours as they wished.

1909 The International Ladies' Garment Workers Union (ILGWU) leads a general strike in New York City. Thirty thousand garment workers walk off the job. Although the strike fails, the ILGWU is established as a major union.

Middle Class and Underclass

There are two very different chapters to the female story of jobs and money in the twentieth century. The first is one of a growing female middle class that is enjoying greater occupational and economic opportunities than ever before. This prosperity is an indication that equality is alive for educated, motivated women. The second chapter is more somber, though. It tells of an increasing number of women who are disadvantaged and disconnected from the mainstream of American life.

Despite increasing opportunities for upper- and middle-class females, as a whole women trail men in wealth, income, and many other measures of social and financial status. Women continue to be primarily employed in lower-paying and part-time jobs or earn lower wages than men who have similar jobs. It comes as little surprise, then, that the poverty rate for women who are maintaining families remains substantially higher than the poverty rate for any other population group.

Women's increased workload outside the home, however, has not involved a decrease in their workload inside the home. Married women with jobs perform 73 percent of household chores while full-time housewives do 83 percent.

Unemployment

Unemployment rates were higher for women than for men throughout the

Women continue to demand equal pay for their work.
Photograph by Freda Leinwand. Used by permission.

1960s and 1970s. Since women had just started entering the labor force in large numbers, they were often the first to get laid off or fired when businesses needed to reduce staff (the saying in business is, "Last hired, first fired"). However, by the 1980s, unemployment rates for women were nearly the same as for men.

Inequality in Income

Women's incomes have yet to gain equality with men's. Recent studies have found that women with similar levels of education, occupation, and experience tend to earn less than their male coun-

Timeline: Women's Work

1911 The Triangle Shirtwaist Factory fire in New York City kills 146 young women, mostly immigrants.

1913 Elizabeth Gurley Flynn organizes a strike by mill workers in Paterson, New Jersey, protesting increases in hours without increases in pay. The strike fails.

1919 Lena Madeson Phillips founds the National Federation of Business and Professional Women's Clubs to promote opportunities for women in professional and white collar jobs. The group focuses on the right of married women to remain in the workforce.

1921 The Women's Bond Club is founded in New York City for women working in the financial industry.

1923 The U.S. Supreme Court strikes down minimum wage laws for women.

1938 The Fair Labor Standards Act establishes a minimum wage for *all* workers and prohibits (bans) child labor in businesses engaged in interstate commerce (trade between states).

1941 World War II and its need for male soldiers increases the demand for women workers.

1945 Women make up one-half of the U.S. labor force but are paid only about one-half of what male workers receive doing the same job.

1962 Dolores Huerta helps found the United Farm Workers Union.

1963 Mary Kay Ash takes $5,000 from her savings account and founds Mary Kay Cosmetics. The company's sales go on to exceed $1 billion, and the firm is listed as one of the one hundred best companies to work for in America.

1963 The President's Commission on the Status of Women issues its *American Women* report. Among other actions, it

terparts. Generally, women earn about 73 cents for every $1 that a man earns. Women's incomes are often still considered supplements or family bonuses rather than money necessary for the family's survival.

Data on income from the U.S. Department of Commerce confirm those findings. In 1992 the average income of year-round full-time working women was $22,167 compared to $31,012 for working men.

Poverty

Women were 51.3 percent of the U.S. population in 1990, but they made up 57.7 percent of all persons living in poverty. Analysts today talk of a disturbing new phenomenon called the "feminization" of poverty. This phenomenon calls for federal and privately funded child-care centers for working women, equal employment opportunities, paid maternity leaves, equal pay laws, vocational training, and the promotion of women to high-level jobs in government.

1963 The U.S. Congress passes the Equal Pay Act of 1963. To this day, the Act remains difficult to enforce.

1964 The Civil Rights Act of 1964 is passed and prohibits discrimination in employment based on race or sex.

1967 President Lyndon Johnson signs Executive Order 11375. It broadens affirmative action by prohibiting gender discrimination in jobs. Employers who do business with the U.S. government cannot discriminate against women in hiring.

1977 Chicago legal secretary Iris Rivera refuses to make coffee for her boss. She is fired, but her act launches a movement to improve working conditions for office workers.

1993 Major U.S. companies having at least one woman director is 69 percent. The figure has risen to 81 percent by 1995.

1993 Women hold 8.3 percent of the 6,274 seats on corporate boards of directors. By 1995 the figure has risen to 9.5 percent.

1994 Women make up 46 percent of the U.S. workforce, but are concentrated in low-paying service jobs such as clerical work and domestic service.

1996 The American Bar Association releases its report on gender bias in the legal profession and states that "discrimination continues to permeate [be found throughout] the structures, practices, and attitudes of the legal profession."

has been brought about by the increase in the number of families consisting of a mother and her children with no husband (or second income) present.

Family Structure and Family Income

Between 1970 and 1990, an astounding 99 percent increase in the number of families living in poverty were families headed by women. Nearly one-quarter of all American families with children under age 18 are headed by single mothers.

By 1991, 11.5 percent of all families had income below the poverty level. More than one-third (35.6 percent) of families maintained by single white women were poor. The poverty figures are even higher for black and Hispanic

Money Talk

Each year *Working Woman* magazine compares women's salaries with those of men. According to *Working Woman*'s 1996 report, women's salaries were starting to catch up to men's and, in some cases, even exceeded men's. It was more typical, though, for women to earn 5 to 15 cents less per dollar than men working in similar jobs. In some cases, women's earnings had declined from the previous year. The author of the article, Diane Harris, said: "One of the big problems facing women is not that they get paid less when they have the same job with the same experience. The problem is that women are clustered in traditional female lower-paying jobs."

Here are some of the results of the survey:

- Where women in university administration (dean of arts and letters, for example) earn $126,117, men earn $104,172.
- Where women engineers with five to six years' experience earn $49,100, men with the same amount of experience earn $50,000.
- Where women in financial services (sales representative) earn $26,936, men earn $48,932.

The survey also listed the American women executives who earn the most. Their yearly earnings ranged from a high of $9.49 million to a low of $2.72 million.

---

female-headed families. About one-half of these families live in poverty.

There are also wide differences in income between elderly men and women. Twice as many elderly women live in poverty as elderly men. Elderly black women have the highest poverty rate of all.

The Role of Government

Many of the government programs that address the needs of poor and working women were developed during the Great Society era of the 1960s. Among these programs were the Equal Pay Act of 1963, the Civil Rights Act, and affirmative action legislation.

Equal Pay Act of 1963

On the recommendation of President John Kennedy's Commission on the Status of Women, the U.S. Congress passed the Equal Pay Act of 1963. The act provided for equal pay for men and women in jobs that required equal skills, responsibility, and effort. The act has been difficult to enforce, however, because the meaning of the terms "skills," "responsibility," and "effort" is open to debate.

The problem is made more complicated because most women do not work in the same jobs as men. Many jobs continue to be almost all female or all male. Although "female jobs," such as those of teacher, secretary, nurse, and day care worker, may require skills and training that are comparable to "men's jobs," they continue to be lower paying. As a result, some women have chosen to move into so-called "men jobs." However, studies show that women in these "men's jobs" are still paid less than the men preforming the same jobs.

Civil Rights Act of 1964

When the Civil Rights Act of 1964 was first proposed to Congress, it was intended to ban discrimination based on race. Many prejudiced people objected to the proposed act. U.S. Representative Howard W. Smith was one such person who wanted the act defeated. He facetiously proposed an amendment that would prohibit discrimination based on race and sex, thinking that Congress and the American people would find his proposal so ridiculous that the Civil Rights Act would not pass.

President Lyndon Johnson was firmly behind the Civil Rights Act, however, so he began to pressure Congress. He also enlisted the help of two women members of Congress, Representative Martha Griffiths of Michigan and Senator Margaret Chase Smith of Maine. These women were known as the "Conscience of the Senate." In spite of tremendous opposition, the Civil Rights Act,

The Gender Gap in Earnings

The table below shows some recent figures on how women's earnings compare with men's.

Year	Profession	Median Income Women	Men
1994	Advertising	$38,500	$73,400
1989	Architecture	$29,451	$40,110
1994	Computer Programming	$31,616	$37,596
1994	Engineering	$48,555	$59,750
1995	Lawyers (1-5 yrs experience)	$30,806	$37,500
1995	Lawyers (10-20 yrs experience)	$68,466	$90,574
1989	Music	$18,653	$22,988
1994	Nursing	$34,476	$32,916
1989	Painting	$18,762	$24,320
1989	Photography	$17,381	$25,456
1992–93	Teaching	$53,233	$60,321
1989	Writing	$25,101	$33,837

Source: Working Women magazine, January 1994 and 1996. National Endowment for the Arts Research Division Report, No. 29, 1994. U.S. Equal Employment Opportunity Commission. American Institute of Chemical Engineering.

complete with its provisions banning employment discrimination on the basis of race or sex, was passed into law. The new law also provided for the establishment of the Equal Employment Opportunity Commission (EEOC), to make sure the Civil Rights Act is obeyed.

Margaret Chase Smith

mative action results in "reverse discrimination" because it denies opportunities to qualified whites and men.

In 1996 President Bill Clinton suspended federal affirmative action programs for three years. Women and minority business owners expressed their concerns that the removal of those programs would result in the loss of jobs worth billions of dollars. They also believed it would threaten the survival of their businesses.

Women in the Workforce: Some Background

From American colonial times, a woman's work was in her home. She performed a variety of tasks, such as food cultivation and preparation, the manufacture of clothing, teaching her own children and perhaps others', cleaning, home and furniture repair, and so on. The rare early exception was domestic service (such as maid work or housecleaning).

From colonial days until the late 1940s, domestic service was the largest occupation for women who worked outside their own home. Working conditions were hard, but the work was appealing because food, clothing, and shelter were often provided by employers. However, domestic servants were at the mercy of their bosses, who sometimes mistreated them. As industry grew in the cities, many men and women left domestic service to work in the mills.

Beginning in the early 1800s, the introduction of power machinery for the

Affirmative Action

Johnson, happy with his success in pushing through the Civil Rights Act, followed it in 1967 with Executive Order 11246. That order established a policy of affirmative action to end discrimination in hiring and was also meant to persuade companies to hire more minorities and women. Affirmative action policies usually require that employers set goals for hiring and promoting minorities and women.

Affirmative action has always been controversial. Its supporters say it is the only way to make up for past discrimination. Its critics say, however, that affir-

manufacturing of clothing resulted in the transfer of women's work from the home spinning wheel to the textile (fabric) mills. In the early days of factory work, most men were still involved in farming, so factories had to hire women. By the 1830s, thousands of women worked in the textile mills, making that industry the second largest occupation for women who worked outside their homes. Although factory work made women specialists in one particular task, it took away their freedom. Factory workers sold their labor instead of using it for their families.

Women working in textile mills spun and wove cloth, sewed garments, and also did piecework (work paid for by the piece) in their homes. Working conditions varied greatly. Some textile workers were fairly well paid while others, especially in large cities, worked in sweatshop conditions. Gradually, however, men replaced women in the spinning trade, one of the most highly paid of the jobs in textiles.

Wages Were Low

Working women had no choice but to accept the low wages they were offered, since most had to earn income to support themselves or their families. Employers excused the low wages they paid single women by pointing out that these women had no one to support but themselves. Married women, they declared, should be paid low wages because they had husbands to support them. Those women who did piecework at home in order to generate income while staying at home

Window on the World: Labor Force Participation Trends

Worldwide, the highest labor participation rates (that is, the number of women in the labor force as a percentage of the population aged 15 to 64) have been in Scandinavian countries (Norway, Sweden, and Denmark). The lowest rates have been in Greece, Ireland, Italy, Portugal, and Spain. Still, by the end of the twentieth century, most women in the majority of the world's countries are segregated into the lowest paid jobs.

with their families made about 30 cents a day. Employers justified this low pay by saying such women could work at their leisure in the comfort of their homes.

The Lowell Mill Girls

Young women who moved to the cities to work in the mills expected to leave the mills as soon as they were married. Women worked these jobs because they earned more money than they could earn on the family farm or in domestic service. In the mills women also had the support of other women and were not as isolated as domestic servants. However, employers could and did take advantage of mill girls because they were reluctant to protest at first.

Title page of the Lowell Offering

male factory workers earned. Lowell made his work package more attractive to women by providing living quarters together with educational and recreational benefits. The girls lived in dormitories with a house mother, and the parents of the girls who came to work for Lowell were reassured that their daughters were moving into a wholesome atmosphere.

At first the mill girls enjoyed their experience. They edited and produced their own newspaper, the *Lowell Offering,* in which they said about the work: "It is easy to do and does not require very violent exertion, as much as our farm work does." Gradually however, the workers grew less satisfied with their thirteen-hour workdays and the poor ventilation in the mills. During the 1840s the Lowell mill girls joined with other groups who were fighting for a ten-hour work day. The mill girls were also a major force behind the first labor union for women in industry, the Female Labor Reform Association.

The Lowell mill girls were paid $2 a week. From that amount, $1.25 was paid back to the mill owner for providing them a place to live. In the fourteenth annual report of the Massachusetts Bureau of Statistics of Labor (1883) and her book titled *Massachusetts Women in the Suffrage Movement,* Harriet H. Robinson, a Lowell mill girl herself, wrote about her experiences in the mill:

> [The main reason girls worked in the mill] was to secure the means of education for some *male* member of the family. To make a *gentleman* of a brother or a son, to give him a college education.... I have known more than one to give every cent

One of the most famous mills was the one built in 1813 by Francis Lowell in Waltham, Massachusetts. Lowell kept costs low by hiring women, who would work for about one-half the amount that

Working Women in the Wild West

Mary Mathews was a widow living with her young son in Buffalo, New York. In 1869 she headed west to Nevada to try and settle the tangled business affairs of her recently deceased brother. She spent ten years in Nevada, where she became a business owner and a real estate investor and was involved in a number of lawsuits, all unusual activities for a woman of the time. Upon her return to New York, she wrote a book describing her adventures.

In Nevada, Mathews worked as a seamstress, nurse, laundress, baby sitter, and letter writer. She started her own school, in which a dozen students each paid her 50 cents per week. When she had finally managed to save $500, she bought her own home. Next she built a lodging house with a store below it. "As fast as I got a room papered, I furnished and rented it, until the whole house was full," she wrote. In her lodging house, Mathews served as maid and did all the cooking herself.

Seeing that there was money to be made in Nevada, Mathews invested in stocks and real estate. She wrote about her experiences in an article titled "Ten Years in Nevada, or Life on the Pacific Coast," excerpted from *Let Them Speak for Themselves:*

In the West, she explained, "I can make more money in three months than I can in the East in a year; and I never saw the time while there that I could not borrow from $1,000 to $2,000 on one day's notice; and the parties lending it would never think of asking me about my indebtedness [how much money she already owed], or how much property I owned, if it was a small sum of $200 or $300, or less. My word was always quite sufficient for them."

Mathews's conclusion that the West was more friendly to women in business has been echoed in the writings of other women of the period.

of her wages, month after month, to her brother, that he might get the education necessary to enter some profession.... There are many men now living who were helped to an education by the wages of the early mill-girls.

Robinson later added that "these men . . . sometimes acquired just enough learning to make them look down upon the social position in which their women friends and relatives were forced to remain."

By 1860, in part because of their demands for better pay and working conditions, the mills were no longer employing native-born women from the American countryside. Instead, most of

Window on the World: The Maquiladora Factory System

Sweatshops are alive and thriving all around the world. Many of them help boost the profits of large U.S. clothing companies. In Latin America, which is made up of all of the Spanish-, French-, or Portuguese-speaking nations south of the United States, the system is called the *maquiladora* factory system. Factories such as these employ mostly women.

These women report that their bathroom visits are timed to insure that they earn every one of their 56 cents per hour. When large orders for garments arrive from the United States, the workday stretches to 18 hours or longer.

American companies located on the Mexican border employ *maquiladoras*. Although many Mexican men are too proud to work for the United States, their wives, sisters, and daughters will because they need the money. This situation can create tension in Mexican homes.

the workers were immigrants, mainly from Ireland. By then, few of the workers had any good things to say about their work experience.

Sweatshop Girls

Meanwhile, the garment industry was expanding, notably in New York City. The workers there were mostly immigrant women from southern and eastern Europe who were poorly paid. They labored up to fourteen hours per day in enclosed and extremely hot spaces. Working conditions were terrible and strikes became more common. A young Polish girl described her experience in *The American Worker in the Twentieth Century:*

> I did not know at first that you must not look around and talk, and I made many mistakes with the sewing, so that I was often called a 'stupid animal.' But I made $4 a week by working six days in the week.

Women working in these conditions believed it was time for the garment industry to organize in greater numbers. By doing so, workers hoped to force employers to grant better working conditions.

The National Women's Trade Union League Is Formed

During twenty-five of the forty years between 1870 and 1910, the United States was dominated by economic problems. Widespread unemployment and poverty were the result, and no government aid programs were in place.

Working conditions during these years were often harsh, and labor unions such as the American Federation of Labor (AFL) were formed to help make conditions better. Few working women were members of trade unions, though. The unions considered female members to be of little importance and even possible threats to men's wages. To the rescue of working women came Mary Kenney O'Sullivan and Leonora O'Reilly.

O'Sullivan lived at Hull House with Jane Addams in Chicago. Hull House was dedicated to helping poor working women improve their lives. In 1880 O'Sullivan had organized the Woman's Bookbinder Union. After her husband, also a labor activist, was killed in an accident, O'Sullivan returned to union work in Boston, where she met O'Reilly.

O'Reilly had worked in the garment industry since childhood, and in 1897 she helped form the United Garment Workers Union. The two women met at an AFL meeting in 1903 and learned that the union had nothing to offer women, so they decided to form their own union. The result was the National Women's Trade Union League (NWTUL). Its motto was "The Eight Hour Day; A Living Wage; To Guard the Home." The league supported working women's strikes by organizing picket lines and running relief kitchens. The group was especially important during the garment industry strikes between 1909 and 1911.

The National Women's Trade Union League Holds a Convention

At its first convention, the National Women's Trade Union League proposed six goals. They were:

- equal pay for equal work
- women's suffrage (the right to vote)

Although the invention of the typewriter in 1870 opened up a whole new career opportunity for women, working conditions continued to be unfair.

- full unionization for all women workers
- an eight-hour work day
- a mandatory minimum wage
- all of the economic benefits asked for by the AFL

After the Triangle Shirtwaist Factory fire (see box on p. 416), the League conducted an investigation into the conditions that had led to the fire. As a result of its investigation, laws were put into place requiring companies to maintain safety precautions. The League operated until just after World War II.

The Triangle Shirtwaist Factory Fire

A year and a half before the Triangle Shirtwaist Factory fire in 1911, more than eighteen thousand shirtwaist makers (mostly women) walked off the job, protesting fifty-nine-hour work weeks, low wages, and dangerous conditions. (A shirtwaist is a type of woman's tailored shirt that resembles a man's dress shirt.) Three months later the strike failed, and the workers returned to face the same conditions.

On March 25, 1911, one of the few male employees at the Triangle factory dropped a cigarette into a pile of trash and started a fire. The blaze quickly spread through the several floors of the company. Since it happened to be a Saturday—payday at the factory—all the doors were locked to prevent any workers from leaving even a minute early to celebrate their one day off.

While some women managed to escape, 146 of them were not so fortunate. More than 50 bodies were found piled up behind the locked doors. Dozens of women jumped out the windows. Some died when they hit the sidewalks; others were impaled (pierced) on the iron fences that surrounded the building.

In the court hearing that followed, the all-male jury let all company managers and owners go unpunished. One juror said it was the jury's opinion that the young women who died were not very smart and probably caused their own deaths from panic.

Rosie the Riveter

During World War II (1939–45), women began to take an active part in the U.S. workforce. Because millions of men were off fighting in the military, women were needed to work in factories and the booming war industries. By 1942, 2.5 million women were working in factory and shipyard jobs that had previously been reserved for men. Experts estimated that another 6 million women workers would be needed by the end of 1943. It was during this time that "Rosie the Riveter," a character in a popular song, came to stand for the woman who rolled up her shirt sleeves and went to work for the war. Inequalities between men and women would continue to exist, however, as women earned less than men in factories.

Attitudes After the War

After World War II, in spite of their tremendous contributions, attitudes about the proper role and place of women remained traditional. They were supposed to be wives and mothers. Indeed,

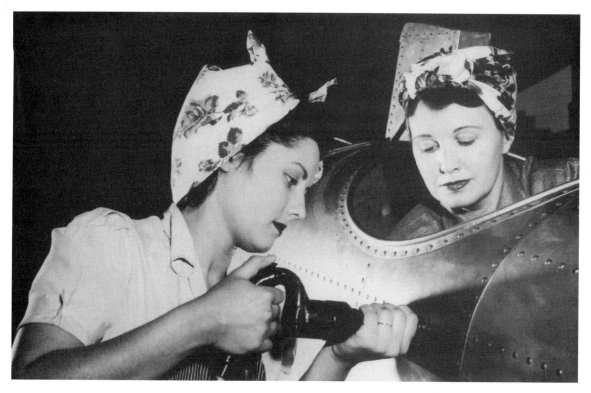

Rosie the Riveter became a popular symbol for working women during World War II.

society expected that they would be delighted to return to their roles, since technology had given homemakers many laborsaving appliances (washers and dryers, blenders, canned food).

Women did return to their domestic world with enthusiasm. The postwar years saw women marrying younger, having more babies, and failing to pursue careers in spite of their education. Despite the loneliness and isolation of the suburbs, becoming a suburban housewife was a role to which many women aspired after the war.

But the American economy was changing. The servant class disappeared as women who might have been forced to do that type of work found more agreeable work. It gradually became harder to support a family on only one paycheck. Finally, more and more women, especially married women, entered the labor force. They were expected to have a career and to take care of home and family.

Society still expects women to take primary responsibility for homemaking and child rearing, whether they work outside the home or not. For this reason, women often train for work that allows flexibility, so they can combine their work and family responsibilities. For instance, they may choose to become teachers so they have their holidays and summers to spend with their children. However, this type of work tends to be low paying.

Businesses' Response to Women in the Labor Force

Part-Time Work

Part-time work has long been an option offered by businesses to working women. Part-time work allows businesses to control labor costs by adjusting the size of their workforce. In good times, businesses hire more part-time workers; in bad times, they lay them off.

Women accept part-time jobs because these jobs allow them to balance their responsibilities at work and home. Part-time work is not a perfect solution, however, because employers usually pay part-time workers lower wages and offer them no benefits (such as medical insurance and paid sick days).

Flex Time

In recent years, many businesses have been experimenting with flexible time schedules (also known as "flex time") to help women and men find answers to the problems of having to combine work and family responsibilities. Rigid systems that require all employees to report to work at the same time every day create problems for parents who work. Flex time allows parents to coordinate their workday with their children's schedules and with other responsibilities.

Help With Child Care

More and more mothers of young children are entering the workforce. In March 1992, 70 percent of working mothers with preschool children worked full time, and it is expected that the numbers will increase. Parents cannot feel secure on the job if they are concerned about how their children are being cared for, and business will not thrive unless employees feel secure.

The demand for good child care is growing faster than the supply. Some employers have responded by offering money to parents to help pay for child care. A few employers even operate their own child-care facilities. In general, though, business has been slow to admit that care of children ought to be a responsibility shared by parents, business, and government.

The Glass Ceiling

Beginning around 1970, more women began to enter the corporate world than ever before. But by 1995, many of the women who had achieved the greatest success in the business arena talked of giving it up. These women were part of a trend highlighted in a 1995 issue of *Fortune* magazine. Eighty-seven percent of women responding to the survey said they were considering making a major career change because they found the corporate world so unfriendly. These women had encountered the phenomenon known as the glass ceiling.

In many cases, the men who control large businesses are still very unwilling to allow women to reach the highest ranks. The glass ceiling is an invisible barrier that keeps women from reaching the top levels of large businesses. These top ranks continue to be the domain of white men.

As we approach the year 2000, however, two out of three people entering the labor force will be minorities and women. Businesses must break their own glass ceiling barriers if they wish to compete in an increasingly diverse world. If not, they will find themselves at a great disadvantage.

How to Succeed in Business

Kathleen B. Cooper, chief economist of Exxon Corporation, delivered a speech as part of the Greater Dallas (Texas) Chamber Distinguished Women Leaders Lecture Series in June 1994. The speech was titled "What Do I Recommend for Young Women?" In it Cooper thought back to how different things were from when she was in high school. She said:

> One very positive change that is worlds apart from 20 to 30 years ago is the college guidance that is provided to bright young women.... When I graduated [high school], I do not remember my teachers even asking if I planned to attend college—let alone encouraging ... me to attend the best possible. That, despite the fact that I was near the top of my class and involved in everything. Yes, indeed, things have changed!

In her speech, Cooper discusses statistics showing that "women represent nearly half of the labor force and 40 percent

What Is It About Those Wellesley Women?

Wellesley College, a distinguished college for women, was founded in 1875. In 1995 the media reported on an interesting phenomenon. More than any other college in the country, Wellesley was turning out women who shattered the glass ceiling. Graduates of Wellesley were overrepresented in high places in America's major corporations. About one-third of Wellesley's graduates go into the business world.

Wellesley prides itself on its bright students, its strong and popular economics department, and its excellent teachers. Professor Carolyn Shaw Bell taught at Wellesley from 1950 to 1989. "She used to tell us that we should brag," a former student said, "that we should let people know what we can do." Wellesley also points to its programs that encourage networking among graduates and between graduates and students as additional keys to success for its alumni.

of manager positions but less than 5 percent of senior management positions and corporate board memberships." She offers the following advice to young women thinking of entering the business world:

> First of all, I recommend that they think *very* hard about whether they want to run the show. And just because the sta-

tistics are disheartening now should not discourage them from setting their sights high. Once those sights are set high, careful planning, hard work, and a mentor or two along the way will help her progress toward her goal. In other words, she must always be looking for the next assignment to shoot for as well as assignments two and three years down the road. She'll have to continually re-evaluate her plan as her career may take unexpected turns, but she must never stop looking for that next job and striving for that ultimate goal.

Government Responses to Women in Business

The Glass Ceiling Act

When the American public first became aware of the glass ceiling in the early 1980s, the U.S. Department of Labor became involved in identifying what was causing it. In 1991, the Department of Labor issued its *Report on the Glass Ceiling Initiative* to inform the public of the problems. That same year Senator Robert Dole introduced the Glass Ceiling Act in Congress, and it was signed into law as part of the Civil Rights Act of 1991. The act established the Glass Ceiling Commission to conduct a study and prepare recommendations on "eliminating artificial barriers to the advancement of women and minorities" to "management and decisionmaking positions in business."

The Glass Ceiling Commission released two reports. The first was a factfinding report, and the second consisted of recommendations for dismantling employment barriers. Although the Glass Ceiling Commission has since been disbanded, the reports are still available. Research papers, fact-finding, and recommendations of the U.S. Department of Labor's Glass Ceiling Commission are available through the Internet's World Wide Web Server. The access code is http://www.ilr.cornell.edu. Printed copies are available through the U.S. Government Printing Office, telephone (202)512-1800. According to René A. Redwood, former Executive Director for the Glass Ceiling Commission, "When glass ceilings in America are forever shattered, we will have come a long way to achieving the full promise of our nation by making its bounty equally available to all."

The Family and Medical Leave Act

The first bill U.S. President Bill Clinton signed into law was the Family and Medical Leave Act in 1993. The act symbolizes the U.S. government's belief that working adults need and deserve help in balancing work and family responsibilities. The act provides workers with the right to take an unpaid leave of absence from the job when members of their family or they themselves are ill. Terms of the act require that workers be placed in the same or an equivalent job when they return to work. Before this law was passed, employers could—and did—fire people who were forced to take time off to care for ill family members. Since women are most often caretakers for ill family members, those firings affected them most. Unfortunately, even today in some businesses, women who take advantage of family-friendly policies are thought to be lacking a serious commitment to their jobs.

U.S. Department of Labor Initiatives

According to the U.S. Department of Labor, about two-thirds of all people who enter the workforce between 1990 and 2000 will be women. What jobs will they find? The Department of Labor predicts that jobs requiring high levels of skills and education will be the high-growth occupations. While only 14 percent of new jobs will be available to workers who do not have a high school education, 58 percent of women workers will have no more than a high school diploma by the year 2000.

A key issue for women, then, is job training: where to find good training and how to find the support services that trainees need, such as affordable housing, child care, and transportation. Many companies spend little or no money on job training. The Department of Labor recognizes the problems and has shifted its emphasis to encouraging the training of all Americans to be highly skilled workers in a high-wage workforce. Some of its programs are described below. For more information, the publication titled *1993 Handbook on Women Workers: Trends and Issues* and many other publications are available by writing the Women's Bureau, U.S. Department of Labor, 200 Constitution Avenue, Washington, D.C., 20210 (telephone 202-523-8913). U.S.

Department of Labor data is also available through a World Wide Web site on the Internet. The homepage, http://stats.bls.gov, may be accessed by using a Web browser.

Job Training Partnership Act

The federal government has been active since the 1960s in providing training and employment programs for disadvantaged or unemployed workers. The Job Training Partnership Act of 1982 was designed to enlist the help of businesses in preparing people for entry into the labor force. Between 1984 and 1989, the percentage of trainees under this act who were female increased from 51 percent to 55 percent.

The 1990 Carl D. Perkins Vocational and Applied Technology Act is another example of a federal government training program. The Perkins Act provides funding for single parents, displaced homemakers, and unwed mothers for training in traditionally male occupations.

The Women's Bureau of the U.S. Department of Labor

Up until the beginning of the twentieth century, little was known about female workers. Then the U.S. Congress ordered an investigation into the conditions of working women and children. The result was a nineteen-volume report, which took four years to prepare and was released in 1911. It was titled *Women and Child Wage-Earners in the United States*.

Without proper training and education, women will continue to be clustered in low-paying jobs such as clerical work.

As a result of that report, the Women's Bureau of the U.S. Department of Labor was established in 1920. The bureau's job was to formulate "standards and policies for promoting the welfare of wage-earning women . . . and [advance] their opportunities for profitable employment."

Today, among other things, the Women's Bureau concerns itself with improving women's access to training and to occupations of their choice. An example of a project developed with Women's Bureau funding is a training and reference manual to help state high-way agencies find and train women to work on highway construction projects (which tend to be very well paid and have long excluded women). The Women's Bureau has also initiated several projects focusing on building science and math skills among women and minorities.

Small Business Administration Loans

Women still have a problem obtaining money (capital) to start a business or to help keep a business running. Loans are harder to come by because of unfounded myths about women, such as the belief that women are less likely than men to repay loans.

In March 1996, *Working Woman* magazine reported on their study of small, female-owned businesses. Their study found that "women's businesses are not only solid credit risks—they are *as good as or better risks* than men's firms *across a broad array of industries.*"

Between 1990 and 1994, U.S. business firms owned by women increased 42.6 percent, from 5.4 million to 7.7 million businesses. Many of these women obtained start-up funds and other assistance from the Small Business Administration or SBA (established in 1953). The SBA's Women's Prequalification Loan Program assists women in a variety of ways, including offering "a quick response to loan requests of $250,000 or less." To learn more, consult the "U.S. Government" section in your telephone directory, or call 1-800-8-ASK-SBA.

Current Trends

Women–Owned and Women–Headed Businesses

Many women have responded to what they see as the unfriendliness of big business by starting their own companies. By the late 1990s, female-owned businesses were growing at two times the rate of male-owned businesses. And many of the smaller companies that were opening were family-owned businesses, where all workers, including women, were needed and used.

In 1995, a Chicago company called George A. May International conducted a survey of 895 people who headed small or midsize companies. Nearly one-half responded that it was highly likely or somewhat likely that their next head would be a woman. Manufacturing companies, however, were the most hostile to women. In the survey, 39 percent of heads of these companies said in the survey that they strongly oppose a woman as head of the company.

Networking

The word "network" used as a verb was coined by women in the 1970s. Network means to have good connections with other women and to provide information, help, and personal or professional support for one another. An example of a networking organization is the National Association for Female Executives, based in New York City. This organization boasts more than two hundred thousand members who help one another by sharing information and resources. The group also offers loans to businesswomen and publishes *Executive Female* magazine, in which female executives tell stories of working life. The association's address is 127 West 24th Street, New York, NY 10011; telephone (212)645-0770; fax (212)633-6489.

Working Women Count Honor Roll

The Women's Bureau of the U.S. Department of Labor sponsored a 1994 survey of 250,000 working women. In the survey, women identified three areas of the working world in which they would like to see changes to improve the lives of working women and men. Those areas were:

- improving pay and benefits
- building a family-friendly workplace
- valuing women's work through training and advancement.

Based on this list, the Women's Bureau launched the Working Women Count Honor Roll. According to Robert Reich, head of the Department of Labor for the Clinton Administration, the purpose of the Honor Roll is "to recognize businesses, organizations and individuals that make a real commitment to the changes women and their families need." To qualify for the Honor Roll, a business must establish a program to advance women's interests in one or more of the three ways mentioned above. A number of companies have pledged to do so, and the Women's Bureau hopes that their efforts will catch on with other businesses.

Sweatshops Still Exist

There is a French saying, *Plus ça change, plus c'est la même chose,* which means, "the more things change, the more they stay the same." This saying proves true with sweatshops, which most people assume disappeared long ago.

In 1995 the news media reported that more than forty-five hundred sweatshops were still operating in New York City, a center of the garment manufac-turing industry. It was also reported that more than fifty thousand people, most of them Asian and Hispanic women who spoke little or no English, were employed in those sweatshops.

The women sweatshop employees said that during their employment, working conditions, hours, and pay had gotten worse rather than better. Some workers said that they often would not get paid for several weeks. Reich was quoted as saying: "there are sweatshops operating illegally and exploiting [mistreating] workers" all around the United States.

Sex Discrimination and Harassment at Work

Sex discrimination in employment has been against the law since the Civil Rights Act of 1964 was passed. Sex discrimination includes sexual harassment. A woman is sexually harassed when she is forced to choose between putting up with unwelcome sexual comments or actions from bosses or coworkers or losing her job or chance for advancement.

Even though it's against the law, sexual harassment still exists. It is especially high in areas where women make up a minority, such as in the highly paid skilled trades (electrician, plumbing, carpentry), the military, and protective services (such as the police force).

Some say that the gap between men's and women's earnings is one form of sexual discrimination. Critics argue that the gap in earnings is caused by women having less education and job experience than

Sweatshops continue to be a problem in the United States.

men, holding less-skilled jobs, and taking time out from work to care for children. A recent study by the U.S. Department of Education answers that argument.

The U.S. Department of Education studied both male and female members of the high school graduating class of 1972. The women they studied had better grades in high school and college, but they earned less than the men. By 1985, the men in the study had average earnings of $25,022. The women in the study who did not have children had average earnings of $18,970, while those with children earned $15,016. Even when the women worked in the same occupation and had been there for the same length of time without taking time out for family responsibilities, the men were paid more.

Activists are urging that laws be passed or strengthened at the state level to prohibit sex discrimination in employment. Those activists say there are too many gaps in the Civil Rights Act; as a result, companies can avoid obeying the law. State laws, they say, have a greater chance of being successfully enforced and might cover types of discrimination not mentioned in the Civil Rights Act (such as discrimination against people who take time off for family responsibilities).

Iris Rivera: A Different Kind of Heroine

Iris Rivera, a Chicago legal secretary, was fired in February 1977 for refusing to make coffee for her boss. Rivera offered three reasons for refusing this then-common request:

1. "I don't drink coffee.

2. "It's not listed as one of my job duties.

3. "Ordering the secretaries to fix the coffee is carrying the role of homemaker too far."

On February 3, 1977, fifty secretaries staged a protest during their lunch hour in the center of Chicago's business district. Another group, Women Employed, took the opportunity to educate the public about the methods used to make female clerical workers feel inferior. As part of their program, Women Employed offered lessons on how to make coffee (Step 5: "Turn the switch to on."). They also presented Rivera's boss with a bag of used coffee grounds. In the end, Rivera got her job back.

Women Employed and a similar organization, Nine-to-Five, were started in the 1970s in an effort to change public attitudes, employers' practices, and laws for working women. They were also instrumental in popularizing the idea of equal pay for equal work. By 1987 more than forty states and fifteen hundred local governments had in place some type of so-called "comparable worth" policy.

Diversity Policies

As we noted earlier, the modern U.S. workforce is much different from the old workforce. This new workforce is no longer dominated by white men. More women, minorities, and foreign-born people are entering the workforce at a steady pace. At the same time, the actual number of people entering the workforce is declining because fewer babies are being born.

Companies that wish to remain competitive are not just sitting back and waiting to see what happens with this new kind of workforce. Instead, they are actively looking for, hiring, encouraging, and training women and minorities. These companies' actions are referred to as "diversity policies."

Take Our Daughters to Work Day

Many young people, especially girls and members of minority groups, have not been exposed to the business world. It is difficult for girls to form career goals when they do not know what options are open to them.

In 1993 the Ms. Foundation for Women launched Take Our Daughters to Work Day. Parents were encouraged to take their daughters or other girls of their acquaintance to work with them so the girls could see what the world of work was like. Take Our Daughters to Work Day was a response to research findings that young girls often receive less attention in school and in programs for youth, that adult expectations for girls are lower than for boys, and that girls tend to like or dislike themselves based on their physical appearance.

Research has shown that if girls are helped before these attitudes take root, they can grow up more confident, healthy, and eager to fulfill their dreams.

The first Take Our Daughters to Work Day was successful beyond its creators' imagination. By its second year, twenty-five million people were participating. Then the critics, however, declared Take Our Daughters to Work Day was "reverse discrimination," meaning it discriminated against boys. As a result, some companies then hosted boys and girls on the same day, noting that—as they had feared—the boys demanded attention and the girls shrank back.

One group of girls who spent Take Our Daughters to Work Day at the *New York Times* newspaper published an editorial about their experience. They wrote: "Bringing boys into this program would eliminate its significance. It would be just like any other day in this world. When women truly have equality in opportunity and expectations and can enter the workplace with a feeling of confidence equal to men's, that is when sons may be invited to take part in this day."

Women in the World of High Technology

For thousands of years, what separated men's and women's work was physical strength. In the Information Age, knowledge is what matters.

Analysts say that one of the most important trends affecting companies and employees today is technology. Women are in a good position to take advantage of this trend. The steps they can take to prepare themselves include:

• being able to write clearly and concisely

• having a college degree, preferably a master's degree, with knowledge of finance and business management

• being technologically knowledgeable

• having foreign language ability

For too long women's employment opportunities have been limited by the scope of their education. Many have avoided learning about money and management, while many are limited by insufficient knowledge of the English language. English is one of the primary languages used in international trade. Anyone who deals with customers in other countries must excel in reading, writing, speaking, and understanding English. However, many businesspeople have found success by speaking the language of their customers, so it is also important to develop the ability to communicate in two or more languages.

16

The Family

Changes in Society

The Reasons Behind Family Life

Unlike others in the animal kingdom, human children require much help to grow to adulthood. Horses are able to run within hours of being born, and infant monkeys can cling to their mother's fur when they are only days old. However, human children are born helpless and remain this way for several years. To survive, human children rely on others who will provide them with food, shelter, protection, and love.

For thousands of years, human families have been the source of that food, love, and shelter. The family unit has existed since the times when cave dwellers were painting pictures of bison and mammoth hunts on the walls of their homes. In earliest times, humans were rovers who formed bands to follow the animals they hunted for food. Even as humans discovered farming and began to settle down, they continued to live in family groups. Men continued to hunt while women farmed and cared for the

Fact Focus

- In 1990, there were about 66 million families in the United States.

- Only 37 percent of American families fit the "nuclear" family definition (married couple with children).

- Nearly 1 in 8 American families was headed by a single parent in 1991, twice the number as in 1970.

- In the 1990s in the United States, adult children live in their parents' home longer due to inflation, housing costs, delayed marriages, and lower wages.

- In 1990, 1.2 million divorces were granted in the United States. (The number of marriages was 2.4 million.)

children. As people acquired more possessions, however, the family unit gained an economic aspect. A family's property (land and goods) could be passed on from one generation to the next.

Early human families lived in larger groups called villages. These villages provided protection and a chance to share farming and child-care duties. This village-type of life has continued into modern times. Most people live in neighborhoods of some type, whether it is a single-family home on a city block, an apartment in a huge complex, or a farm in the country.

Families and communities are important because they are the first places where children learn about the world. They learn about relationships through watching their parents and siblings interact. In earlier times, the family also provided a learning experience for children as they watched their parents farm or tan leather or operate a blacksmith workshop. By being a part of a neighborhood, children learn about being a member of society.

In the past, a family was usually made up of a husband, a wife, and their children. Today however, the U.S. Bureau of the Census defines a family as two or more persons related by birth, marriage, or adoption who reside together. Some trends in modern society have a direct impact on the U.S. family. The trends listed below have changed the face of the family unit:

- The marriage rate fell almost 30 percent between 1970 and 1990.

- Americans are delaying marriage (in 1991, the average age for men was 26 and for women 24).

- The divorce rate increased by almost 40 percent between 1970 and 1990.

- In 1990, more than 1 in 4 children was born to an unmarried mother.

- About one-half of U.S. children will spend some part of their childhood in a single-parent home.

- More women and more mothers work outside the home.

While people's tendency to live in groups has remained constant, our division of labor is changing drastically as we

Profile of American Families: 1990

This table presents a profile of the American family in 1990. In 1970, more than 40 percent of the American population lived in a two-parent family. Within twenty years, only 25 percent did.

[Number of families in thousands.]

Family type	American families with children under age 18	
	Number	**Percent**
All Races		
Married-couple families	52,317	46.9%
Single female	10,890	60.6%
Single male	2,884	40.0%
White		
Married-couple families	46,981	45.9%
Female householder	7,306	57.5%
Male householder	2,303	40.8%
Black		
Married-couple families	3,750	52.6%
Female householder	3,275	68.2%
Male householder	446	38.8%
Hispanic Origin		
Married-couple families	3,395	64.5%
Female householder	1,116	66.8%
Male householder	329	35.9%

Source: "Women in the U.S. Work Force," *Women's Voices: A Polling Report,* a joint project of the Ms. Foundation for Women and Center for Policy Alternatives, 1992, p. 26.

approach the dawn of the twenty-first century. The biggest single change is that more women are working outside the home, a fact which has greatly affected family life.

Modern women's ability to earn money outside the home has had several major consequences for society. Perhaps because many women can support themselves, they are marrying later. These

Window on the World: Muslim Family Life

Muslims are people who follow the religion called Islam, which started in the Middle East around A.D. 630. Muslim family life is based on a patriarchal structure. That is, the father and other older male family members make the decisions for the female and younger family members. While she is unmarried, a woman's father cares for her. If her father dies, an older brother or uncle steps in to make decisions such as whom the woman will marry. When she marries, her husband assumes the decision-making role. If she is a widow, and her son is old enough, he becomes the head of the household.

Traditionally, Muslim men practice polygyny, which allows a man to have as many wives as he can support. In earlier times, these women lived together with their children in a separate part of the house called a harem. When they went out in public, the women wore veils, which left only their eyes and hands uncovered. These veils protected the women from the unwanted advances of men. While at home, they could go without a veil but only in the harem. Today, men in only a few of the 21 Arab countries actually practice polygyny, but many Muslim women still wear their veils when in public.

Since Muslims place a strong value on family life, the extended family is an important part of everyday life. Grandparents, aunts, uncles, cousins, and other less directly related relatives comprise the Muslim family.

women also have no children at all or fewer children than women of previous generations, and when they do have children, they tend to continue to work outside the home. The percentage of women working outside the home rose from about 15 percent in 1940 to almost 55 percent in 1994. If these working women experience unhappiness in their marriage, they feel more freedom to seek a divorce.

Types of Families

Many sociologists believe that women's economic freedom has had a major role in creating a new, broader definition of the "typical" American family. This family may be:

Pre-Children Families: In earlier times, marriage and children automatically went together. Today, a couple may marry with the intention of not having children immediately. They may wait several years before beginning a family. This couple forms a "pre-children" family.

Married/No Children Families: Some couples choose to marry but do so with the intention of never having children. Their decision may be based on income, unhappy previous experiences with fam-

The traditional nuclear family consists of two parents and their children.

ily life, a commitment to a career, or health reasons.

Nuclear Families: Nuclear families consist of a married couple and their children. These children may be the biological offspring of the parents or they may be adopted children. Nuclear families usually live together in a home or apartment. Despite the recent changes in society, in 1992, families with children are still the

Window on the World: Hopi Family Life

The Hopi are a Native American tribe who live in the states of Arizona and New Mexico. Unlike most other communities, the Hopi are a matriarchal society, meaning the oldest woman in each family has the authority and makes decisions for the whole family.

The Hopi also trace their family heritage through their mother's line. The most important male figure in the life of Hopi children is their mother's oldest brother. Because he is of the mother's line, he is the male authority in the family.

most common form of family (34.2 percent) in the United States.

Single-Parent Families: A single-parent family consists of one parent and his or her children. The parent may be single because of divorce, the death of a spouse, or because she or he never married. In 1991, 1 in every 4 American children (about 16.6 million children) lived in a single-parent home. This number has tripled since 1960.

Dual-Custody Families: Some divorced parents share custody of their children. This means that the children spend part of the week, month, or year living in the mother's home, and the other time is spent living in the father's home. These children essentially have two homes and two separate home lives.

Stepfamilies: Stepfamilies are created when a divorced or widowed parent remarries. The new spouse becomes the child's stepfather or stepmother, and the child becomes that new spouse's stepchild. Some experts believe that 1 in every 3 Americans is a stepparent, and that rate will rise to 1 in every 2 Americans by 2000.

Blended Families: Blended families add children to the stepparent arrangement. Blended families are not new to American society. In earlier times, when the death rate was high due to illness and poor nutrition, a surviving spouse often remarried. Today, remarriage most often occurs because of the high divorce rate. A blended family is created when a parent with children marries a person who also has children. The new relations are called stepbrothers and stepsisters. Statistics show that 1 of every 6 American families is a blended family.

Extended Families: Almost everyone has some type of extended family. This term refers to your relatives who do not live in your home. These relatives may include grandparents, aunts, uncles, and cousins. In some cultures, godparents and their families are considered relatives and part of a person's extended family.

Empty-Nester Families: Empty-nesters are parents whose children have grown up and left home. The children may be attending college in another location, may have married and established their own home, or may be living as single

Types of American Families: 1970–1992

This table shows types of U.S. households in 1970, 1980, and 1992.

Type	Percent of all households		
	1970	**1980**	**1992**
Married couples, with children	40.3%	30.9%	25.5%
Married couples, without children	30.3%	29.9%	29.3%
Other types of families, with children	5.0%	7.5%	8.7%
Other types of families, without children	5.6%	5.4%	6.7%
Men living alone	5.6%	8.6%	10.0%
Women living alone	11.5%	14.0%	15.0%
Other nonfamily households	1.7%	3.6%	4.7%

Source: Selected from *Population Profile of the United States: 1993,* Special Studies Series P23-185, Figure 15. U.S. Bureau of the Census. "Children" refers to their own children under age 18.

persons. Empty-nesters tend to be middle-aged (fifty years and older) or elderly people. In the latter part of the twentieth century, the empty-nester couple was increasingly transformed into a nuclear family once again as adult children moved back home because of job loss, divorce, or in order to save money for a home.

Cohabiting Families: Cohabitation is a term that covers a variety of family types. Most commonly it refers to couples who live together in a sexual relationship but are not married. Europe has a higher rate of cohabiting couples than the United States. Cohabiting couples may be male-female, male-male (homosexual), or female-female (lesbian). The percentage of cohabiting families has doubled from 15 percent in 1960 to 30 percent in 1991. The law in most states does not recognize these couples as legally related to one another. However, some cohabiting couples have challenged the legal system and their employers over issues such as health care benefits, life insurance, and inheritance of property. Sometimes these cases are decided in favor of the cohabiting partners.

The U.S. Census Bureau also uses cohabitation to describe roommate situations and households which contain two unrelated families. For instance, two divorced mothers may decide to live in the same house to share expenses and

Interracial families continue to be a small minority in the United States.

babysitting resources. These types of arrangements are sometimes called communal families.

Interracial Families: Interracial families are families in which the husband and wife are of different races. In the United States, about 1 in 4 interracial marriages occurs between a black person and a white person. The majority of black-white interracial marriages occur between an African American man and a Caucasian woman. About one-half of interracial marriages occur between a Caucasian man and a woman of another race (Hispanic, Asian, Native American or African American). The children of

interracial marriages are often called biracial ("bi" means "two"). While interracial marriages are more common today than in the past, they still make up only 2 percent of U.S. marriages.

Elderly Families: Throughout the world, more people tend to get married than remain single. In industrialized nations such as the United States, Japan, and most of Europe, women outlive men by a number of years. This means that more women will end their lives as widows (women whose husbands have died). For this reason, elderly families are often single person families. Some elderly people live in institutions such as nursing homes or special apartment complexes. In 1990, about 5 percent of all people aged 65 and older lived in one of these facilities.

The Impact of Divorce

Until recently, people who were unhappily married often chose to remain together rather than divorce. Divorce is the legal ending of a marriage. While divorce is common in modern-day societies, this was not always the case. For example, some societies would not legally recognize divorce (as late as 1995, the Republic of Ireland still did not). Other societies allowed only the husband to begin divorce proceedings. Since most societies in history regarded the marriage bond as unbreakable, only kings and other highly placed wealthy people could win a divorce. Often these divorces—now referred to as annulments if the marriage is invalidated rather than ended—required official sanction (approval) from the pope (the head of the Roman Catholic Church) or some other religious leader.

Divorce became more common around the time of the Industrial Revolution (mid-1800s). However, divorced people still were not accepted in polite society—especially divorced women, who were seen as wicked and immoral. Even into the mid-1900s, many people regarded divorce as a form of failure and a sign of a poor character.

Many times, before a divorce trial began the judge would talk to the unhappy couple with the aim of resolving the problems and saving the marriage. Sometimes the judge recommended marriage counseling. Despite such efforts, some divorces proved inevitable. If the judge had decided to grant a divorce, he would consider alimony. Most often alimony was paid by an erring ex-husband to his injured ex-wife. The alimony was money to support her, since she had lost her husband's income. Many ex-husbands saw alimony as society's punishment for committing adultery—a common reason for ending a marriage.

Today, most divorces result from unresolved problems between the husband and wife. The conflict might be over how to spend the family's money, or sometimes results from one partner changing, as when a woman decides to pursue schooling and a job after being a stay-at-home mother. Other times the conflict begins when one spouse begins an extramarital affair. In blended or stepfamilies, conflicts can arise over the discipline of children and how much attention the children receive from each of the parents.

Not all divorces, however, are entirely negative experiences. Many experts agree that sometimes an unhappy couple creates so much tension and psychological stress that they and their children experience a feeling of relief when the divorce finally occurs.

Current Trends

Between the early 1960s and the early 1980s, the divorce rate in the United States soared. At its peak, almost one

Many of today's marriages end in divorce.

of every two American marriages ended in divorce. This high divorce rate was attributed to several changes in society. For example, in the 1960s, cohabitation became more socially acceptable. This casual attitude toward marriage led many Americans to question the permanence of the marriage union. The Women's Liberation Movement of the 1970s also affected marriages by bringing more women into the workplace. Women with jobs had fewer fears about leaving unhappy marriages. Around the same time, divorce became more socially acceptable; it was no longer regarded as a sign of a flawed character.

Sometime during the 1980s, the U.S. divorce rate leveled off. This leveling off is believed to have been caused by several key changes in society. For example, people are marrying later, so they are spending more time choosing a partner, and women are earning more money, so they feel free to forego marriage altogether. In the past, many women married partly for financial reasons since a husband provided a home and income.

How Women Experience Divorce

Ideally, divorced women who win custody of their children usually have two sources of income: their job or alimony and the money the father pays for the care of his children, known as child support. In reality, however, the child support payments are often inadequate or are missing altogether. The U.S. Bureau of the Census reported in 1985 that yearly child support averaged only $2,215. In 26 percent of cases, a parent refused to pay child support, and in another 26 percent of cases, only partial child support was paid. The term "deadbeat dad" was coined for fathers failing to pay child support

It is not surprising then, that divorce often results in a lower standard of living for women and children. Divorce may mean a move to a more affordable home, a decrease in discretionary income (spending money), and delays in repairing and replacing major items such as cars or refrigerators. It may also mean doing without vacations and major home repairs such as roofs and plumbing systems.

Custody

Now that society is no longer so judgmental about divorce, most states have enacted what are called "no fault" divorce laws. Neither spouse has to prove that the other committed some offense to prompt the divorce. Instead, one spouse files paperwork at the local county office, and the divorce proceedings begin. The majority of problems during divorce proceedings now come from disagreements about the division of property or the custody of children the couple might have. Most states evenly divide the property (money from the sale of the house, money in the bank, household furnishings, cars,

etc.). The question of custody, however, is less easily solved.

Until the late 1800s, custody of children was almost always awarded to the father because he was the head of the house and the provider of food, shelter, and clothing. The law also declared that the children were his property, and he was entitled to them. Then attitudes about custody began to change. They were influenced by studies which showed that the female of most species seemed to have a built-in maternal instinct. Based in part on this recognition of the "mothering instinct," judges began to award custody of children to their mothers.

By the 1950s, it was rare that fathers received custody of their children. But again changes in society led to changes in laws and customs. Today, a judge determines custody based on several considerations: the parent's character, his or her income, the child's preference, and the state of the home in which the child will be living.

Issues for Modern Families

Child Care

Seventy-five percent of American women with children six years and older have jobs outside the home. This means that child care is a major issue for single-parent families and for families where both parents work. Child care is more of an issue for the parents of young children under age ten because these children require constant care and supervision.

Children's Champion: Marian Wright Edelman

Marian Wright Edelman, an African American educator and child's rights activist, was born in 1939 in South Carolina. At the time of her birth, the American South was still a segregated society. Blacks and whites did not mix socially and went to separate schools and churches. Edelman was the daughter of a Baptist minister who taught her and her four siblings that education, hard work, and service to the community were important.

Edelman absorbed that lesson well. After graduating from high school, she entered Spelman College in Atlanta, Georgia. The college was devoted to educating African American women. Edelman, an excellent student, had decided on a career as a language teacher.

However, in her senior year at Spelman College, Edelman became active in the Civil Rights movement. She embraced Martin Luther King Jr.'s method of using civil disobedience and nonviolence to make a point about the unfairness of racism. During a sit-in at the Atlanta City Hall, Edelman and thirteen other students were arrested for disturbing the peace.

The event changed Edelman's life and focus. She decided to become a lawyer and fight racism from within the legal system. She attended Yale University Law School on a scholarship and continued her civil rights work. After graduation, she moved to Mississippi, and at age 26, Edelman became the first black woman to pass the Mississippi bar exam and qualify as a lawyer. She went on to head the NAACP (National Association for the Advancement of Colored People) Legal Defense and Education Fund in Mississippi from 1964 to 1968. Of this time, Edelman wrote:

"I realize that I am not fighting just for myself and my people in the South, when I fight for freedom and equality. I realize now that I fight for the moral and political health of America as a whole and for her position in the world at large."

In 1973, Edelman founded the Children's Defense Fund (CDF), a nonprofit child advocacy organization that is based in Washington, D.C. Its purpose is to make sure that U.S. government laws and policies take into consideration the needs of children and families.

The United States is one of the few industrialized nations that has no government-run child-care system. Some countries have centers supported by the government, where the child can be dropped off and picked up. Other countries offer lower taxes and other incentives to companies that offer on-site day care to employees with children. Still, other countries offer generous tax breaks to

One of the first concerns of the CDF was the high rate of teen pregnancy among black girls. Edelman saw that the practice was leading to another generation of poverty as these young girls depended on government support to raise their children.

As Edelman describes it, the CDF's mission is to teach the nation about the needs of children and encourage preventive investments in children before they get sick, drop out of school, suffer too-early pregnancy or family breakdown, or get into trouble with the law. The CDF has become an effective voice nationwide in the areas of adolescent pregnancy prevention, child health, education, child care, child welfare, mental health, and family support systems.

In 1987 Harvard University Press published a book titled *Families in Peril: An Agenda for Social Change*. The book was based on a series of lectures that Edelman delivered while she was teaching at Harvard. She has also earned numerous awards for her leadership and dedication to children and families.

families to help pay for child care. Child-care workers thus are well paid and can support themselves by caring for children. In Sweden and Finland, for example, the government provides preschool during the full workday for children aged four and five, and almost total coverage for children aged two and three. These longer hours mean a less stress-filled workday for parents.

For some women, child care is performed by a relative or friend in his or her home.

In the United States, however, only government workers are offered government-subsidized child-care centers, and businesses receive only small tax breaks for running on-site day care. And child-care workers are among the most poorly paid of American workers.

As a result, American families have become very creative in devising child care. A whole range of child-care options is used. Some are:

- The child is cared for by a relative who comes to the child's home.
- The child goes to a relative's home for care.
- The child is cared for by a neighbor.
- The child is in a church- or school-run nursery or day care center.
- The child is in a public day care center or nursery school.
- The child splits his/her time among several places, sometimes going to a

grandparent's house or day camp or being in a latch-key program at school.

One criticism made of the U.S. child-care system (or lack of it) is that it does not guarantee that children are cared for in a safe and healthy environment. For instance, if the child is cared for in the home of a friend or relative, that person need not be trained in first aid, nutrition, child development, or discipline methods. Also, the premises do not need to be inspected or licensed for cleanliness and safety.

Another problem with the U.S. child-care system is that it is not supportive of working parents. The day care arrangements can become nightmarish if a child is sick or a parent must work late or travel out of town.

A third flaw is the lack of attention given to older children, who often spend long hours without adult supervision. These children are usually age ten and older and are called "latch-key" kids because their parents entrust them with a key to the family home. When a "latch-key" kid is dismissed from school, he or she goes home to an empty house, and it may be several hours before the parent arrives home. Often these arrangements work well. The child does homework and chores. But sometimes these arrangements lead to trouble because the child may be lonely or lack the discipline to study or work on a hobby.

Fathers and Child Care

The U.S. Bureau of the Census reports that more than ever before fathers are the primary caregivers for their young children.

As more women enter the workforce, more fathers become the primary caretakers of their children.

In 1988, only 15 percent of children under age five were cared for primarily by their fathers while their mothers worked outside the home. In 1991, that figure had risen to 20 percent. If those fathers were jobless, that figure rose to 56 percent.

Socialization

Socialization is the process of teaching a person how to behave in a certain way. For instance, a baby who grows up in a middle-class white home will behave differently and have different attitudes from a baby who grows up in a wealthy Hispanic or black family.

Children learn more than cultural and economic messages at home. They also learn messages about how to behave as a boy or girl and, later, as a man or woman. One of the ways children learn this message is by watching their parents. For instance, children learn about the division of labor in the home by seeing who holds the outside job, and who does the housework, the yard work, the child care, the community or school volunteer work, and the care of elderly relatives. If these jobs and chores are split between the parents, the child learns that it is appropriate for both men and women to do them. If the outside work is done by the father and the mother does all the other chores, the child gets a different message.

One 1994 study found that women employed full-time outside the home do 70 percent of the housework while full-time homemakers do 83 percent of the housework. This study suggests that while both partners may have full-time jobs, the woman still does the large majority of housework. Some believe that this uneven sharing of household chores is left over from the days when more women were stay-at-home wives and mothers. These types of chores became regarded as "women's work." An uneven sharing of chores may be a source of friction for couples.

Elderly Care

Statistics show that most American women will be caregivers at some point in their lives. Either they will have children and/or they will care for their elderly parents. Care of the elderly is time-consuming and stressful, even when the elderly person lives in an institution such as a nursing home. The elderly parent still needs help paying bills, handling medication, and dealing with the nursing home staff. The elderly parent also needs love and attention. Often this need must be met by those relatives who live the nearest to them. As a result, the visiting often rests on the same two or three relatives. Stress and guilt often result from trying to juggle the elderly parents' affairs and visiting schedule while meeting the demands of the caregiver's own job and family.

Homelessness

Homelessness became an issue in the 1980s, at a time of economic prosperity in America. However, much of this prosperity stopped at the upper and middle classes. The lower class found fewer jobs, and lower paying jobs resulted from the corporate mergers (the joining of two companies) and downsizing (actions taken by a company to cut its staff) that were occurring at such a rapid rate. Also during these years, many social programs found that their federal grants had been cut and that they could offer fewer services.

Many experts believe that joblessness and the lack of social services have contributed to create the phenomenon we know as "homelessness." When home-

Women and children are becoming the largest group of homeless people.

lessness was first brought to the attention of Americans in the 1980s, the majority of the victims appeared to be single men. Often these homeless men had a history of substance abuse and mental illness. For this reason, it was easy for many Americans to believe that these men could find a home if they were willing to stop their use of drink or drugs and find work.

Later, the face of the homeless seen on nightly television news was that of women and the elderly. Eventually, Americans saw entire families living out of their cars or in cardboard shacks. Finally, Americans received the message about the extent and seriousness of the homeless problem.

In the mid-1990s, Americans continue to deal with the homeless in much the same way they did in 1980. Americans support government-run programs with tax dollars, give to charities that run shelters and soup kitchens, and learn about the homeless through television, magazines, and newspapers.

Even with these programs, the homeless problem will remain embedded in American society for a long time. Those children growing up in cars and shacks often do not attend school regularly. Their poor education will not prepare them well for the work world. They often suffer from poor nutrition and rarely receive the immunizations (vaccines) that they should. This means potential long-term health problems, which will affect their ability to work and mean that the government will need to support them.

Domestic Violence

Domestic violence is the verbal and physical abuse of any family member by another family member. The large majority of victims are wives, ex-wives, girlfriends, ex-girlfriends, and mothers. The children of these women are often victims as well. Domestic violence is not a new phenomenon. It appears throughout history and is the topic of many famous novels and plays.

By the mid-1990s, domestic or family violence had become a topic commonly discussed in newspapers, television talk shows, movies, political speeches, and conversations throughout America. The incidence of family violence had not grown, but the country's awareness of it had. In the past, domestic violence was considered a private matter, one best left to the family to resolve. Even when there was clear evidence that women and children were being harmed, those in authority often turned a blind eye to the situation. These authorities included police who may have been called to the scene of a domestic argument, hospital workers who treated injured wives or children, and teachers and counselors who saw bruises and cuts on students at school.

This attitude did not mean that the authorities were indifferent (uncaring) to the pain and suffering of battered wives and children. The attitude was simply an outgrowth of the old and mistaken notion that the man is the master of his family and his home. His wife and children were considered his property to discipline as he saw fit.

Then came the women's movement in the 1970s. Women and their supporters began to question the validity of the idea that a man could abuse his family without interference from outside society. Members of the women's movement called attention to the number of wives who had suffered injuries or even had been killed by abusive spouses or boyfriends. They cited the numbers of children who lived in violent homes, and pointed out that children from this environment often grew up to become batterers themselves. Children practice what they see; if they see violence, they often become violent. Statistics show that 20 to 40 percent of chronically violent teenagers come from abusive homes.

Women participating in the women's movement began to open shelters where women and children could stay during violent episodes at home. These activists also offered legal help if a woman decided to separate from or divorce her abusive spouse. Some of the shelters offered counseling to cope with the grief, despair, and guilt that come with battering. Abused women also found help in training for jobs if they needed to return to work.

With the help of the women's movement, society began to reevaluate its attitude toward abusive husbands and battered wives. The legal system began to prosecute (take to court) husbands and boyfriends who threatened or harmed their mates and/or children. Schools, hospitals, and neighbors began to report to the police any incidents they saw that appeared to be battering.

Today, women, children, and even men are still abused in episodes of family violence. In 1992, the U.S. Surgeon General ranked domestic violence as the leading cause of injury to women age 15 to 44. One expert estimated that family violence resulted in health care costs between $5 and $10 billion annually.

Kentucky Offers Help to Battered Wives

The state of Kentucky runs 15 shelters for women and children who are fleeing from a violent home. In 1994, those 15 shelters helped 2,346 women and 3,120 children. Another 31,225 people were given help through crisis telephone lines run by the shelter staffs. The Kentucky system of shelters has been cited as a national model by Bonnie J. Campbell, director of the new federal Violence Against Women office.

Kentucky has taken other steps to help the victims of abuse. In 1992, it reformed its domestic violence laws and won the praise of U.S. Attorney General Janet Reno. Some of the reforms meant that the courts were open 24 hours a day to provide legal help to keep abusive spouses out of the house and away from the intended victims. The reforms also gave the police more freedom in following up evidence of domestic abuse.

In 1994, the National Council of Juvenile and Family Court Judges published the Model Code. This 49-page document outlines how communities, police, and courts should respond to family violence. It covers how to keep victims safe, how to handle abusers, how to obtain and enforce a restraining order (a legal order that keeps an abuser or a stalker away from his/her victim), and how to prevent domestic violence. The states do, however, have some choices in how strictly they interpret these national guidelines.

Blaming the Victim

Unfortunately, societal attitudes have not entirely caught up with the changes in laws and penalties. Like the abusers, many members of society believe that a woman provokes a battering. Tragically, many abused women also believe that they deserve the abuse they receive. The abuser may rationalize his abuse as disciplining a nagging wife. Society may also rationalize it this way, while the woman may view it as her punishment for not being a perfect wife.

Whatever the rationalization, everyone involved needs to understand that violence is not an acceptable way to solve family problems. Studies have shown that violence in the home often leads to violence in society, since people tend to solve problems the same way they solve them at home. Blaming the victims of violence allows the cycle to continue. The way to break the cycle is for the victim to leave the abusive home or for both the victim and the abuser to enter counseling or therapy.

Special Concerns of African American Families

Many observers have claimed in recent years that the African American family is in a crisis, the major reason being the growing numbers of poor, female-headed families. In 1970, 68 percent of African American families were headed by a married couple. By 1980, that figure had fallen to 56 percent. By 1990, only one-half of black families were headed by a married couple, and the percentage continues to fall. One advantage of the two-parent family is that it often means more income and a better standard of living. Another advantage of the two-parent family is that children often receive more supervision and guidance and have better role models.

The average African American household contained 2.9 persons in 1990, compared with 2.6 persons for white households. Even though they had a lower income, black female-headed households contained an average of one more person than white female-headed households.

In 1960, 65 percent of black women age 30 to 34 were in an intact marriage (living with their husband). By 1990 that figure had fallen to 39 percent. Over that same period, the percentage of black women who were divorced grew from 8 to 12 percent, and the percentage never married grew from 10 to 35 percent.

While similar divorce patterns have occurred for white women, the change has been more dramatic for African American women. Although there are many reasons why women do not marry, analysts point to the fact that black women outnumber black men in the age group when most people marry and start families (between 20 and 49 years old). So, fewer black women may be getting married because there are not enough eligible black men.

Only one-half of African American families are headed by a married couple.

Others believe that there is less social and economic support for black men in the American culture. Black men are not encouraged to support families in the same way white men are. Fewer black men being employed in our society may also account for the low marriage rates among African Americans.

Black Children

In 1990, 55 percent of all black children lived in a single-parent household, 51 percent with their mothers. Contrast this to the 19 percent of white children who lived with only one parent.

Twenty-seven percent of all African American children live with mothers who have never married. Those black children who are not living with their mother are more likely to live with a grandparent than are either white or Hispanic children. What does this mean for black children? These types of families—female-headed or grandparent-headed—are more likely to be poor. Nearly two-thirds of the black households headed by single women are poor and live in central cities, more than one-quarter of them in public (government supported) housing.

Families in Poverty

While the *percentage* of poor black families is higher than that of whites, there is a higher *number* of poor white families in the United States. In fact, American children are more likely to be poor than the children of other industrialized nations. For instance, the poverty rate among children rose from 14 percent of the population in 1969 to 20 percent in 1987. That means that 20 out of every 100 American children live at or below the poverty level.

What does the face of poverty look like? Poor children are more likely to have:

- health problems (including low birth weight)

- problems at school because of poor nutrition and health care

- high delinquency rates (skipping school)

- high rates of teenage pregnancy

In response to this poverty, the U.S. government offers several welfare programs to aid families. One such program, Aid to Families with Dependent Children (AFDC), offers unmarried, unemployed mothers government money to care for their children. Other welfare programs include food stamps and Medicaid (a government health care program).

Some Americans complain, however, that the United States spends too much money on these welfare programs.

For example, in 1993, the federal government spent $13.8 billion on welfare programs, and state governments spent $11.4 billion.

The U.S. government does have some success stories when it comes to helping American families. The Women, Infants, and Children (WIC) program and the Head Start preschool program offer health and educational services to poor families and children.

However, critics of welfare claimed victory in August 1996 when President Bill Clinton signed a bill ending the current welfare system. The most significant change to the welfare program is that the state governments will now be responsible for public assistance instead of the federal government. Other provisions of the bill include: limiting welfare benefits to five years or less, forcing recipients to find work, and ending most aid to nonresidents.

Families continue to be a vital part of society, even if today's families don't resemble those of the past. Just as their predecessors did, today's women play an important role in families. However, modern women face many different problems than women of the past. The high divorce rate, child-care issues, and elderly care are just some of the issues that face these modern women and their families. Society must recognize the problems of modern women and be willing to help them so that families can continue to give children the foundation they need.

Health: Women's Bodies and Minds

Physical Differences Between Men and Women

Men and women are alike in most observable ways. They have arms, legs, eyes, ears, hair, teeth, and noses. The most visible difference between women and men is that women have breasts, which usually means that clothing hangs a little differently on them. Other dissimilarities include women tending to have slightly broader hips, and men tending to be taller. But these are slight variations on common characteristics. The main difference between men and women is that women are able to conceive, carry, and deliver children while men cannot. This ability to carry children occurs after a girl reaches puberty.

Puberty

A girl baby is born with about four hundred thousand immature eggs, or ova, in her ovaries. During puberty the girl's body begins its preparation for childbearing. Inside, the ovaries and uterus

Timeline: Significant Events in the History of Women's Health

1070 Trotula of Salerno writes *Passionibus mulierum curandorum* ("The Diseases of Women").

1322 Italian physician Jacaba Felicie is charged with illegally practicing medicine. Her protest that male doctors do not understand female conditions goes unanswered.

1853 England's Queen Victoria uses chloroform while giving birth to her eighth child. Her act removes the stigma of using pain-relieving anesthesia during childbirth.

1953 The Kinsey Report, the first study of American women's sexual habits, is published.

1960 Women in America begin to use silicone implants to enlarge and reshape their breasts.

1970 Breast cancer rates among women in industrialized nations begin to soar. The reason is uncertain.

1990 The United States sees a growth in the number of family practitioners, doctors who combine primary care with knowledge of women's health needs.

begin to grow larger, and she will experience her first menstruation cycle or "period." The cycle is repeated each month until she reaches the age of menopause (usually in her fifties). The stages of the menstruation cycle are:

- A signal from the brain releases a hormone (a chemical that produces a specific effect on targeted cells and organs).

- The hormone causes an egg within the ovary to begin to mature or ripen.

- At the same time, the uterus begins to build a lining of tissue to nurture a fertilized egg.

- About midway through the cycle, the mature egg bursts from the ovary and enters the fallopian tube.

- While the egg is in the tube it may be fertilized if sperm from a man is present (if sexual intercourse has occurred without the use of birth control measures).

- If the egg is fertilized it will travel down the fallopian tube and nest in the lining of the uterus (meaning pregnancy has begun). The lining of the uterus will develop further and no period will occur until the pregnancy is over.

- If the egg is not fertilized, it will travel down the fallopian tube, through the cervix, and exit the body through the vagina. Within a few days the uterus will begin shedding its extra tissue and the woman will experience menstruation. The tissue is a combination of blood and clotted material.

Some girls and women experience a set of symptoms called PMS, or premenstrual syndrome, before they begin their periods. The symptoms of PMS may include cramping, irritability, headaches, and water retention. In severe cases, doctors may prescribe medication. Other women, however, cope by using home remedies that include reducing the amount of salt and caffeine in their diet before a period, since salt can cause bloating and the caffeine in coffee, tea, chocolate, and soda may increase the discomfort a woman feels.

Some cultures regard menstruation as an unclean process. These cultures may require women to undergo a ritual bath after the period ends or may require her to wait for a week to resume sexual relations. Some societies throughout history feared menstruating women because they thought the vagina was a huge mouth with sharp teeth that caused bleeding. In these societies, men would not have sex with a woman during her period.

Sexuality

While the girl's body is experiencing many changes inside, her external appearance is also changing. Her breasts are growing and her hips may begin to broaden. She may experience a growth spurt leaving her with arms and legs that seem too long and awkward. She may feel dissatisfied with her appearance and uncomfortable with these changes.

Late in the process, girls and boys also experience puberty on a very personal level. They think about their bodies, and they may worry about their attractiveness to the opposite sex.

At some point, most people begin to have sexual relations. Many times this occurs later in a person's life, when she or he is married or in a committed long-term relationship. However, some people begin to have sex during their teenage years.

Scientists have called the sexual urge one of the strongest that people feel. All animal species feel the need to procreate (create new life) because this is how the species survives. Humans are no exception. From the teen years until death, most humans experience a need to have sex.

Human sex is complicated by the fact that humans are intelligent creatures. They bring to the sexual act much more than the need to procreate. They bring a need for love, acceptance, closeness, and commitment or bonding.

Medical Visits

Because the human body has many complex systems, it is important that both women and men have a complete physical examination once a year by a physician. The following section briefly describes the process that a woman experiences during her annual visit to her doctor.

Pelvic Exams

A doctor who specializes in female anatomy and diseases is called a gynecologist. A doctor who specializes in

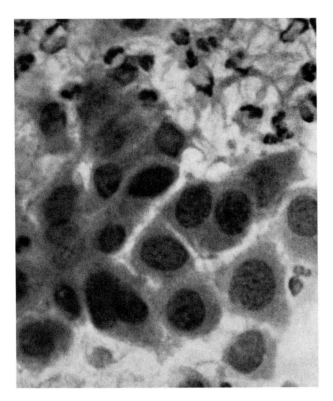

Microscopic view of a pap smear showing cancerous cells.

ually active. The doctor also takes the girl's vital signs (height, weight, blood sample, etc.). By doing this, the doctor is trying to gain an overall impression of the girl's health and habits.

The next step is a breast exam. The doctor will examine the girl's breasts and teach her how to do a self-exam so she can repeat the process at home. The doctor is feeling for any lumps or thickening in the breast tissue that may signal a problem such as breast cancer. Ordinarily a girl's breast feels firm and as if it is filled with a bag of sand or gravel. A lump has a different feel. It may be a larger size grain or may have a different texture or consistency. The doctor will encourage the girl to do the exam every month about midway through her menstrual cycle. Most breast tumors and cancers are found through this type of examination.

After the breast exam, the doctor will do a pelvic exam. The doctor uses an instrument called a speculum to gently open the vagina. Then the doctor inserts a swab to take a sample of cells from the cervix. These cells are spread on a slide for later examination under a microscope. This is called a pap smear. The doctor then looks around, noting the color of the tissue, any swelling, or other symptoms. When this is done, the doctor removes the speculum. The next part of the exam consists of the doctor feeling the girl's stomach and lower abdomen to judge the size and position of the internal organs.

The exam is now over. If the doctor has noticed any abnormal signs, she

treating pregnant women is called an obstetrician (ob-sta-tri-shun). Many times, a doctor will combine these specialties and be called an OB/Gyn. In many American health care programs, women are allowed to choose two principal doctors who will be responsible for treating them: one will be a primary care or a general care physician, the other will be an OB/Gyn.

When a girl is a teenager, she should make her first visit to an OB/Gyn. In this visit, the OB/Gyn will talk with the new patient and begin keeping a record of the girl's medical history by asking how regular her periods are and whether she is sex-

or he will talk with the girl either at the end of the exam or when the test results come back. American doctors recommend that women have a yearly pelvic exam and pap smear. These procedures are useful in the early detection of cancers and other reproductive problems.

Birth Control

Many fine books exist that discuss birth control methods in great detail. We offer a general listing of the most commonly used ones, and refer you to *Our Bodies, Ourselves* (see box) or a similar book for more detail and opinions about effectiveness and comfort. Some of the less discussed methods and options are covered in more detail here.

Birth control limits the number of times that a woman is exposed to the possibility of pregnancy. Practicing birth control puts a woman or a couple in charge of when pregnancy occurs. In the early 1900s, birth control pioneer Margaret Sanger called this concept "voluntary motherhood."

Women limit their pregnancies for a number of reasons. Some choose never to have any children. Others do so because their health is poor. Some limit the number for economic reasons. Whatever the motivation, U.S. women have had access to safe and reliable birth control only since the 1930s. Before then, women typically had a large number of children, since little was known about the reproductive system and methods to limit pregnancy. Today women have many options from which to choose. Doctors freely discuss birth control methods, and most public schools teach about sexuality and reproduction.

Virginity

A virgin is a person who has not had sexual relations. A virgin may be a boy or a girl. In some societies, the virginity of girls is highly prized; only girls who are virgins are accepted as marriage partners. However, in the United States many young people feel the pressure to have sex from a sex-oriented society which uses ads, billboards, television programs, and movies to promote sex. Pressure also comes from peers, who believe that only "nerds" or "babies" do not have sex. During the 1990s, though, many young people in the United States decided to resist this pressure to have sex. These people call themselves "voluntary virgins" and openly admit that they have chosen to postpone their first sexual experience.

Celibacy/Abstinence

A celibate is a person who has made a personal commitment not to engage in sexual activity. Many religious people such as priests and nuns have chosen to remain celibate. They believe celibacy will help them concentrate on worshiping God and serving humankind.

Abstinence is the voluntary giving up of sexual relations. A person may be sexually active and then decide to enter

Our Bodies, Ourselves

In the mid-1900s, medicine was still a male practice, with most doctors and medical researchers being men. As a result, the American view of medicine and health took on a male perspective.

The publication of *Our Bodies, Ourselves* in 1969 helped change that. *Our Bodies, Ourselves,* written by the Boston Women's Health Collective, is a long, detailed account of health from a woman's point of view. It covers diseases, conditions, and feelings often overlooked by the male medical community. *Our Bodies, Ourselves* is billed as a "self-help" book because it gives women information that helps them care for themselves. The book also gives women the confidence to ask their doctors questions about female prob-lems and to persist until they receive a satisfactory answer.

By the mid-1990s, *Our Bodies, Ourselves* was in its third printing. It is still considered by many the most thorough discussion of women's health care written for a nonprofessional audience.

The Boston Women's Health Collective is a nonprofit organization based in Somerville, Massachusetts. It is devoted to education about women and health and maintains projects on midwifery and reproductive health. You can contact the collective at:

Boston Women's Health Collective
Box 192
West Somerville, MA 02144

a period of abstinence. Their reasons may vary from waiting to fall in love with another person to waiting for medication to clear up a sexually transmitted disease.

Pregnancy

Pregnancy occurs when a sperm meets and enters a mature egg. During the nine-month human gestation (development) period, the fertilized egg continually multiplies its cells; thus, a baby grows from two tiny cells (sperm and egg) at conception into a multibillion-cell complex creature. Along the way, the cells become differentiated; some grow into nerves, others into hair, and still others into organs. At the same time, the complex intermingling of the parents' genes (cells that carry hereditary information which is used to create new cells) is determining the child's complexion, height, athletic ability, intelligence, and thousands of other characteristics.

The stages of pregnancy are covered in many health and medical books in your local public or school library. This section focuses on some of the side issues associated with pregnancy.

Fetal tests

During pregnancy, most American women make regular visits to their OB/Gyn or primary care physician. The doctor weighs the woman and takes her blood pressure. Her stomach is measured to see how much the fetus has grown and, later in the pregnancy, a Doppler sound device can help her hear the fetus's heartbeat. The doctor also prescribes special vitamins rich in the nutrients that fetuses need to grow.

Most doctors also prescribe a series of tests for pregnant women. Some of the tests are to determine the mother's state of health. For instance, there is a condition that some pregnant women develop called gestational diabetes. Its symptoms can be detected by a simple blood test and then treated so that a woman can safely deliver her child. Many of the prescribed tests are to determine the fetus's state of health.

Three-part Series

A three-part series of tests is administered to women early in their pregnancies to search for symptoms of conditions that require further testing. The tests are conducted by taking blood and urine from the mother. The AFP (alpha fetal protein) screen measures the amounts of a particular protein in the mother's blood. If this protein is present in too-high or too-low quantities, it can indicate that a

Teens and Pregnancy

Some experts call it an "epidemic." They are referring to the number of teenage girls who become pregnant each year in the United States. About 1 in every 10 girls (1.1 million) became pregnant in 1996. The vast majority are unmarried and do not have a lasting relationship with the father of the child.

Many communities and schools have begun programs to try to reach young girls before they become pregnant. The programs talk about birth control, sexuality, and self-image. Some experts believe that girls become pregnant because they are afraid they will lose their boyfriend's love if they reject his sexual advances. Others believe that girls are looking for a companion, someone to feel close to, and they believe a baby will fulfill this need.

fetus is distressed in some way. Unlike a test, which gives concrete results, a screening points only to the possiblity of a problem. The doctor can then follow up a screening with a test.

The second part of the series is called an estriol test, which measures the amount of estrogen in the mother's urine. This level indicates whether the pregnancy is progressing as it should. The third part is called the HCG (human chorionic gonadotrophin) test, which shows the development of fetal growth.

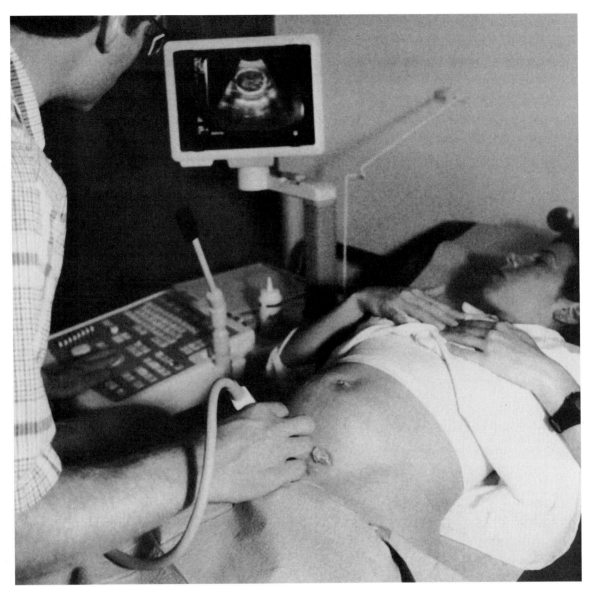

A woman undergoing an ultrasound

Amniocentesis

Amniocentesis involves using a needle to withdraw some of the amniotic fluid from the woman's abdomen. The fetus is supported from shocks by floating in amniotic fluid in the uterus. A laboratory test of a fluid sample is used to reveal whether there is abnormal development among the fetus's cells. Diseases such as Downs' syndrome and spina bifida can be detected through amniocentesis. Downs' syndrome produces mentally handicapped children; spina bifida refers to the incomplete closing of the spinal column. A child can live into adulthood with Downs' syndrome but usually has a shorter, painful life with spina bifida. Some parents use amniocentesis to help them make a decision about whether a fetus should be aborted.

Ultrasound

Ultrasound is a method that gained acceptance among OB/Gyns in the 1970s. It uses sound to help create a picture of the fetus's dimensions. By bouncing sound waves off the abdomen of the pregnant woman, the ultrasound "hears" dense tissue and skips over less dense fluid. The image created helps the OB/Gyn determine the size and health of the fetus.

Midwives

Midwives have been attending births since the earliest days of humankind. A midwife is a person who knows about and is skilled in caring for pregnant women. A midwife, usually a woman, is also present at the birth and helps care for the child after the delivery. In ancient times, a midwife gained her reputation by the number of healthy children she successfully delivered. In later times, a midwife was expected to help with difficult deliveries. A midwife also had knowledge of herbal medicines and teas which she used to treat childbed fever and colicky infants, who suffer from stomach distress.

Today, midwives are usually registered nurses who attend a special program to qualify as nurse-midwives. In 1992, the United States's 4,000 registered nurse-midwives attended 185,000 births, about 5 percent of the babies born in the country that year. The modern nurse-midwife, like her historical counterpart, develops a special bond with her patients, and she is the person the pregnant woman sees on most of her pre-delivery visits. The nurse-midwife teaches new mothers how to care for their infants, including how to breast-feed and bathe the baby.

Post-Partum Depression

When a woman undergoes pregnancy and childbirth, her body experiences huge surges in its production of hormones (chemicals that spark reactions in certain cells and organs). After delivery, it takes time for a woman's body to absorb any extra hormones. For many mothers, especially those experiencing a first child, childbirth is a traumatic event that causes both an emotional and a physical upheaval in her life.

The hormone imbalance is often accompanied by the fatigue that comes with nursing and caring for a child. Some mothers experience fear and confusion. They feel unprepared to cope with caring for another life. Others are career women who are now home and alone for a large part of the day. They feel lonely and isolated. Whatever the feelings and their source, sometimes these feelings last and develop into a serious emotional condition called post-partum depression. "Post-partum" means "after delivery."

Breast-Feeding or Formula?

The 1950s were a time of great strides in technology. Americans were beginning their space program, developing computer models, and learning about science at every level. It was during this decade that many doctors got on the technology bandwagon and encouraged their pregnant patients to consider feeding their new babies formula (artificial milk) instead of breast milk. Breast-feeding was wrongly thought to be unsanitary and old-fashioned. Formula was considered a better product because it was vitamin-fortified and made in sterile factories.

But doctors and mothers soon learned that formula could not replace breast milk from a health point of view. The breast-feeding experience helped mothers and infants develop feelings of closeness and affection. Breast-fed babies were also given immunity to some diseases when they absorbed the antibodies present in their mother's milk. Some babies just did not like formula, or they developed allergies and digestive problems (Breast milk is now known to be the most easily digested food for infants.).

By the 1990s, the medical community had gathered enough research to state that breast-feeding is the preferred source of nutrition for new babies. Many doctors still recommend formula but suggest that it be used to supplement a diet of breast milk. With this breast milk-formula approach, if a nursing mother is ill or absent, her infant will be used to the taste of formula and will be accustomed to taking a bottle from another person.

Post-partum depression can begin immediately after delivery and last for weeks, months, or years. A seemingly healthy mother may even find herself spiraling into depression when her child is several months old. Although some women never experience post-partum depression or "baby blues," it has been recognized as a problem among women for thousands of years. In early times, a female relative was present for the birth and then stayed with the new mother for several weeks after. The relative's stated reason for being there was to help with household chores. Her other reason was to offer support, comfort, and advice when the new mother experienced the "baby blues."

When post-partum depression is severe or prolonged, a new mother's doctor may suggest she enter counseling to vent her feelings and fears. But since post-partum depression also has a chemical source (the imbalance of hormones), the doctor may feel the need to prescribe medication to combat the symptoms.

If left untreated, post-partum depression can have serious consequences. A woman who is desperately unhappy may act out her feelings on herself, her child, or others around her. In the past, American society expected that motherhood would make a woman happy. We realize today that motherhood can take some getting used to. Fortunately, we are freer to recognize and talk about negative experiences such as post-partum depression.

Birth Control Methods

Before listing the commonly used methods for birth control, some cautions should be offered.

- Birth control methods are effective in preventing pregnancy only if they are used during each sexual experience. Hit-and-miss applications often result in pregnancy.

- Even when used properly, birth control methods can fail and pregnancy can occur because the materials that make up the birth control device can be punctured or torn.

- No method can protect 100 percent against the spread of sexually transmitted diseases (STDs), including AIDS. Even condoms have a failure rate of 8 to 12 percent. That exposes not only the women to pregnancy, but both partners to possibly deadly diseases.

- The following list is very basic. It cannot and should not be used as a "how to" for selecting or using birth control.

Natural Birth Control

For many years, the Roman Catholic Church has preached against the use of birth control. The Church believes strongly that interrupting the chance for life is a decision that God, not humans, should make. The exception has been the rhythm method, which the Catholic Church has approved for use by its members. The method is based on the idea that a woman experiences a fertile period each month, a week-long period in which she can become pregnant. If a woman keeps track of her menstrual cycles, she has some idea of when her next one will start. The fertile period usually occurs sometime between the eleventh and sixteenth day after the start of the last period; many couples abstain from intercourse during this time. The rhythm method has worked for many couples but has failed for many others.

Today the sympto-thermal method is preferred by the Catholic Church and other religious groups that object to artificial birth control. The sympto-thermal method is often mistaken for the old rhythm method, but it is much more sophisticated. The sympto- portion of the name refers to the fact that there are definite signs that occur throughout a woman's monthly cycle. These symptoms include changes in the amount, color, and texture of the mucus found around the cervix. To use the method, women have to become acquainted with how this mucus changes during the cycle.

The thermal part refers to the fact that a woman's body temperature rises slightly when she ovulates (releases an egg). Ovulation begins a woman's fertile period. When the temperature drops again, the fertile period is ended.

Many woman like this method of birth control because it teaches them about their bodies. They also like the fact that it does not expose their bodies to artificial devices or chemicals. The method also helps women who want to become pregnant. In fact, many couples having difficulty conceiving use the sympto-thermal method to find the fertile period.

Others criticize the method for being imprecise and unreliable. The charge of being imprecise is one that is often heard when natural methods and remedies are used. Since Americans live in a medical society, we have learned to become skeptical about methods other than those prescribed by the medical community. However, when it comes to reliability, many doctors and health care workers believe that the sympto-thermal method ranks among the top pregnancy preventers if used consistently. The Planned Parenthood Federation of America reports that, when used properly, the sympto-thermal method has an 80 to 97 percent effectiveness rate.

Not everyone has the right personality to use the sympto-thermal method, however. It takes a woman who is willing to take charge of her body, who can chart a temperature each morning, and who can resist her own and her partner's sexual urges during her fertile period.

Artificial Birth Control

Artificial birth control devices have been used for thousands of years. The first were crude condoms and small balls placed in the uterus. In the twentieth century, chemical birth control methods were developed. The section below briefly describes the most used methods in the United States.

Condoms

Condoms made of animal skin and cloth have been used throughout history. Today they are a thin sheath made from latex or a natural material. It has a reservoir or pocket at the tip to collect the sperm. The condom acts as a barrier. When it works well, a condom will prevent sperm and sexually transmitted diseases from entering another person's body. However, if a condom has even a tiny puncture, pregnancy or STDs can result.

Diaphragm

A diaphragm is a small rubber disk that a woman inserts over her cervix. Like a condom, a diaphragm is a barrier that blocks semen from entering the uterus. Its effectiveness rate is improved when a woman also uses a spermicidal (sperm killing) foam or jelly. Women should be fitted for a diaphragm by their doctor. The Planned Parenthood Federation of America reports that, used properly, diaphragms have an 82 to 94 percent effectiveness rate.

IUD

IUD stands for intrauterine device. It is a device that is inserted through the cervix to expand in the uterus. Common IUDs are shaped like a "T" or a "7." Once inserted an IUD can remain in place and be effective for years. It is unclear exactly why IUDs work to prevent pregnancy. Two common theories are that the presence of the IUD irritates the lining of the uterus enough so that a fertilized egg cannot attach and grow. Instead it passes out through the cervix and the woman menstruates. The other theory is that the IUD acts as a spermicide, killing sperm before they can fertilize the egg. IUDs are between 97 to 99 percent effective in preventing pregnancy, according to the Planned Parenthood Federation of America.

Spermicides

Spermicides are materials or devices that kill sperm. Common spermicides come in the forms of jellies, creams, and foams. The creams and jellies are packaged in a tube and the foam in a can with an applicator for spraying it into the vagina. They are considered more effective when combined with another method such as a diaphragm.

The Pill

The birth control pill works because it uses hormones to convince a woman's body that she is already pregnant. A woman takes the pill for about 28 days and then stops and has a period. While the pill has a high effectiveness rate and is easy to use, it continues to raise health concerns, especially among long-term users. According to the Planned Parenthood Federation

Birth control became available to more women with the development of the birth control pill.

of America, the pill—when taken consistently—is between 97 and 99 percent effective in preventing pregnancy.

Norplant

This method, introduced in the 1990s, consists of surgically inserting six tiny tubes under the skin of a woman's upper arm. Over a period of five years, the tubes release enough artificial hormone to prevent the release of fertilized eggs. Norplant is more than 99 percent effective in preventing pregnancy, according to the Planned Parenthood Federation of America.

Roe v. Wade

Until 1972, abortion was illegal in the United States. Then the U.S. Supreme Court settled a court case called *Roe* v. *Wade*. Jane Roe was a pregnant women who argued that her right to privacy meant that she should legally be able to seek an abortion. Her lawyer claimed that the medical community and the police had no right to interfere in this personal health decision. The Supreme Court agreed, and today a woman in her first trimester of pregnancy can obtain an abortion in any state. However, some states do have restrictions that include not using Medicaid (government health care) funds for abortion.

Female Condom or Pouch

The female condom is a thin material pouch that is spread inside the vagina before intercourse. The pouch is a barrier that prevents sperm from entering the uterus. It also helps protect against spreading sexually transmitted diseases. Planned Parenthood Federation of America states that female condoms prevent pregnancy about 75 percent of the time.

Sponge

A woman places the sponge over her cervix before engaging in intercourse. The sponge acts as a barrier and a spermicide by preventing sperm from entering the womb and the chemicals imbedded in it kill the sperm with which it comes in contact. Sponges have been known to cause toxic-shock syndrome, however, and are no longer sold in the United States.

Withdrawal

Withdrawal is a common but unreliable method. It occurs during intercourse, when both parties are focusing on pleasure. This method relies on the man to remove his penis from the woman's vagina before he ejaculates (releases sperm).

Sterilization

Sterilization is using surgery to tie off or remove reproductive organs. It is a method for interrupting sperm or eggs from reaching their end points (penis or ovary). In a man, an out-patient surgery ties off the tube that carries the sperm from the testes to the penis. In a woman, a major surgery is required to tie off (usually with a laser scalpel) her fallopian tubes. Sterilization is more than 99 percent effective in preventing pregnancy, according to the Planned Parenthood Federation of America.

Abortion

Abortion is not a birth control method in the strictest sense. Birth control is used to prevent pregnancy, while abortion is used to end a pregnancy once it occurs. A woman may choose to end a pregnancy for a number of reasons. It may be an unplanned or unwanted pregnancy. There may be financial or health reasons to end it. The woman may not have a committed partner to be with her to raise the child. The pregnancy may be the result of incest or rape. Or the fetus might be found to have major health problems.

Abortion has been legally available in the United States since the early 1970s. Prior to the Supreme Court ruling called *Roe* v. *Wade* that legalized abortion, doctors who performed abortions and the woman whose child they aborted could be arrested and tried for murder if they were caught.

Abortion is rarely an easy choice for a woman and is often just as distressing for her partner. It involves strong emotions before, during, and after the process. Many health facilities offer support groups for women who choose abortion.

Women's Diseases

Women contract and develop many of the same diseases that men do. However, some diseases are only developed by women because they revolve around a woman's reproductive organs. Other diseases are seen in much greater percentages among women. This section gives a brief description of some of the major diseases that afflict women. More detailed discussions of each, as well as diseases that are contracted by both men and women, are available in library reference books and medical encyclopedias.

Cancer

Cancer is the rapid growth and spread of abnormal cells. Cancer can be

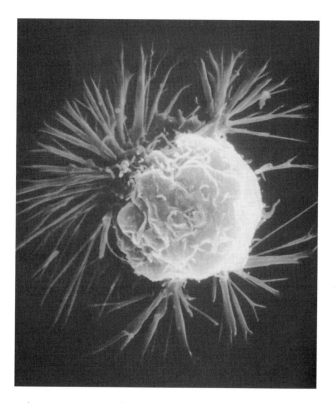

A breast cancer cell

caused by heredity, the environment, or behavior. Heredity means we have inherited a tendency to develop the disease from our parents. Environmental causes include chemicals that are present in air, water, and soil pollution. Behavior includes introducing toxins (poisons) into our body through smoking, drinking, or misusing drugs. Sometimes these toxins are also carcinogens (car-sin-o-jens), meaning they cause cancerous cells to develop.

Cancers are always treated as soon as they are diagnosed because they grow and spread rapidly. Methods for treating cancer include surgery, chemotherapy,

Window on the World: Israel

In the 1970s, Israel, like other industrialized nations, saw a significant rise in the number of breast cancer cases. However, unlike other nations, Israel took aggressive steps to tackle their incidence rate. One such step was to outlaw the use of organochlorine-based pesticides (such as DDT). Ten years after the phase-out, statistics showed a drop in new cases of breast cancer. While the Israeli experience is not proof, it is a dramatic example of how environmental pollution may affect public health.

and radiation therapy. Surgery involves identifying and cutting out the infected site, along with some surrounding tissue. Chemotherapy involves taking strong medicines designed to kill the cancer cells. Unfortunately, the medicines are so strong that they often make the patient violently ill and include side effects like hair loss. Radiation therapy involves using large, focused doses of radiation to burn out infected sites. Sometimes both chemotherapy and radiation therapy are recommended following cancer surgery so the doctor can be sure that all the cancerous cells have been or are being treated.

Cancer sometimes returns after treatment. However, if a woman remains cancer-free for five years, she is considered to have been cured of the disease.

Breast Cancer

Since the early 1970s, the incidence of breast cancer among American women has skyrocketed. In the 1950s, 1 in 20 women developed breast cancer. In the early 1990s, the rate was 1 in 9. Doctors are unsure why the incidence has increased. Many believe that it is the price we pay for living in an industrialized society, where pollution is a fact of life. Others, however, believe that it is a result of long-term use of products such as the birth control pill. Still others believe it has more to do with childbirth. For example, research shows that women who give birth to at least one child have lower incidences of breast cancer, possibly because childbirth stimulates the lactation process. Women who give birth at a younger age (late teens to middle twenties) have an even lower incidence of breast cancer. Some researchers believe the high breast cancer rate is the direct result of American women marrying later in life and delaying the birth of their first child.

Breast cancer is detected through a breast self-exam or by a mammogram. A mammogram is an X ray that shows any shadows or dark lumps in the tissue of the breast. Traditionally, most doctors recommend that women have a baseline mammogram taken in their early forties and a yearly mammogram taken after they reach fifty years old.

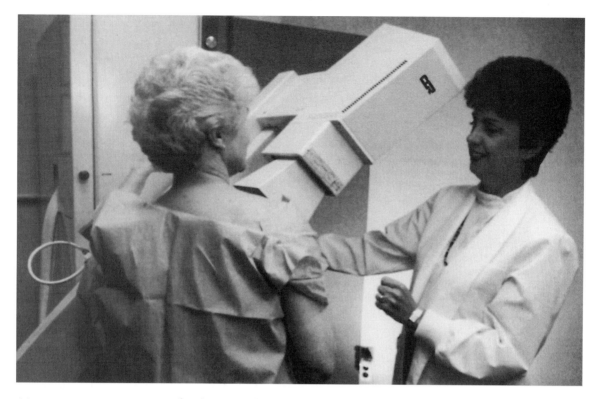

Mammograms are important for detecting the presence of breast cancer in women.

If a lump is detected, the doctor schedules a biopsy. During a biopsy, the area is frozen and the doctor uses a needle to withdraw a small amount of tissue from the lump. The tissue is then sent to a laboratory that examines it and determines whether cancerous cells are present. If they are, the doctor and the woman have several choices of action, depending upon the size and location of the lump.

Cervical cancer

Cervical cancer is usually found during a pelvic examination. The pap smear will reveal unusual or abnormal cells, and the doctor will perform a biopsy. If cancer is detected, the usual treatment is a hysterectomy. A hysterectomy (his-ter-ec-tomy) is the surgical removal of the uterus and cervix. In a complete hysterectomy, the ovaries and fallopian tubes are removed as well. In the 1990s, cervical cancer was killing American women at a rate of about 4,400 annually.

Ovarian cancer

Ovarian cancer is difficult to detect and has an extremely high mortality (death) rate. This means that most women are diagnosed in the late stages of the disease and die soon after. More women

Progress on Breast Cancer Treatment

The treatment for cancer (including breast cancer) was the same in 1995 as it was in 1945. The treatments are surgery, radiation, and chemotherapy. Some breast cancer survivors, bitter about their choices, refer to them as "slash, burn, and poison."

While a cancer diagnosis is still frightening, many people are benefiting from variations on the surgery/radiation/chemotherapy response. For instance, the medical and scientific communities have developed reconstructive surgery, which includes using natural tissue or silicone implants to recreate a missing breast. A newer type of surgery, the lumpectomy, tries to preserve as much of the woman's natural breast as possible.

Other researchers are focusing on vaccines that will possibly prevent people from developing cancer. Still others are looking at the patterns in society that show which people will become ill with cancer. This study is called epidemiology (epi-dee-me-ology), because it helps predict where epidemics will break out.

of color develop ovarian cancer, and they have an even lower survival rate.

Some in the medical community want to include a routine rectal exam in the annual pelvic examination because the rectal exam is the one effective way to detect problems in the ovaries. A blood test introduced in the 1990s is another tool in diagnosing ovarian cancer. In early stage ovarian cancer, the patient undergoes a complete hysterectomy.

In the United States, 1 in 70 women will develop ovarian cancer in their lifetimes and 3 of 5 who do will die from it.

Uterine Cancer

Cancer of the lining of the uterus most often occurs in menopausal or postmenopausal women. Its symptoms include heavy vaginal bleeding. Uterine cancer is detected through a biopsy and treated by a hysterectomy.

Endometriosis

The endometrium is the lining of the uterus. Endometriosis is an inflammation or infection of that lining. It is a painful disease that many women experience. It occurs when uterine tissue grows in the abdominal cavity (the woman's lower body where her female organs are located). While no one can say for certain what causes endometriosis, some researchers believe it occurs from an incomplete shedding of the uterine lining that builds up during a woman's menstrual cycle. Researchers believe that instead of traveling out through the vagina with the menstrual flow, this tissue instead backs up and out through the fallopian tubes. Once in the abdominal cavity, it can attach itself and continue to grow on any organ it finds.

Symptoms of endometriosis include heavy menstrual bleeding, severe cramping, lower back pain, fatigue (tiredness), and inability to conceive (infertility). Endometriosis is first diagnosed through a pelvic exam. The doctor then orders a laparoscopy. This is a small incision made near the woman's navel. The doctor inserts a small tube through the incision. The tube acts as the doctor's eyes, allowing the doctor to see inside the woman's abdomen. Treatments include hormone drug treatment and surgery.

Pelvic Inflammatory Disease

Often called PID, pelvic inflammatory disease is a painful inflammation of the woman's abdomen. The inflammation or soreness can result from an infected ovary, an ectopic pregnancy (in which the fertilized egg grows in the fallopian tube), or an untreated sexually transmitted disease. Sometimes PID remains undiagnosed for years, and the condition worsens to the point where the woman needs a hysterectomy.

Bladder/Urinary Tract Infections

Many women suffer from recurring bladder and/or urinary tract infections (UTIs). The sign of a bladder infection is a frequent need to urinate. The sign of a urinary tract infection is pain or burning during urination. Some doctors believe that women develop these infections because of poor bathroom habits (wiping from the back to the front, thus bringing fecal infections into the urethra area. The urethra is the opening from which women urinate.) Most doctors, however, believe that it is the close location of the urethra

to the vagina and anus that introduces bacteria. Holding urine and failing to change wet clothes or bathing suits are also notorious causes of UTIs. Treatments include warm baths, drinking lots of fluids to flush out the bacteria, and antibiotics to kill any remaining bacteria.

Yeast Infections

Yeast infections can grow in any warm, moist body cavity (mouth, underarm). In women, they can and often do grow in the vagina. Signs of a yeast infection are vaginal itching and a thick white-yellow discharge from the vagina. Treatments include over-the-counter antibiotic creams and doctor-prescribed medications.

Anemia

Anyone can suffer from anemia, but women suffer from it four times more often than men. Anemia occurs when the amount of iron in the blood is too low. Many women are borderline anemics, suffering from slightly low blood iron all their lives. Low blood iron leads to feelings of fatigue and weakness. Traditional remedies for anemia include eating iron-rich foods such as liver and red meats or taking iron-rich vitamin tablets.

Toxic Shock Syndrome

Toxic shock syndrome was first identified in 1980. It occurs when a type of staph bacteria is introduced into the woman's system. Most often, toxic shock syndrome is associated with the improper use of super-absorbent tampons. Recently some cases have been linked to the use of contraceptive sponges (a birth control method no longer on the market) and diaphragms. Symptoms include a high fever and a sunburn-like rash that peels. Treatments include removing any device present in the vagina and immediately calling a doctor. Speed is critical because the disease spreads very quickly. Antibiotics are often prescribed as treatment.

Lupus

Lupus occurs when a person's body begins to develop antibodies that attack the person's own organs instead of outside germs. Lupus attacks nine times as many women as men, and about 1 in every 500 Americans. Although serious cases of lupus can affect every organ in the body and can lead to death, many people live a long life after a lupus diagnosis. Treatment includes low exposure to sunlight and stress and the use of aspirin, ibuprofen, or a steroid treatment when inflammation or swelling occurs.

Osteoporosis

While osteoporosis is not just a woman's disease, it does appear more frequently in women. "Osteo" means bone. "Porosis" means porous or full of holes. A person with osteoporosis has brittle bones. It is a condition seen mostly in the elderly, and it is caused by a lack of calcium in the diet. A person with brittle bones suffers broken bones more easily and those broken bones take longer to heal. Sometimes doctors recommend that their elderly patients add milk or calcium pills to their diet so that they avoid developing osteoporosis.

Sexually Transmitted Diseases

Sexually transmitted diseases or STDs, as they are commonly called, are diseases that are passed from one person to another during sexual intercourse or foreplay (fondling and touching). STDs include gonorrhea, syphilis, chlamydia, genital warts, genital herpes, crabs and lice, and AIDS. Each year, 12 million Americans will contract some type of STD, with chlamydia being the most prevalent.

Some STDs cause external symptoms such as bugs that are visible on the skin or sores or discharge. Others have symptoms that are internal: itching, irritation during urination, or pelvic pain. Some have no symptoms at all.

Certain STDs can be detected through the woman's yearly gynecological exam, while some are detected by the woman herself. Others remain undetected and cause long-term health problems that may lead to infertility or a hysterectomy. These diseases are treated in a variety of ways: medication, creams, or suppositories (pills that dissolve in the vagina or anus). A few STDs are incurable, most notably AIDS and genital herpes. AIDS will eventually lead to death, and at a faster rate for women than for men. Genital herpes does not kill, but the person will suffer periodic outbreaks and be contagious throughout her life.

Women and AIDS

AIDS stands for acquired immunodeficiency syndrome and is the name for the disease believed to be caused by the HIV virus. The fatal disease affects the body's immune system and leaves it unable to fight off illnesses such a pneumonia. In the United States, women make up about 15 percent of the AIDS cases.

While the spread of AIDS is slowing in the United States, other parts of the world are experiencing great leaps in the numbers of people infected. Asia, Thailand, and Myanmar (formerly Burma) report that as many as 2 percent of their adult population are stricken with AIDS. That means that 2 of every 100 adults (people aged 15 and older) have this incurable disease. The rate is also very high in India and Malaysia.

The Asian experience echoes the experience of sub-Saharan African countries (countries located south of the Sahara Desert) such as Botswana, Uganda, and Zimbabwe. As many as one-quarter of the adults in these countries will die from AIDS. Doctors working with the United Nations predict that 12 million Asians will be infected with the AIDS virus by the year 2015. Without a cure, these 12 million people will die, but not before they have spread the disease to others.

Many developing countries in Asia and Africa are using education programs to teach people about AIDS and how it is spread. It was this increased public awareness and knowledge that led to the slowing of new AIDS cases in the United States. Unfortunately, these techniques have not proven entirely effective in the United States. Women are now the fastest growing group with AIDS diagnoses, and almost 75 of every 100 women diagnosed with AIDS are women of color.

While no method protects you 100 percent against getting an STD, your chances can be lessened by:

- Knowing your sexual partner
- Using a condom (male or female variety) during sex
- Not having sex with a partner who has symptoms of an STD
- Washing with an antibacterial soap before and after sexual activity
- Using a barrier form of birth control such as a diaphragm or cervical cap

Substance Abuse

Substance abuse is the catch-all name for the misuse of alcohol, tobacco products, and drugs (including prescription and illegal street drugs).

Alcohol includes any beverage with an alcohol content. These beverages range from wine coolers to beer to mixed drinks. According to the U.S. Department of Health and Human Services, about 1.6 million women in the United States can be classified as heavy drinkers. Heavy drinkers are defined as people who have consumed five or more drinks per occasion on five or more days during the past month.

Tobacco products include cigarettes, snuff, and chewing tobacco. About one-quarter of American women (22.5 percent) are cigarette smokers, and the rate has been increasing by about 3 percent each year since the 1980s. While smoking levels have remained constant among adults (about 26 percent smoke), the levels continue to rise among teenagers. Statistics show that teens who smoke are likely to continue and remain permanent smokers in adulthood. This is tragic when it is clear that smoking is the single most preventable cause of death in the United States. Each year, some 420,000 people die of smoking-related diseases.

Common prescription drugs that are misused include amphetamines (uppers), barbiturates (downers), and tranquilizers like Valium. Street drugs include cocaine in all its forms, heroin and other opiates, LSD and other psychedelics, and marijuana or "pot." Treatments for substance abusers include hospitalization, medication, counseling, and support groups.

Mental Health

Nearly one-half of the American population will develop some type of mental illness during their lifetime, if you take into account alcoholism and fear of public speaking (a mild phobia). While women do not suffer from a different set of mental illnesses, they do suffer from certain illnesses at a higher rate than men. For instance, twice as many women as men suffer from depression.

In many cases, the mental illness is triggered or worsened by society's expectations of how women should feel, behave, and look. For instance, women are still expected to put their emotional needs last, after the needs of their husbands and children. They are expected to behave as nurturing caregivers who are also strong and assertive. In addition, they are expected to be thin, well-groomed, and smiling. These expectations can create a great deal of stress, both on the women and in their relationships with others as they strive to be this perfect person. Some therapists call these expectations the "superwoman" or "supermom" syndrome.

It has been more than thirty years since women became more conscious of these unrealistic societal expectations. (A famous book by Betty Friedan called *The Feminine Mystique* was published in 1962, questioning why so many American women appeared to be unhappy when they had "everything.") During those thirty years, women have found or developed many ways to help themselves, and many have started seeing counselors who have a feminist viewpoint. They may also attend support groups whose members have experi-

A Woman's Diet

This table shows what adult females actually eat (actual consumption) and how much they think they eat (perceived consumption). It then shows how much they should eat. The information was gathered from 2,000 households for the National Live Stock and Meat Board.

Food group	Servings		
	Actual consumption	Perceived consumption	Recommended consumption
Fats, oils, sweets	3.2	1.8	use sparingly
Milk, yougurt, cheese	1.0	2.3	2-3
Meat, fish, dry beans, etc.	1.9	2.8	2-3
Vegetables	2.0	2.4	3-5
Fruits	1.0	2.3	2-4
Bread, cereal, rice, pasta	4.6	2.7	6-11

Source: Selected from "Women's and Men's Diets Compared to the Pyramid," *Eating in America Today: A Dietary Pattern and Intake Report/ Edition II (EAT II),* commissioned by the National Live Stock and Meat Board.

ences similar to theirs. They read about their illnesses, symptoms, and treatments. They try self-help programs that improve their physical health and mental outlook. Following are some of the more common mental illnesses that women experience.

Post-Traumatic Stress Disorder

Both men and women can suffer from post-traumatic stress disorder. According to a 1995 study by the University of Michigan, about 8 percent of all adult Americans will experience at least one episode of the disorder sometime in their lives. Post-traumatic stress disorder occurs after a person undergoes a very frightening or stressful experience. Among those suffering from the disorder are soldiers returning from combat, survivors of cave-ins and other natural disasters, and rape victims. In the U.S. population, rape is the most common cause of the disorder. About twice as many women as men suffer from it. Symptoms include anxiety, depression, tears, anger, and irritability. Treatments include counseling and support groups.

Anorexia Nervosa

Teenage girls are the largest group suffering from anorexia nervosa ("an-o-rex-ia ner-vo-sa"). This is a disease in which a girl's perception of her body does not match her actual body image. For instance, a girl may look in the mirror and see an overweight, unattractive person. In reality, she is severely underweight. Girls suffering from anorexia refuse to eat. In severe cases a girl may starve herself to death (in her weakened condition she is susceptible to any germ she is exposed to). Treatments include forced feeding, nutrition counseling, support groups, and therapy.

Bulimia

Bulimics are people who eat and then force themselves to vomit before the food can be digested. Their purpose is to limit their weight gain. Bulimics often suffer throat and dental problems from the acidic matter that they routinely throw up. Treatments include counseling and support groups.

Compulsive Eating

Compulsive eaters are people who go on eating binges. They may eat a full meal and then eat a carton of ice cream, a package of cookies, and a box of doughnuts, for example. Their eating has little to do with physical hunger. Treatments include counseling and nutrition plans.

Self-Mutilation

One type of self-mutilation is trichotillomania (tri-co-til-o-mania), compulsive or uncontrolled hair pulling. It occurs when a woman or girl has uncontrollable urges to hurt herself. To do so, she pulls the hair on her scalp, eyebrows, pubic area, or eyelashes. Treatments include medication and counseling. Some eight million American women suffer from this condition.

Other types of self-mutilation include cutting oneself with a razor or knife or applying burning matches to the skin. Self-mutilation can result in scarring, infection, and in extreme cases, hospitalization or death. Treatments include medication and counseling.

Suicide

A suicide occurs when a person ends his or her own life. In many religions suicide is a sin or a crime. Teenagers and the elderly suffer high rates of suicide, in part because both are experiencing life crises. Teens are passing from childhood to adulthood, while the elderly are passing from a work life to a possible life of dependence and inevitably death. Treatments for those experiencing suicidal urges include counseling and support groups.

Aging

As women age, their bodies change in significant ways. The clearest sign of aging is the onset of menopause, when a woman's menstrual cycle shuts down. She is past childbearing age. Other signs of aging are common to both women and men. These include weakening eyesight and hearing, stiffening of the joints, and feeling tired faster. However, aging for women is an issue because in our society women are prized for their good looks. Conditioned by what we see in advertisements and on television, we do not find most elderly women attractive. So when a woman leaves middle age, she may have to cope with feelings of lost sexual attractiveness.

Menopause

Menopause takes place over a period of several years, but typically women experience the beginning of it at some point in their mid-forties to early fifties. They may skip a menstrual cycle, notice a change in the amount of menstrual flow, feel "hot flashes," become moody, and cry easily. All these symptoms are linked to a change in the hormone level in the woman's body. As her time for bearing children draws to an end, her body no longer releases the hormones needed for her eggs to mature, and her ovaries, fallopian tubes, and uterus usually decrease in size.

As menopause ends, so does the production of some useful hormones. Many doctors prescribe ERT or estrogen replacement therapy for post-menopausal women. ERT replaces the lost estrogen and helps protect against heart disease and osteoporosis. It also keeps the woman's testosterone level in check. (Testosterone is a hormone found in abundance in males.) If the testosterone level gets too high, a woman may grow a light beard and experience balding as men do.

Women experience different feelings from men as they age. Photograph by Freda Leinwand. Used by permission.

Does the U.S. Medical Establishment Discriminate Against Women?

Who is the medical establishment? It is the doctors practicing now, the colleges they went to, the hospitals, medical insurance companies, the legal system, and the health care industry. In short, it is the people and organizations that combine to give health care to people.

Many women activists believe that the American health system has a bias against women. These activists point to the research dollars spent and the diseases studied. In 1987, 14 percent of the $5.7 billion National Institute of Health budget was spent on women's health research. (And women make up more than one-half of the U.S. population.) In 1992, $158 million was spent on breast cancer research. In the same year, $1.1 billion was spent on AIDS research. While AIDS is a deadly disease, the number of American women who die of breast cancer each year is far greater than the number of both men and women who die of AIDS.

Surgery

When it comes to surgery, however, women are not neglected. The two most common types of surgery are those performed on women: cesarean section, or C-section (a surgery performed on a pregnant woman who is having difficulty in delivering her child naturally), and hysterectomies (the surgical removal of a woman's uterus). Almost 1 in 4 American babies is delivered by C-section. Many activists believe these figures are unreasonably high. Some critics of the medical establishment allege that some doctors perform the surgery because it is an easier way to deal with women's problems. For instance, performing a C-section allows a baby to be delivered within about forty-five minutes. Trying to help a woman through a complicated natural birth takes more time. And removal of a woman's uterus in one procedure ends what could be a long-term medical problem requiring more treatment.

Diseases

While women undergo surgery at a high rate, they do not receive other treatments at the same high rate. Heart disease, for instance, has been the leading cause of death for women since 1908. It kills 360,000 American women each year. And within a year after a heart attack, 50 percent of women will die, compared with 31 percent of men. Women tend to develop heart disease after menopause, in their fifties or later. Men have heart attacks at a much younger age, so we tend to regard heart disease as a male condition. This perception may lead doctors to ignore or misdiagnose symptoms of heart disease reported by women patients. Perhaps because their problems are detected later, women are almost twice as likely as men to die after a heart attack. Women also tend to survive heart surgery such as bypasses at a lower rate than men.

Drug Testing

Some activists object to the fact that most new drugs and treatments are tested on male subjects. The medical and scientific community generally begin testing with males because their bodies are simpler than women's. They have fewer hormones to cause chemical interactions with the drugs being tested (they believe that women's menstrual cycles might affect the results, for instance). There is also the concern that female subjects may be pregnant and that a drug being tested could harm the fetus. Thus, the results on the male subjects become the baseline, or the norm, for the drug's use.

Diseases Among Women

This table shows 11 medical conditions and how many women suffer from the disease, by age. Figures are per 1,000 total persons (men and women).

[Rate per 1,000 persons.]

Condition	Number of women with condition per 1,000 persons			
	Under age 45	45–64 years	65 to years	75 years+
Arthritis	42.2	315.9	508.7	611.2
Ulcer	13.4	29.5	34.0	26.9
Frequent indigestion	16.9	42.0	43.4	35.7
Diabetes	9.0	59.2	109.2	110.2
Heart conditions	32.9	120.3	220.6	401.2
High blood pressure	30.2	222.1	377.7	374.3
Asthma	53.5	56.6	55.9	32.8
Dermatitis	48.6	50.1	49.0	24.8
Trouble with dry itching skin	20.7	31.5	34.3	49.1
Ingrown nails	17.0	35.9	47.2	75.7
Migraine headaches	60.8	80.6	35.4	21.7

Sources: Selected from "Prevalence of Selected Chronic Conditions, by Age and Sex: 1992," U.S. Bureau of the Census, *Statistical Abstract of the United States, 1994.* Primary source: U.S. National Center for Health Statistics.

But since much drug testing stops once the baseline has been established, few drugs are tested on female subjects. This practice of not extending the drug tests to women has led some doctors and scientists to question whether newly approved drugs and treatments will work equally well on female bodies. These doctors and scientists object to what they call the "male model of medicine" that relies on the male body for determining definitions of health and illness. What is normal for a man may be slightly or greatly abnormal for a woman, they argue. For instance, medications are not given by body weight but by designations such as "adult" or "child." Most women have smaller frames and weigh less than men, but the adult dosage has not been adjusted for their smaller size.

Today, the special nature of women's diseases is beginning to receive attention from the medical community. Several studies are being done, including the $652 million Women's Health Initiative sponsored by the National Institutes of Health, a U.S. government agency. The 15-year study will look at breast cancer, osteoporosis, and heart disease with the hope of ending these major threats to women's health.

Index

*Italic indicates volume numbers;
(ill.) indicates illustrations*

Al-Said, Aminah *3:* 655
Alston, Shirley *3:* 555
Alvarino, Angeles *2:* 386
Amazons *1:* 192
American Academy of Arts and
    Sciences *2:* 371; *3:* 496
American Association of Univer-
    sity Women (AAUW) *2:* 295,
    357, 364; *3:* 679
American Episcopal Church
    3: 751
American National Women Suf-
    frage Association *2:* 247
American Red Cross *1:* 108, 170;
    2: 391
Ames, Jean Goodwin *3:* 711
Amniocentesis *2:* 458
Amin, Qasim *1:* 92
Anderson, Elizabeth Garrett
    2: 391
Anderson, Katherine *3:* 568
Anderson, Marian *3:* 528, 536
Andrews, Julie *3:* 598
Anemia *2:* 469
Angela of Brescia *3:* 719
Angelou, Maya *3:* 496, 517,
    593, 627
Anguiano, Lupe *2:* 282
Anguissola, Sofonisba *3:* 699
Anna Christie 3: 612
Annie Get Your Gun 3: 582, 598
Anorexia nervosa *1:* 221; *2:* 474
Anthony, Susan B. *2:* 246, 249
    (ill.), 250; *3:* 669
Anti-Slavery Society *2:* 355
Antonakakis, Suzana (Maria)
    3: 711
Aphrodite *3:* 720
Apisuk, Chantawipa (Noi) *2:* 332
Appalachian Spring 3: 584
Applause 3: 602
Applebee, Constance *1:* 193
Aquinas, Thomas *1:* 4
Aquino, Corazon *2:* 290 (ill.)
Architectural Tower Structure
    3: 712
Argentina *1:* 9
Aristotle *1:* 5
Arms and the Girl 3: 598
Armstrong, Anne *2:* 262
Armstrong, Lil *3:* 553
Arnould, Sophie (Magdeleine)
    3: 533
Artemis *3:* 720
Arzner, Dorothy *3:* 612, 629
Ashford, Evelyn *1:* 212
Ashford, Rosalind *3:* 568
Ash, Mary Kay *2:* 406

Aspects of Love 3: 600
Astaire, Adele *3:* 600
Astor, Mary *3:* 612
Athena *3:* 721
At Home Abroad 3: 598
At Home in Fiji 2: 395
Atkins, Eileen *3:* 605
Atwood, Margaret *3:* 526
Auel, Jean *3:* 518
Auerbach, Charlotte *2:* 384
Augustine *1:* 3
Aulenti, Gae(tana) *3:* 710
Aung San Suu Kyi, Daw *2:* 285
Auntie Mame 3: 598
Austen, Jane *3:* 519 (ill.)
Austria *1:* 136
Avakian, Arlene *3:* 683
Avery, Margaret *3:* 628
Awekotuku, Ngahuia Te *1:* 53
Aycock, Alice *3:* 712
Ayrton, Hertha *2:* 371
AZT *2:* 376

B

Babashoff, Shirley *1:* 212
Babbit, Tabitha *2:* 400
Baca, Judith *3:* 690, 712
Bacall, Lauren *3:* 594
Bach, Anna Magdalena *3:* 539
Backer-Brondahl, Agathe *3:* 541
Backlash 3: 650
Baez, Joan *3:* 550
Bagley, Sarah *2:* 333
Bailey, Florence Merriam *2:* 382
Bailey, Pearl *3:* 598
Baker, Anita *3:* 556
Baker, Josephine *3:* 604 (ill.)
Baker, Sara Josephine *2:* 386
Balas, Mary Frances *3:* 729
Ball, Lucille *3:* 631, 632 (ill.)
The Ballad of the Harp-Weaver
    3: 506
Ballard, Florence *3:* 568
Ballet *3:* 577
Bandit Queen 3: 623
Banti, Brigitta *3:* 533
Bara, Theda *3:* 610
Barfield, Clementine *2:* 335,
    337 (ill.)
Barnard College *2:* 355
Barney, Tina *3:* 710
Barnum 3: 594
Bartoli, Cecilia *3:* 538
Barton, Clara *1:* 108, 169 (ill.),
    170; *2:* 391
Bascom, Florence *2:* 371

Basinger, Jeanine *3:* 612
Bassi, Laura Maria Caterina
    2: 370
Bateman, Hester *3:* 715
Bates, Daisy *2:* 395; *3:* 524
The Battle Hymn of the Republic
    3: 496
Battle, Kathleen *3:* 537
Battered women *1:* 134;
    2: 446-47
Bauer, Sybil *1:* 96
Bayard, Tania *3:* 676
Baylis, Lillian *3:* 581; 602
Beach, Amy Marcy Cheney
    3: 541
Beard, Annette *3:* 568
Beard, James *3:* 673
Beauchamp, Lila M. *2:* 401
Beauvoir, Simone de *3:* 522
Beauty and the Beast 3: 515
Becher, Hilla *3:* 708
Beck, Simone *3:* 685
Beecher, Catherine *2:* 349, 354;
    3: 677 (ill.)
Bejart, Madeleine *3:* 602
The Belle of Amherst 3: 594
Bell, Gertrude *2:* 395
The Bell Jar 3: 513
Bell, Vanessa *3:* 696, 702
Benedict, Ruth *2:* 372
Benoit, Joan *1:* 215
Bergen, Candice *3:* 637
Berghmans, Ingrid *1:* 211
Bergman, Marilyn *3:* 602
Berkowitz, Joan B. *2:* 371
Bernadette of Lourdes *3:* 725
Bernhardt, Sarah *3:* 590, 591 (ill.)
Bernstein, Aline *3:* 715
Bertholle, Louise *3:* 685
Bethune, Louise Blanchard
    3: 710
Bethune, Mary McLeod *1:* 107,
    109, 110 (ill.); *2:* 267, 284
The Betsy Ross House
    1: 104 (ill.)
Bewitched 3: 632
Bhutto, Benazair *2:* 288; *3:* 747
Bianconi, Patricia *2:* 401
Billingsley, Barbara *3:* 631
Bird, Isabella *2:* 395; *3:* 503
Birth control (see: contraceptive
    use)
Birth control pill *2:* 463 (ill.)
Bishop, Katharine Scott *2:* 384
Biswas, Seema *3:* 623
Black, Frances *3:* 547
Black, Mary *3:* 547
Blackbirds 3: 604

D

Etheridge, Melissa *3:* 566 (ill.)
Etiquette in Society, in Business, and at Home 3: 686
Eustis, Dorothy Harrison Wood *1:* 102
Evangelical and Ecumenical Women's Caucus *2:* 301
Evans, Edith *3:* 592
Evans, Marian *3:* 520
Eve *3:* 717
Eveleth Taconite Company *1:* 153
Everson, Carrie *2:* 400
Evert, Chris *1:* 206
Evita 3: 598
Exposing of infants *2:* 344

F

Factory girls *2:* 333 (ill.)
Fair Labor Standards Act *1:* 124; *3:* 671
Fairy tales *3:* 515
Fallaci, Oriana *2:* 272, 274; *3:* 663
Faludi, Susan *3:* 514, 634, 650
Families in Peril: An Agenda for Social Change 2: 441
Family *2:* 433 (ill.)
Family planning (see: Contraceptive use)
Family and Medical Leave Act *1:* 125, 157; *2:* 420
The Fannie Farmer Cookbook 3: 681
Farmer, Fannie Merritt *2:* 357; *3:* 680
Farrand, Beatrix Jones *3:* 675
Farrell, Suzanne *3:* 581
Fashions for Women 3: 629
Fatal Attraction 3: 622
Fathers and children *2:* 443 (ill.)
Fatimah *3:* 738
Faulkner, Shannon *1:* 143 (ill.), 186; *2:* 364
Fawcett, Farrah *3:* 633
FBI (see: Federal Bureau of Investigation)
Federal Age Discrimination Act *1:* 124
Federal Bureau of Investigation (FBI) *2:* 286
Feinstein, Dianne *2:* 269
Felicie, Jacaba *2:* 452
Felton, Rebecca L. *2:* 266
Female Anti-Slavery Society *2:* 241

Female attorney *2:* 299 (ill.)
Female college students *2:* 366 (ill.)
Female Condom *2:* 464
Female gold miner *1:* 34 (ill.)
Female medical students *2:* 359 (ill.)
Female office worker *2:* 415 (ill.), 422 (ill.)
Female Political Association *2:* 254
Female soldiers *1:* 181 (ill.)
Female teacher *2:* 361 (ill.)
The Female World 3: 673
The Feminine Mystique 1: 21; *2:* 258, 472; *3:* 513
Feminist Writers' Guild *2:* 294
Fernando, Chitra *3:* 522
Fernea, Elizabeth Warncock *3:* 523
Ferraro, Geraldine *2:* 269-70, 270 (ill.), 280
Fetal tests *2:* 457
Field, Sally *2:* 334; *3:* 621
Filatova, Maria Yevgenyevna *1:* 210
Film noir *3:* 618
Finatri, Suellen *2:* 396
Finland *1:* 19
Fiorentino, Linda *3:* 610, 618
The Firebird 3: 574, 578
Fitch, Nancy M. *2:* 400
Fitzgerald, Ella *3:* 553
Flagstad, Kirsten Malfrid *3:* 535
Flannery, Kathryn *2:* 325
Flex time *2:* 418
The Flower Drum Song 3: 598
Flynn, Elizabeth Gurley *2:* 406
Fontanta, Lavinia *3:* 699
Fonteyn, Margot *3:* 574, 580
Food and Drug Act *3:* 679
Fort, Cornelia Clark *1:* 107
Fossey, Dian *2:* 382
Foster, Jodie *1:* 139; *3:* 624, 630, 631 (ill.)
Foster, Meg *3:* 634
The Fountainhead 3: 514
The Four Marys 3: 583
The Four Temperaments 3: 577
Foxy Brown 3: 627
Francis, Clare *2:* 395
Francis, Connie *3:* 561
Frank, Anne *3:* 512
Frankenstein 3: 519
Frankenthaler, Helen *3:* 702
Franklin, Ann *3:* 651
Franklin, Aretha *3:* 528, 555
Franklin, Rosalind *2:* 372

Frau Holle *3:* 516
Frederick, Pauline *3:* 643
French, Evangeline *3:* 732
French, Francesca *3:* 732
French, Julia Blanche *2:* 402
Freud, Sigmund *1:* 14
Frey, Viola *3:* 694
Friedan, Betty *1:* 21; *2:* 257 (ill.), 258, 262 (ill.), 273; *3:* 513
Fritchie, Barbara *1:* 100
From Hollywood to Hanoi 3: 626
Frontier couple *1:* 30 (ill.)
The Frugal Housewife 3: 676
Fugitive Slave Act *3:* 501
Fuller, Loie *3:* 582-83
Fuller, Lucia *3:* 701
Fuller, Margaret *3:* 661, 662 (ill.)
Funny Girl 3: 562, 597
Funny Lady 3: 621

G

Gadgil, Sulochana *2:* 377
Gaea *3:* 720-21
Gaia hypothesis *2:* 381
Gamble, Cheryl *3:* 556
Gandhi, Indira *2:* 274–75, 275 (ill.)
Gannon, Nancy *2:* 339
Garbage *3:* 568
Garbo, Greta *3:* 608, 612-13
Garden, Mary *3:* 535
Gardner, Gayle *3:* 646
Gardner, Isabella Stewart *3:* 699
Gardner, Julia Ann *2:* 372
Garland, Judy *3:* 561, 615, 687
Garrison, Lucy McKim *3:* 546
Garro, Elena *3:* 525
Garson, Greer *3:* 618
Gauthier, Isabelle *1:* 179
Gayle, Helene Doris *2:* 380
Gaynor, Janet *3:* 608
Geer, Letitia *2:* 401
The Generation of Animals 1: 5
Gentileschi, Artemisia *3:* 690, 698
Gentlemen Prefer Blondes 3: 582, 598, 608
Georgia, Georgia 3: 627
George, Phyllis *3:* 646
Ghana *1:* 12
Ghost 3: 625-26
Gilbreth, Lillian *2:* 388; *3:* 680
Gilda 3: 618
Gillett, Emma *2:* 357

Homelessness *2:* 444, 445 (ill.)
The Home Maker and Her Job
    3: 680
Home Notes Magazine 1: 12
Hopi Indians *2:* 434
Hopper, Grace *1:* 160, 185;
    2: 387 (ill.)
Hopper, Hedda *3:* 614
Horne, Lena *3:* 627
Horney, Karen *2:* 372
Horstmann, Dorothy Millicent
    2: 384
Horton, Gladys *3:* 568
Hosmer, Harriet Goodhue *3:* 711
House of Flowers 3: 592, 598
The House of the Spirits 3: 525
The House on Mango Street
    3: 516
House Un-American Activities
    Committee *3:* 509
Houston, Whitney *3:* 562, 627
Howe, Julia Ward *2:* 341; *3:* 496
How to Be Very, Very Popular
    3: 621
How to·Make an American Quilt
    3: 624, 669
How to Marry a Millionaire
    3: 621
Huerta, Dolores *2:* 282, 334 (ill.)
Hull, Peggy *3:* 642
Human Rights Project *2:* 330
Human Rights Watch *1:* 83
Humphrey, Doris *3:* 582
Hunter, Alberta *3:* 552
Hunter, Clementine *3:* 690, 694
Hunter, Laurie Ann *3:* 544
Hunter-Gault, Charlayne *3:* 646
Hurston, Zora Neale *3:* 511
Hutchinson, Anne *1:* 105; *3:* 719,
    727, 743, 744 (ill.)
Hutton, May Awkwright *1:* 116
Hyman, Libbie Henrietta *2:* 382
Hymowitz, Carol *3:* 668
Hypatia *2:* 370
Hysterectomy *2:* 467-68, 476

I

"I Am Woman" *3:* 548
Ichiyo, Higuchi *3:* 522
I Dream of Jeannie 3: 632
I Know Why the Caged Bird
    Sings 3: 517 (ill.), 593
I'll Fly Away 3: 638
I Love Lucy 3: 631
India *1:* 6; *2:* 352; *3:* 564
·Industrial Revolution *1:* 20;
    2: 360

In My Place 3: 646
Institute for the Study of Matri-
    monial Laws *2:* 300
Institute for the Study of Non-
    Violence *3:* 551
Institute for Women's Studies in
    the Arab World *2:* 297
Institute of Electrical and Elec-
    tronic Engineers (IEEE)
    2: 305
International Ladies' Garment
    Workers' Union (ILGWU)
    2: 298
International Mother's Peace
    Day Committee *2:* 311
International Red Cross
    1: 109, 173
Internet *3:* 665
Interracial family *2:* 436 (ill.)
Invitation to the Dance 3: 578
Ireland *3:* 547
Irma La Douce 3: 602
Irwin, May *3:* 608
Isabella I *3:* 728
Isadora 3: 585
Islam *2:* 288, 432; *3:* 736, 752
Israel *1:* 3, 183; *2:* 466
It 3: 612
IUD *2:* 462

J

Jackson, Barbara Ward *2:* 373
Jackson, Janet *3:* 528, 627
Jackson, Mahalia *3:* 559,
    560 (ill.)
Jackson, Rebecca Cox *3:* 735
Jacobs, Aletta *2:* 330, 392
Jacobs, Mary Belle Austin *1:* 98
Jacobs, Mary P. *2:* 401
Jain, Devaki *2:* 353
James, Naomi *2:* 396
James, P. D. *3:* 521
Jamison, Judith *3:* 583
Jane Eyre 3: 520, 594
Janson, W. N. *3:* 691
Japan *3:* 548
Jarvis, Anna M. *1:* 113
Jaudon, Valerie *3:* 697
Jazz 3: 517
Jefferson, Thomas *1:* 10
Jekyll, Gertrude *3:* 675
Jemison, Mae *2:* 396-97
Jewett, Sarah Orne *3:* 505
Jhabvala, Ruth Prawer *3:* 522
Joan of Arc *3:* 584, 719

Job Training Partnership Act of
    1982 *2:* 421
John, Gwen *3:* 701
Johnny Belinda 3: 617
John Paul II *1:* 22, 86
Johnson, Adelaide *1:* 109, 111
Johnson, Amy *2:* 395
Johnson, Barbara Crawford
    2: 387
Johnson, Hazel *1:* 160
Johnson, Osa *2:* 395
Johnson, Tamara *3:* 556
Joliot-Curie, Irene *2:* 372, 374
Jones, Evan *3:* 670
Jones, Marnie *3:* 571
Jones, "Mother" Mary Harris
    1: 113; *2:* 322-23, 323 (ill.);
    3: 503
Jones, Sisseretta *3:* 534
Jong, Erica *3:* 514
Joplin, Janis *3:* 564
Jordan, Kathy *3:* 647
Jo's Boys 3: 501
Journal of a Resident on a
    Georgia Plantation 3: 590
The Joy Luck Club 3: 517
Joyce, Andrea *3:* 646
Joyce, Eileen *3:* 540
Joyce, Joan *1:* 221
Joyner, Florence Griffith *1:* 215
Joyner-Kersee, Jacqueline *1:* 215
Joyner, Marjorie *2:* 401
Judaism *3:* 740
Judith *3:* 742
Julia 3: 592
Julia Child and Company *3:* 686
Juno award *3:* 540, 559, 567

K

Kael, Pauline *3:* 609, 622, 643
Kahlo, Frida *3:* 702
Kanawa, Kiri Te *3:* 538
Karaindrou, Eleni *3:* 543
Karinska, Barbara *3:* 714
Kasia of Byzantium *3:* 528, 541
Kauffman, Angelica *3:* 700
Keaton, Diane *3:* 630
Keddie, Nikki R. *3:* 523
Keen, Dora *2:* 395
Keene, Laura *3:* 603
Keitner, Karen *3:* 544
Kelley, Beverly *1:* 164
Kelley, Florence *2:* 334
Kelsey, Frances Oldham *2:* 384
Kemble, Fanny *3:* 590

Rankin, Jeannette *1:* 116; *2:* 253, 334, 335 (ill.)

Ran, Shulamit *3:* 544

Rapping, Elayne *3:* 647

Rashad, Phylicia *3:* 637 (ill.), 638

A Raisin in the Sun 3: 513

Rathbun-Nealy, Melissa *1:* 183 (ill.)

Ray, Charlotte B. *2:* 354

Read, Catherine *3:* 700

Ream, Vinnie *3:* 704

Rebecca 3: 593, 742

Rebecca of Sunnybrook Farm 3: 610

Recollection of Things to Come 3: 525

Reddy, Helen *3:* 548, 549 (ill.)

Red, Hot and Blue! 3: 599

The Red Lantern 3: 626

Red Rock West 3: 618

Reece, Gabrielle *1:* 221

Reed, Alma *3:* 659

Reed, Esther de Berdt *1:* 166

Reed, Kim *2:* 339

Reeves, Martha *3:* 568

Reformation *2:* 348

Reich, Robert *2:* 424

Renaissance *1:* 3

Rendell, Ruth *3:* 521

Reno, Janet *2:* 287

Report on the Glass Ceiling Initiative *2:* 420

Reproductive rights *1:* 154

Reproductive Rights National Network *2:* 314

The Republic 1: 4

Resnick, Judith *1:* 107

Resovling Conflict Creatively Program (RCCP) *2:* 337

Restzova, Anfisa *1:* 209

Retton, Mary Lou *1:* 214

Revolt 3: 584

Reynolds, Debbie *3:* 598, 620

Rice, Anne *3:* 518 (ill.)

Richards, Ann *2:* 271, 279

Richards, Ellen Swallow *3:* 679

Richards, Linda *2:* 391

Ride, Sally *2:* 396

Rijnhart, Susie Carson *3:* 733

Rinehart, Mary Roberts *3:* 520, 642, 662

Ringgold, Faith *3:* 696 (ill.)

The River Niger 3: 627

Rivera, Iris *2:* 407, 426

Roberts, Joan *3:* 574

Robinson, Harriet H. *2:* 412

Rock and Roll Hall of Fame *3:* 528, 553, 555-56, 563-65, 570

Rockburne, Dorthea *3:* 697

Rockefeller, Abby Aldrich *3:* 699

Rockefeller, Laura Spelman *2:* 357

Rodeo 3: 577, 582

Rodina, Irina Konstantinovna *1:* 210

Roe v. *Wade 1:* 124, 154; *2:* 464-65

Rogers, Ginger *3:* 600, 601 (ill.), 613

Rogers, Marguerite M. *2:* 373

Roman Catholic Church *3:* 722

Romeo and Juliet 3: 580, 590

Rooke, Emma *1:* 116

Roosevelt, Eleanor *2:* 282, 283 (ill.); *3:* 536, 660, 748

Roosevelt, Franklin D. *3:* 507

Rorer, Sara Tyson *2:* 400

Roseanne *3:* 636

Rose, Ernestine *1:* 127

Rosen, Marjorie *3:* 616, 621

Rosenberg, Tina *3:* 518

Rosie the Riveter *2:* 416, 417 (ill.)

Ros-Lehtinen, Ileana *2:* 269

Ross, Betsy *1:* 104

Ross, Diana *3:* 568, 627

Ross, Nellie Tayloe *1:* 121; *2:* 266

Rossetti, Christina *3:* 520

(ROTC) Reserve Officers Training Corps *1:* 160

Rothschild, Miriam *2:* 382

Rousseau, Jean-Jacques *1:* 10

Rowley, Janet D. *2:* 382

Royall, Anne Newport *1:* 109; *3:* 642

Roybal-Allard, Lucille *2:* 269

Rudkin, Margaret *1:* 98

Rudolph, Wilma *1:* 197 (ill.), 221

Ruehl, Mercedes *3:* 594

Russell, Lillian *3:* 596, 597 (ill.)

Russell, Rosalind *3:* 615

Russia *1:* 22

Russian women *1:* 59 (ill.)

Rutherford, Margaret *3:* 593

Ruyak, Beth *3:* 646

Ruysch, Rachel *3:* 699

Rwanda *1:* 131

Ryder, Winona *3:* 669

Ryskal, Inna Valeryevna *1:* 212

S

Sabin, Florence Rena *1:* 111; *2:* 384

Sabrina 3: 602

Sackville-West, Vita *2:* 395; *3:* 675

Sade *3:* 556

Sager, Carole Bayer *3:* 602

Sager, Ruth *2:* 384

Sági, Ildikó *1:* 210

Sahgal, Nayantara *3:* 522

Sainte-Marie, Buffy *3:* 549

Sally 3: 600

Salter, Susanna Medora *1:* 116

Sampson, Agnes *3:* 727

Sandes, Flora *1:* 173

Sand, George *3:* 521 (ill.)

Sands, Diana *3:* 627

Sanford, Maria *1:* 111

Sanger, Margaret *1:* 103; *2:* 330, 331 (ill.), 393, 455

Sappho *2:* 344

Sarandon, Susan *3:* 623, 624 (ill.)

Sargent, Arlen A. *2:* 249

Sartain, Emily *3:* 701

Saudi Arabian women *1:* 93 (ill.)

Save Our Sons and Daughters (SOSAD) *2:* 335

Sayers, Dorothy *3:* 521

The Scarlet Letter 3: 625

Schaaf, Petra *1:* 209

Schacherer-Elek, Ilona *1:* 210

Schau, Virginia M. *3:* 708

Scherchen-Hsiao, Tona *3:* 543

Schlafly, Phyllis *1:* 21; *2:* 261, 315 (ill.); *3:* 514

Schlessinger, Laura *3:* 648

Schmidt, Birgit *1:* 209

Scholastic Aptitude Test (SAT) *2:* 366

Schopenhauer, Arthur *1:* 13

Schroeder, Pat *2:* 269, 276, 278 (ill.)

Schumann, Clara Wieck *3:* 539

Schumann, Margit *1:* 211

Schwarzbaum, Lisa *3:* 648

Science and Health With Key to the Scriptures 3: 745

The Second Sex 3: 522

Seibert, Florence B. *2:* 376

Selena *3:* 570

Self-help *2:* 456, 473

Self-mutilation *2:* 474

Seneca Falls Women's Rights Convention *1:* 15, 17 (ill.), 104, 128; *2:* 245, 248

Sense and Sensibility 3: 519

W

Waddles, "Mother" Charleszetta *3:* 730 (ill.)
Waiting to Exhale 3: 624
Waitz, Grete *1:* 209
Walker, Alice *3:* 517, 628
Walker, Madame C. J. *1:* 96
Walker, Maggie Lena *1:* 109
Walsh, Maria Elena *3:* 525
Walters, Barbara *3:* 643, 645 (ill.)
Walter, Steffi Martin *1:* 211
Ward, Mary Jane *3:* 734
Ware, Dawn Fraser *1:* 211
Warner, Susan *3:* 496
Wasserstein, Wendy *3:* 518, 605
Watanabe, Akemi *3:* 548
Waters, Ethel *3:* 553, 598
The Way We Were 3: 621
Weber, Lois *3:* 608, 628
Weissman, Michaele *3:* 668
Welfare mothers *2:* 450
Wellesley College *2:* 283, 355, 419; *3:* 649
Wells, Mary *3:* 568
Wells-Barnett, Ida B. *1:* 96, 129; *3:* 658
Welty, Eudora *3:* 510
Wentworth, Patricia *3:* 521
Wertheimer, Linda *3:* 649
West, Dottie *3:* 557
West, Mae *3:* 615
West Africa *1:* 12
West Point *1:* 150
West Side Story 3: 617
Westward women *3:* 674 (ill.)
Westwood, Frances Jean Miles *2:* 268
Wharton, Edith *3:* 506, 675
Wheatley, Phillis *3:* 498 (ill.)
Wheeler, Candace *3:* 695
White, Ellen Gould Harmon *3:* 719, 744
Whitney, Adeline D. T. *2:* 400
Whitney, Gertrude Vanderbilt *3:* 699
Whitney Museum *3:* 697, 699, 702
Whittelsey, Abigail Goodrich *3:* 642
Widnall, Sheila E. *2:* 387
Wier, Jeanne Elizabeth *1:* 117
Wilder, Laura Ingalls *1:* 97; *3:* 503 (ill.), 673
Willard, Emma *2:* 349, 361
Willard, Frances *1:* 111
Williams, Anna W. *2:* 380

Williams, Mary Lou *3:* 570
Williamson, Chris *3:* 571
Wilson, Cassandra *3:* 556
Wilson, Mary *3:* 568
Winfrey, Oprah *3:* 628-29, 629 (ill.)
Winnemucca, Sarah *1:* 129
Winona *1:* 97
Wise Parenthood 2: 392
WISH (Women in the Senate and House) *2:* 275
Witchcraft *3:* 725
The Witch House *1:* 101 (ill.)
Witch trial *3:* 726 (ill.)
Witkin, Evelyn Maisel *2:* 380
Witt, Katarina *1:* 215 (ill.)
Witworth, Kathy *1:* 205
The Wiz 3: 604, 627
The Wizard of Oz 3: 561; *3:* 615
Wöckel, Bärbel *1:* 212
Wollstonecraft, Mary *1:* 11; *3:* 519
The Woman's Bible 1: 17
Woman's Peace Party *2:* 334
The Woman Warrior 3: 517
Women at West Point *1:* 186 (ill.)
Women in developing countries *1:* 54 (ill.)
Women playing field hockey *1:* 194 (ill.)
Women's Business Ownership Act *1:* 128
Women's Educational Equity Act *2:* 365
Women's Equality Day *2:* 260
Women's Equity Action League *2:* 260
Women's Health Initiative *2:* 478
Women's International League for Peace and Freedom *1:* 96; *2:* 316 (ill.), 335
Women's Missionary Society *2:* 309
Women's National Press Association *3:* 642
Women's National Press Club *3:* 643
Women's Sports Foundation *2:* 300
Wong, Anna May *3:* 626
Wong, Jade Snow *3:* 517
Wong-Staal, Flossie *2:* 380
Wood, Natalie *3:* 617
Woodhouse, Sophia *2:* 400
Woodhull, Nancy *3:* 657

Woodhull, Victoria C. *2:* 247, 266
Woodman, Betty *3:* 694
Woodward, Charlotte *2:* 266
Woo, John *3:* 626
Woolf, Virginia *3:* 520
Working Woman 3: 655
Workman, Fanny Bullock *2:* 395
World's Antislavery Convention *1:* 17
World Wall: A Vision of the Future Without Fear 3: 690, 712
World Wide Web *3:* 665
Wright, Frances *1:* 107
Wright, Mary Kathryn (Mickey) *1:* 205
Wright, Patience Lovell *3:* 704
Wright, Teresa *3:* 618
Wuthering Heights 3: 520
Wyman, Jane *3:* 617
Wynette, Tammy *3:* 558

X

Xiaoying, Zeng *3:* 544
Xochitl 3: 584

Y

Yamaguchi, Kristi *1:* 215
Yeager, Jeana *2:* 396
Yeakel, Lynne *2:* 276
Yeast infections *2:* 469
Yentl 3: 630
Young, Ann Eliza Webb *1:* 120
Young, Loretta *3:* 613
Young, Simone *3:* 545
Young, Wanda *3:* 568
Your Arms Too Short to Box With God 3: 604
Yumeki, Myoshi *3:* 600
Yuri, Michiko *3:* 548

Z

Zaharias, Mildred "Babe" Didrikson *1:* 119, 193, 195-96, 195 (ill.)
Zahn, Paula *3:* 646
Zedong, Mao *1:* 15
Zelle, Margaretha *1:* 174
Ziegfeld Follies *3:* 595-96, 595 (ill.), 600
Zwilich, Ellen Taaffe *3:* 528, 543